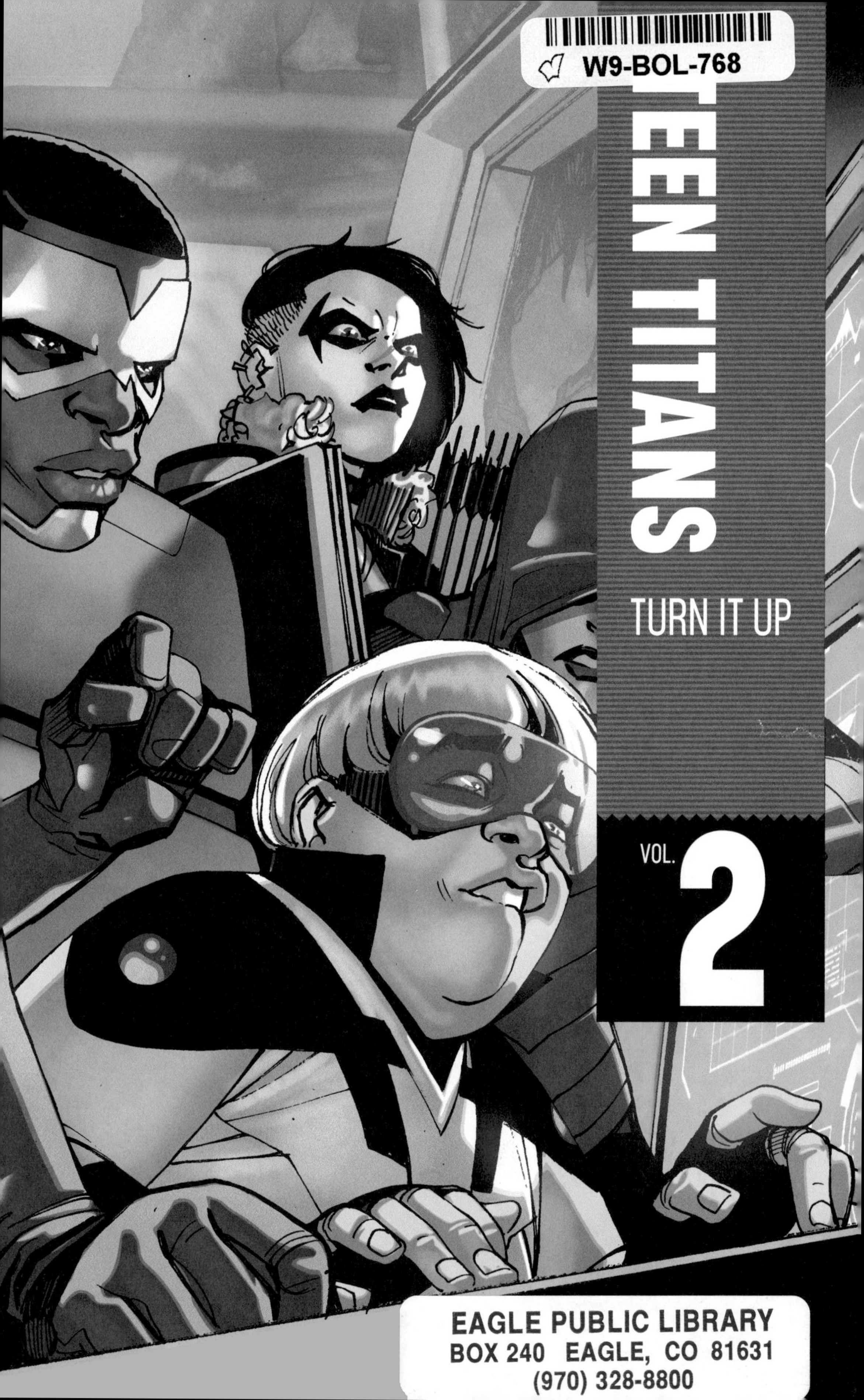
TEEN TITANS
TURN IT UP
VOL. 2

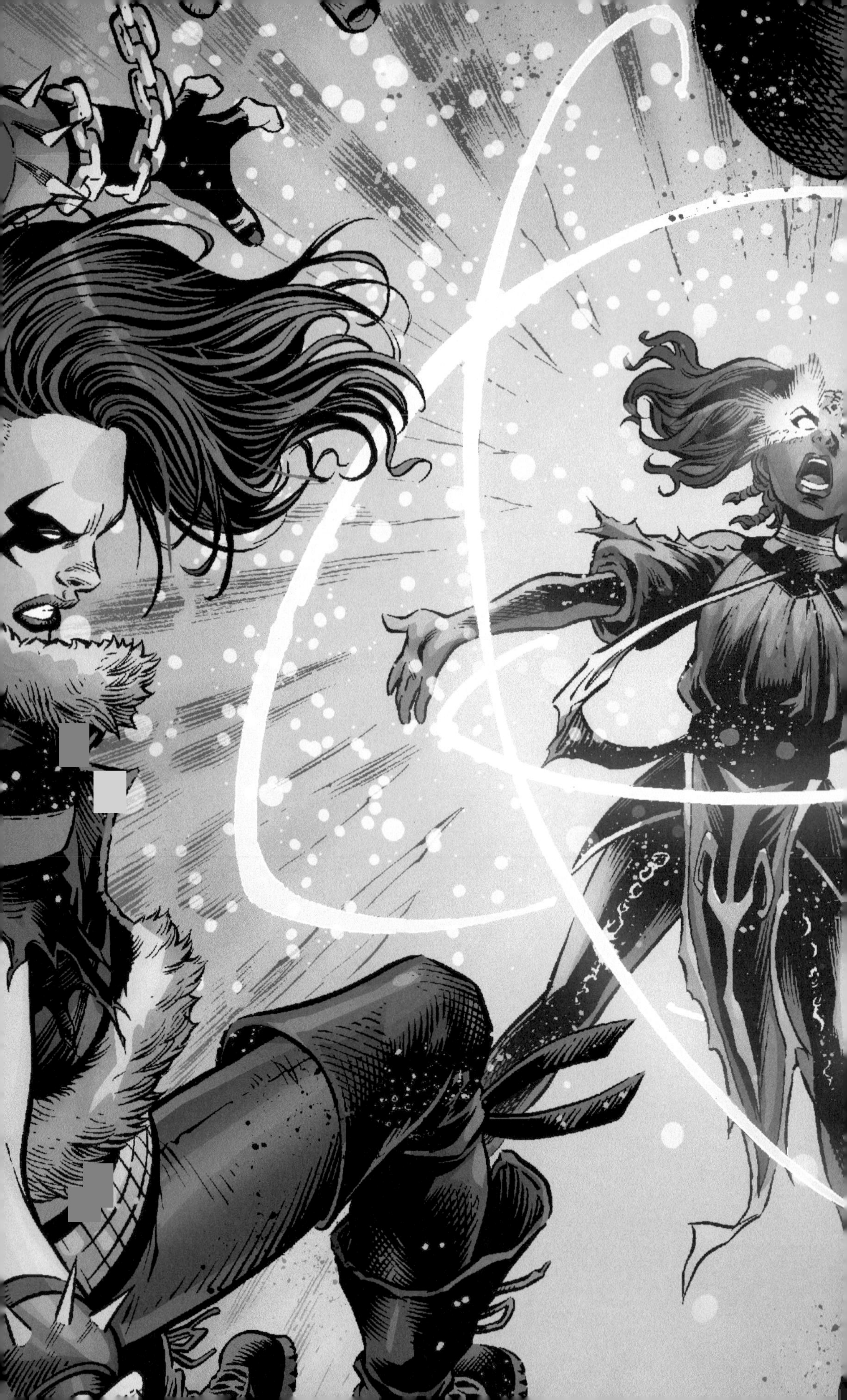

TEEN TITANS
TURN IT UP

writer
ADAM GLASS

pencillers
BERNARD CHANG
ROBSON ROCHA \ RYAN BENJAMIN
MAX DUNBAR \ JOSE LUIS

inkers
BERNARD CHANG \ DANIEL HENRIQUES
RICHARD FRIEND \ CAM SMITH
MAX DUNBAR \ JORDI TARRAGONA

colorists
MARCELO MAIOLO
SUNNY GHO \ HI-FI
IVAN PLASCENCIA

letterer
ROB LEIGH

"CRUSHED" by
ANDREA SHEA writer \ AMANCAY NAHUELPAN artist
TRISH MULVIHILL colorist \ TOM NAPOLITANO letterer

collection cover artists
GIUSEPPE CAMUNCOLI, CAM SMITH
and TOMEU MOREY

SUPERMAN created by JERRY SIEGEL and JOE SHUSTER
By special arrangement with the Jerry Siegel family

VOL.
2

ALEX ANTONE | DAVE WIELGOSZ Editors– Original Series
ANDREA SHEA Assistant Editor – Original Series
JEB WOODARD Group Editor – Collected Editions
ERIKA ROTHBERG Editor – Collected Edition
STEVE COOK Design Director – Books
MONIQUE NARBONETA Publication Design
TOM VALENTE Publication Production

BOB HARRAS Senior VP – Editor-in-Chief, DC Comics
PAT McCALLUM Executive Editor, DC Comics

DAN DiDIO Publisher
JIM LEE Publisher & Chief Creative Officer
BOBBIE CHASE VP – New Publishing Initiatives & Talent Development
DON FALLETTI VP – Manufacturing Operations & Workflow Management
LAWRENCE GANEM VP – Talent Services
ALISON GILL Senior VP – Manufacturing & Operations
HANK KANALZ Senior VP – Publishing Strategy & Support Services
DAN MIRON VP – Publishing Operations
NICK J. NAPOLITANO VP – Manufacturing Administration & Design
NANCY SPEARS VP – Sales
MICHELE R. WELLS VP & Executive Editor, Young Reader

TEEN TITANS VOL. 2: TURN IT UP

Published by DC Comics. Compilation and all new material Copyright © 2019 DC Comics. All Rights Reserved.
Originally published in single magazine form in TEEN TITANS 25-27, TEEN TITANS ANNUAL 1, MYSTERIES OF LOVE
IN SPACE 1. Copyright © 2018, 2019 DC Comics. All Rights Reserved. All characters, their distinctive likenesses
and related elements featured in this publication are trademarks of DC Comics. The stories, characters and
incidents featured in this publication are entirely fictional. DC Comics does not read or accept unsolicited
submissions of ideas, stories or artwork. DC – a WarnerMedia Company.

DC Comics, 2900 West Alameda Ave., Burbank, CA 91505
Printed by LSC Communications, Kendallville, IN, USA. 9/20/19. First Printing.
ISBN: 978-1-4012-9467-0

Library of Congress Cataloging-in-Publication Data is available.

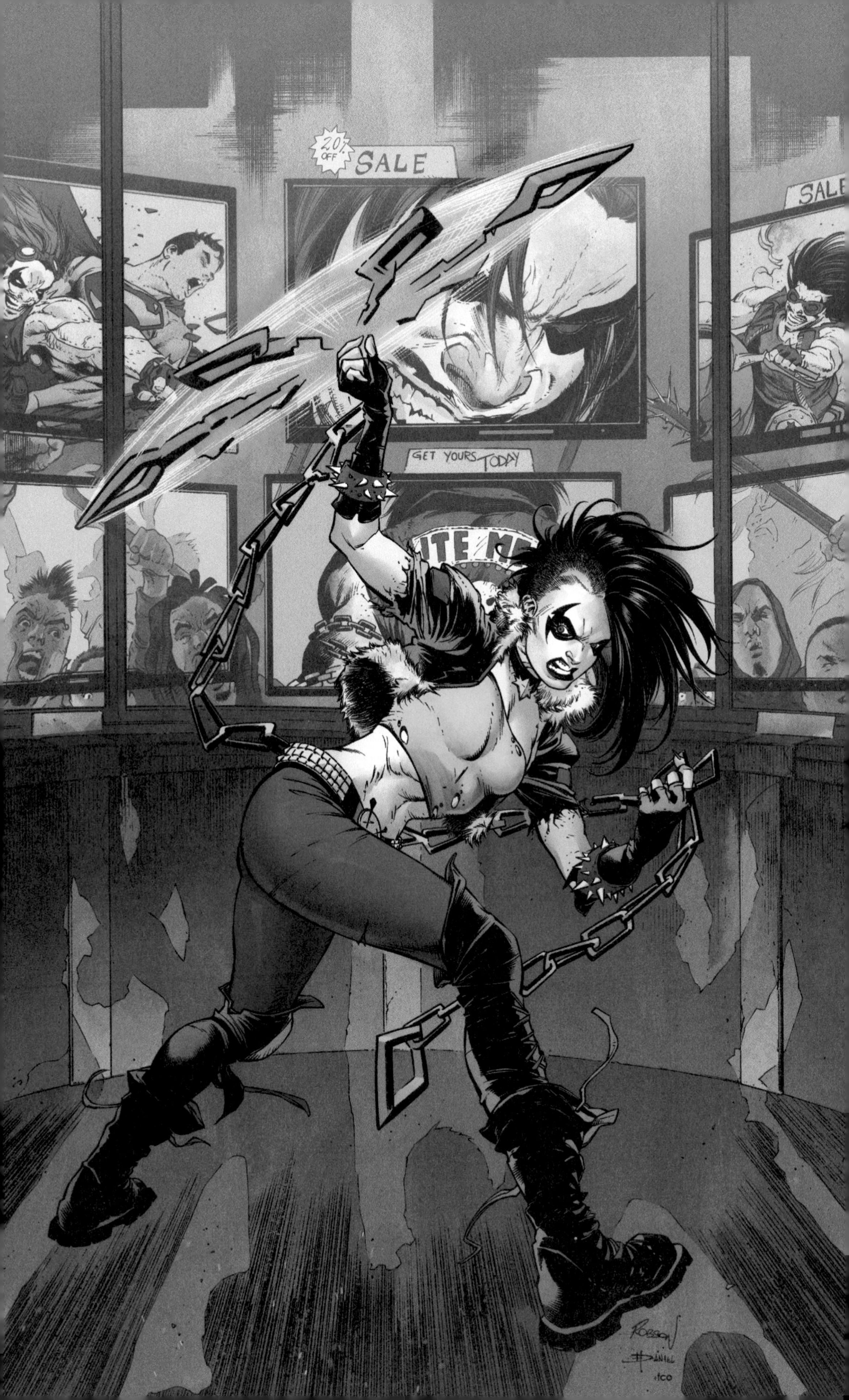

20% OFF
SALE
GET YOURS TODAY

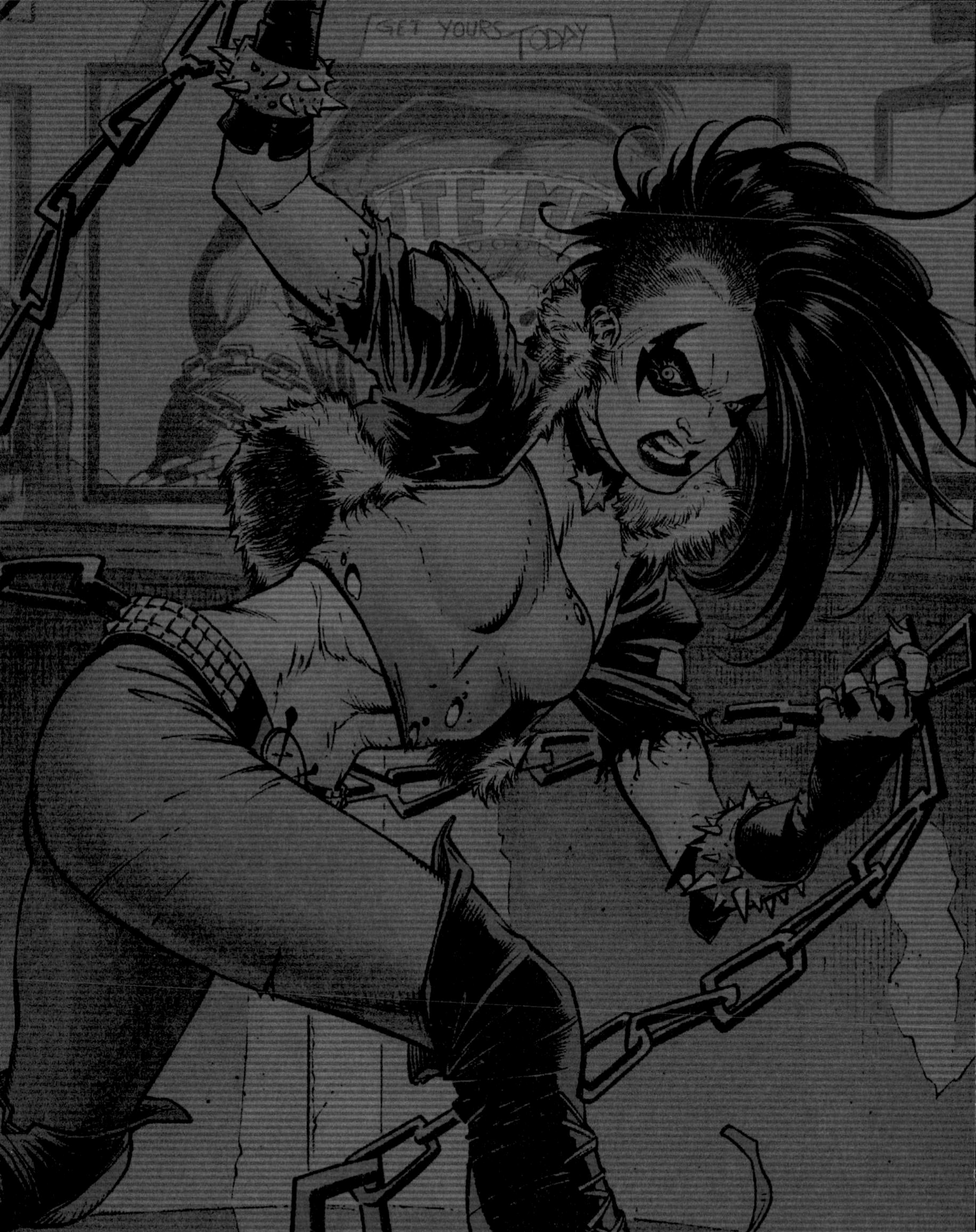
GET YOURS TODAY

TEEN TITANS
#25

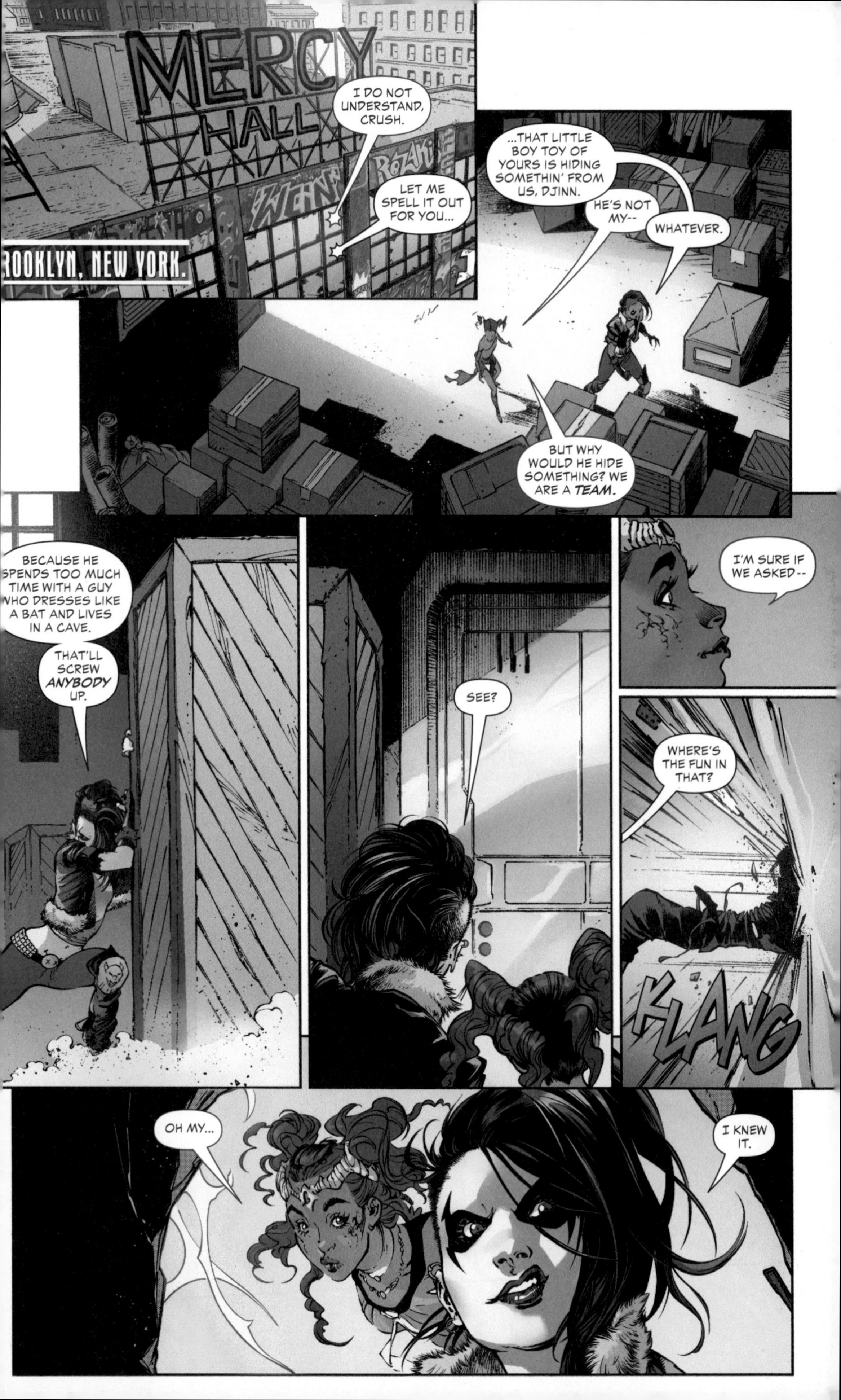
MERCY HALL
I DO NOT UNDERSTAND, CRUSH.
LET ME SPELL IT OUT FOR YOU...
ROOKLYN, NEW YORK.
...THAT LITTLE BOY TOY OF YOURS IS HIDING SOMETHIN' FROM US, DJINN.
HE'S NOT MY--
WHATEVER.
BUT WHY WOULD HE HIDE SOMETHING? WE ARE A TEAM.
BECAUSE HE SPENDS TOO MUCH TIME WITH A GUY WHO DRESSES LIKE A BAT AND LIVES IN A CAVE.
THAT'LL SCREW ANYBODY UP.
SEE?
I'M SURE IF WE ASKED--
WHERE'S THE FUN IN THAT?
KLANG
OH MY...
I KNEW IT.

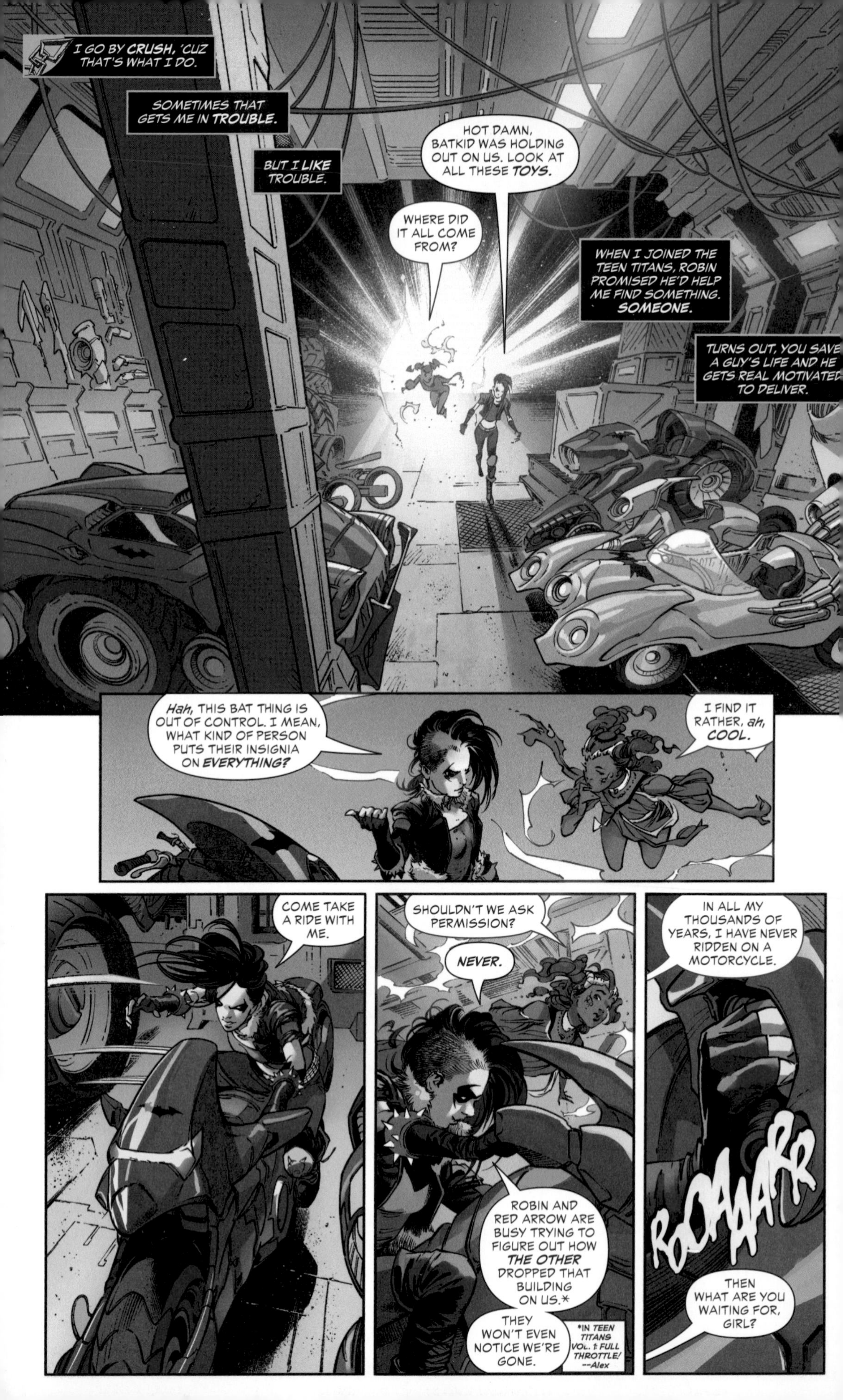
I GO BY CRUSH, 'CUZ THAT'S WHAT I DO.
SOMETIMES THAT GETS ME IN TROUBLE.
BUT I LIKE TROUBLE.
HOT DAMN, BATKID WAS HOLDING OUT ON US. LOOK AT ALL THESE TOYS.
WHERE DID IT ALL COME FROM?
WHEN I JOINED THE TEEN TITANS, ROBIN PROMISED HE'D HELP ME FIND SOMETHING. SOMEONE.
TURNS OUT, YOU SAVE A GUY'S LIFE AND HE GETS REAL MOTIVATED TO DELIVER.
Hah, THIS BAT THING IS OUT OF CONTROL. I MEAN, WHAT KIND OF PERSON PUTS THEIR INSIGNIA ON EVERYTHING?
I FIND IT RATHER, ah, COOL.
COME TAKE A RIDE WITH ME.
SHOULDN'T WE ASK PERMISSION?
NEVER.
ROBIN AND RED ARROW ARE BUSY TRYING TO FIGURE OUT HOW THE OTHER DROPPED THAT BUILDING ON US.*
THEY WON'T EVEN NOTICE WE'RE GONE.
*IN TEEN TITANS VOL. 1: FULL THROTTLE! --Alex
IN ALL MY THOUSANDS OF YEARS, I HAVE NEVER RIDDEN ON A MOTORCYCLE.
ROOAAARR
THEN WHAT ARE YOU WAITING FOR, GIRL?

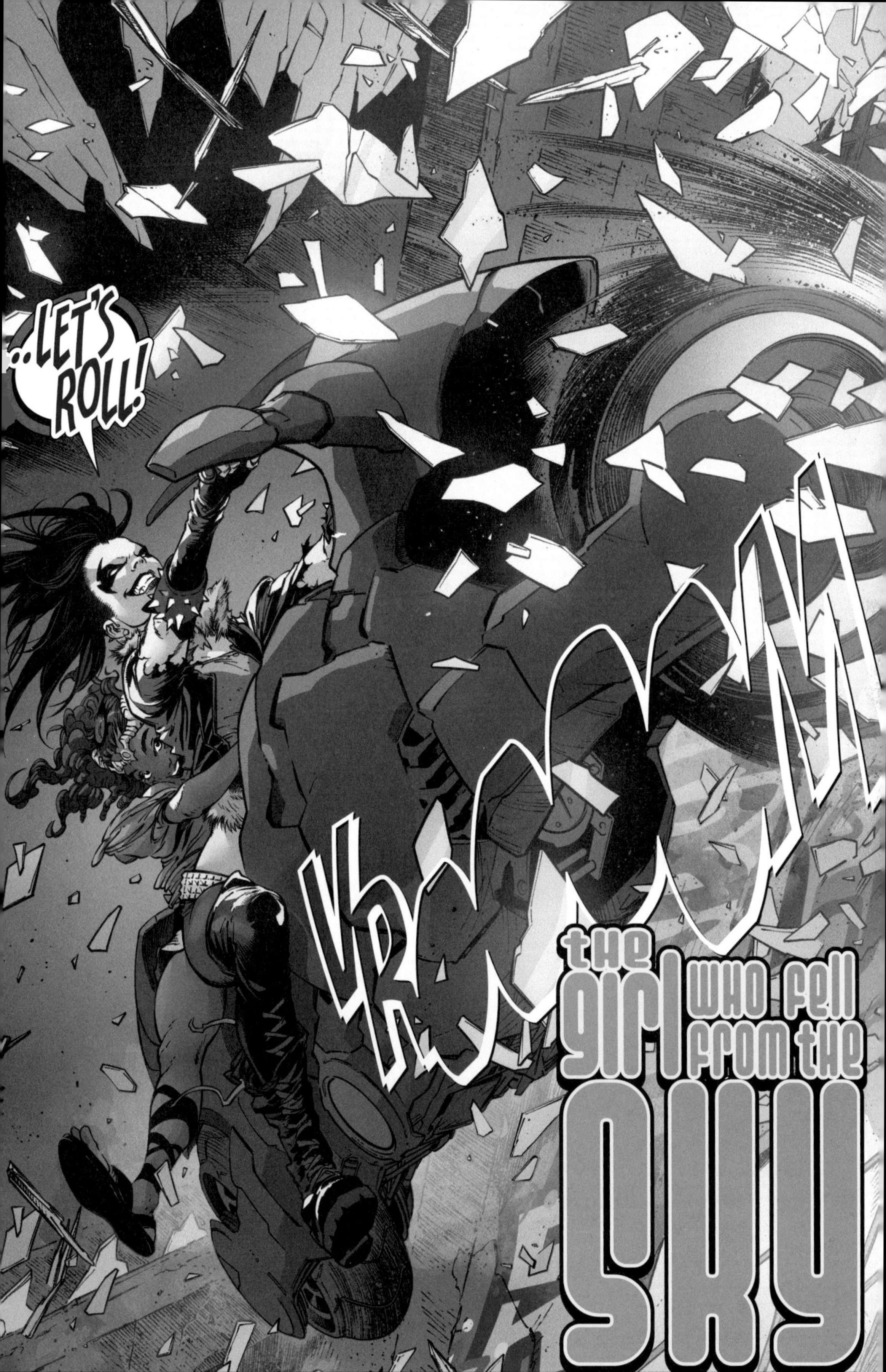
..LET'S ROLL!
THE GIRL WHO FELL FROM THE SKY

ADAM GLASS	ROBSON ROCHA	DANIEL HENRIQUES	SUNNY GHO	ROB LEIGH
writer	guest penciller	guest inker	guest colorist	letterer

ROCHA, HENRIQUES & GHO	ANDREA SHEA	ALEX ANTONE	BRIAN CUNNINGHAM
cover	assistant editor	editor	group editor

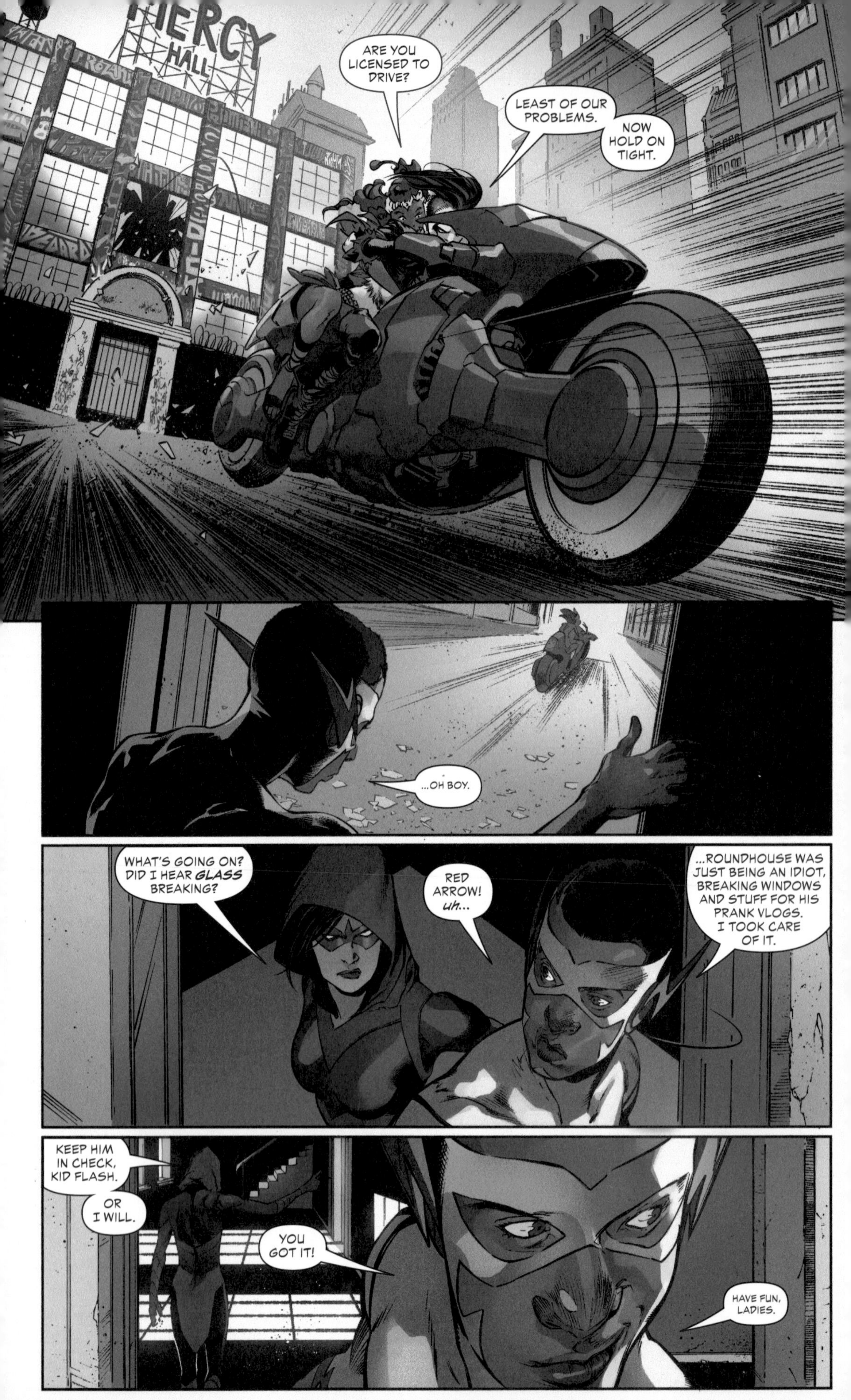

MERCY HALL
ARE YOU LICENSED TO DRIVE?
LEAST OF OUR PROBLEMS.
NOW HOLD ON TIGHT.
...OH BOY.
WHAT'S GOING ON? DID I HEAR GLASS BREAKING?
RED ARROW! uh...
...ROUNDHOUSE WAS JUST BEING AN IDIOT, BREAKING WINDOWS AND STUFF FOR HIS PRANK VLOGS. I TOOK CARE OF IT.
KEEP HIM IN CHECK, KID FLASH.
OR I WILL.
YOU GOT IT!
HAVE FUN, LADIES.

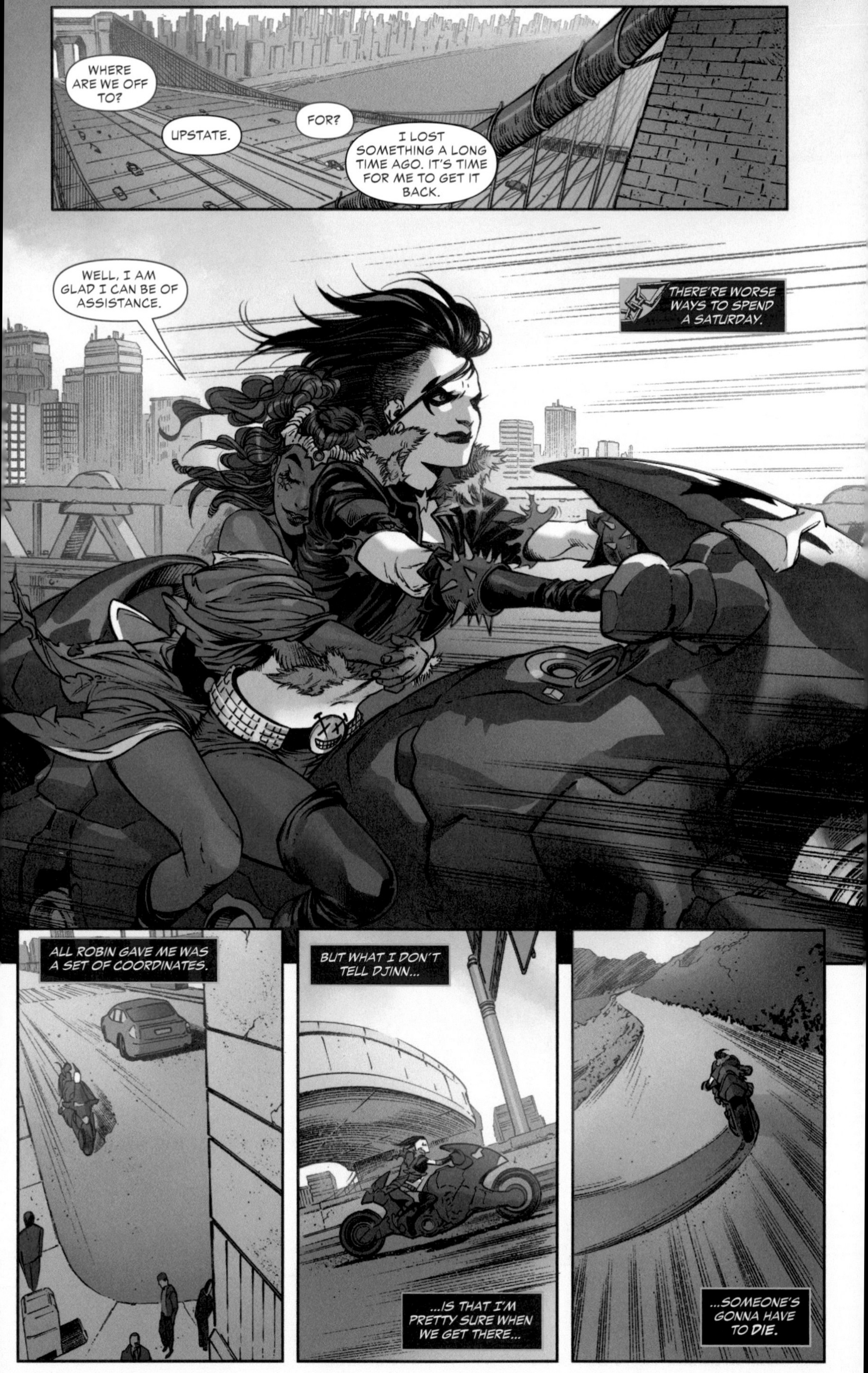
WHERE ARE WE OFF TO?
UPSTATE.
FOR?
I LOST SOMETHING A LONG TIME AGO. IT'S TIME FOR ME TO GET IT BACK.
WELL, I AM GLAD I CAN BE OF ASSISTANCE.
THERE'RE WORSE WAYS TO SPEND A SATURDAY.
ALL ROBIN GAVE ME WAS A SET OF COORDINATES.
BUT WHAT I DON'T TELL DJINN...
...IS THAT I'M PRETTY SURE WHEN WE GET THERE...
...SOMEONE'S GONNA HAVE TO DIE.

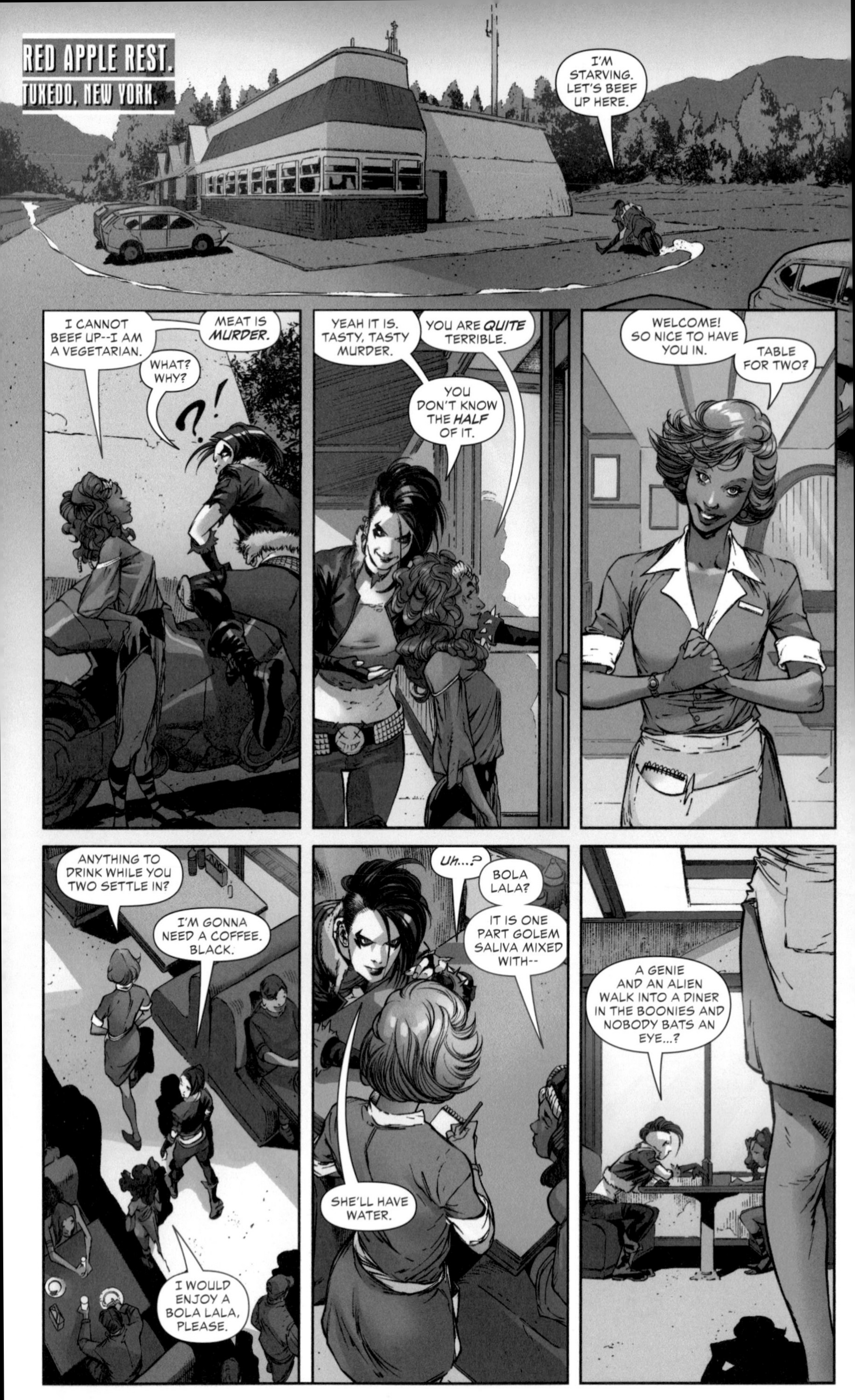
RED APPLE REST.
TUXEDO, NEW YORK.
I'M STARVING. LET'S BEEF UP HERE.
I CANNOT BEEF UP--I AM A VEGETARIAN.
MEAT IS MURDER.
WHAT? WHY?
?!
YEAH IT IS. TASTY, TASTY MURDER.
YOU ARE QUITE TERRIBLE.
YOU DON'T KNOW THE HALF OF IT.
WELCOME! SO NICE TO HAVE YOU IN.
TABLE FOR TWO?
ANYTHING TO DRINK WHILE YOU TWO SETTLE IN?
I'M GONNA NEED A COFFEE. BLACK.
I WOULD ENJOY A BOLA LALA, PLEASE.
Uh...?
BOLA LALA?
IT IS ONE PART GOLEM SALIVA MIXED WITH--
SHE'LL HAVE WATER.
A GENIE AND AN ALIEN WALK INTO A DINER IN THE BOONIES AND NOBODY BATS AN EYE...?

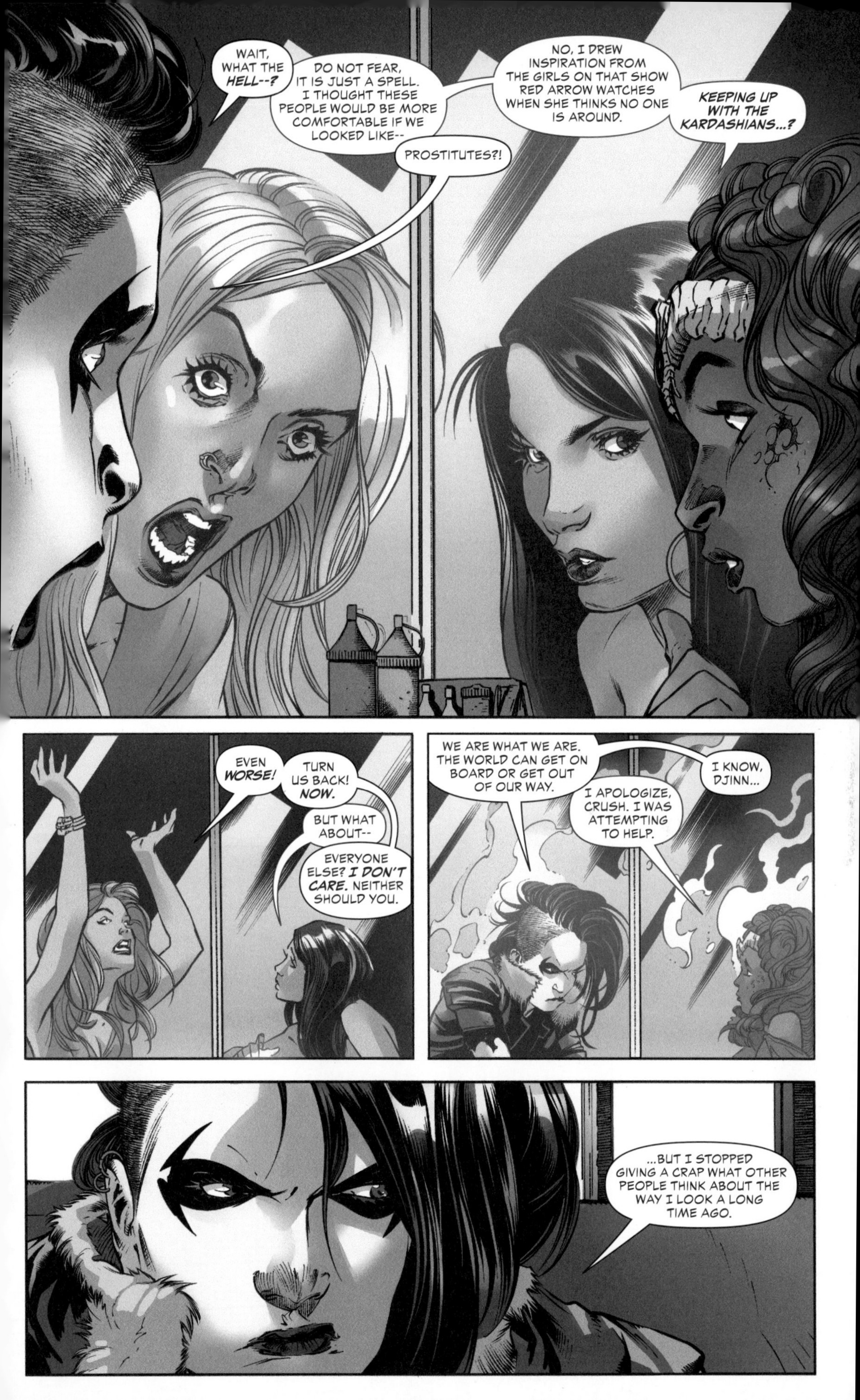
WAIT, WHAT THE *HELL--?*
DO NOT FEAR, IT IS JUST A SPELL. I THOUGHT THESE PEOPLE WOULD BE MORE COMFORTABLE IF WE LOOKED LIKE--
PROSTITUTES?!
NO, I DREW INSPIRATION FROM THE GIRLS ON THAT SHOW RED ARROW WATCHES WHEN SHE THINKS NO ONE IS AROUND.
KEEPING UP WITH THE KARDASHIANS...?
EVEN *WORSE!*
TURN US BACK! *NOW.*
BUT WHAT ABOUT--
EVERYONE ELSE? *I DON'T CARE.* NEITHER SHOULD YOU.
WE ARE WHAT WE ARE. THE WORLD CAN GET ON BOARD OR GET OUT OF OUR WAY.
I APOLOGIZE, CRUSH. I WAS ATTEMPTING TO HELP.
I KNOW, DJINN...
...BUT I STOPPED GIVING A CRAP WHAT OTHER PEOPLE THINK ABOUT THE WAY I LOOK A LONG TIME AGO.

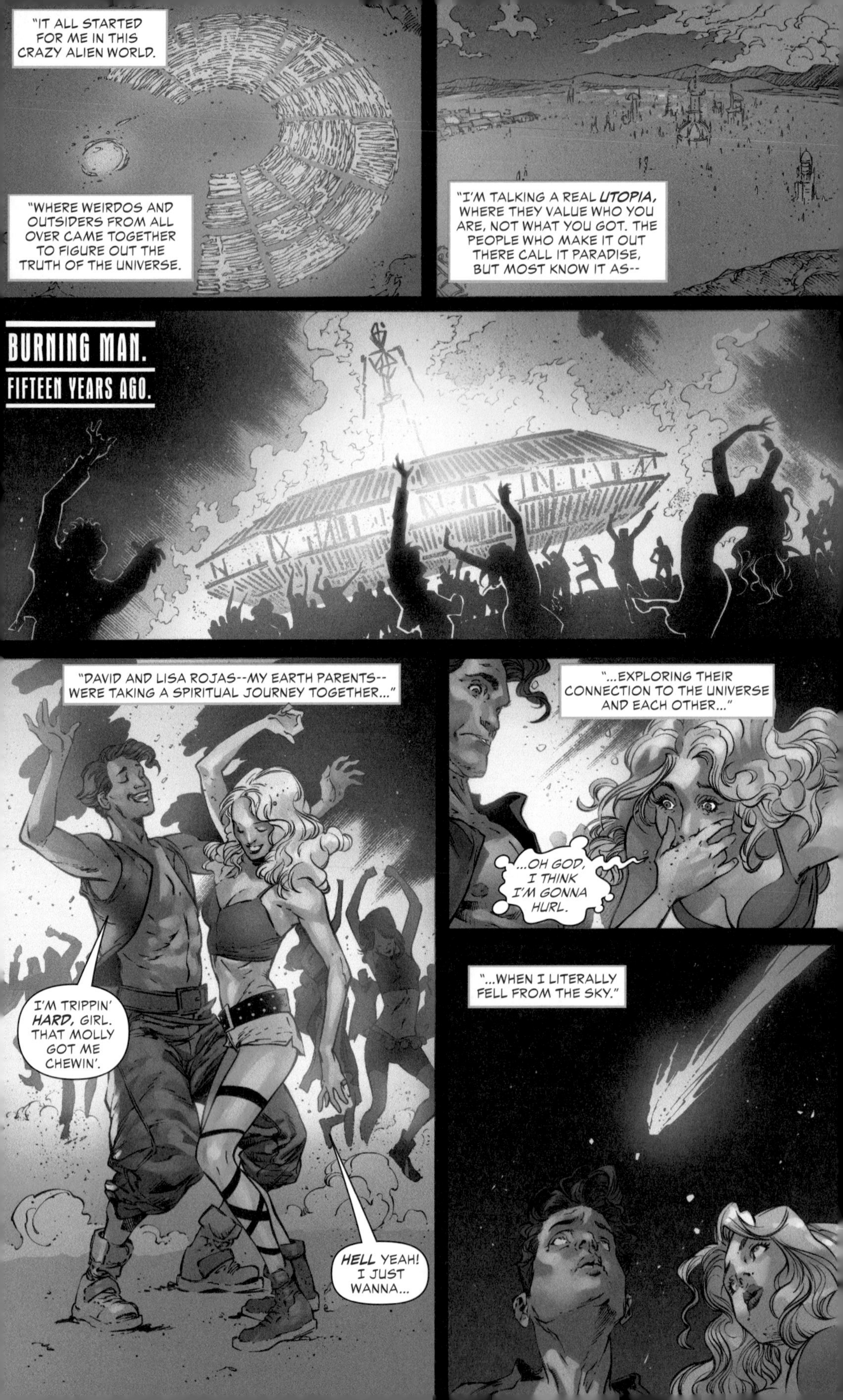
"IT ALL STARTED FOR ME IN THIS CRAZY ALIEN WORLD.
"WHERE WEIRDOS AND OUTSIDERS FROM ALL OVER CAME TOGETHER TO FIGURE OUT THE TRUTH OF THE UNIVERSE.
"I'M TALKING A REAL *UTOPIA,* WHERE THEY VALUE WHO YOU ARE, NOT WHAT YOU GOT. THE PEOPLE WHO MAKE IT OUT THERE CALL IT PARADISE, BUT MOST KNOW IT AS--
BURNING MAN.
FIFTEEN YEARS AGO.
"DAVID AND LISA ROJAS--MY EARTH PARENTS--WERE TAKING A SPIRITUAL JOURNEY TOGETHER..."
I'M TRIPPIN' *HARD,* GIRL. THAT MOLLY GOT ME CHEWIN'.
HELL YEAH! I JUST WANNA...
"...EXPLORING THEIR CONNECTION TO THE UNIVERSE AND EACH OTHER..."
...OH GOD, I THINK I'M GONNA HURL.
"...WHEN I LITERALLY FELL FROM THE SKY."

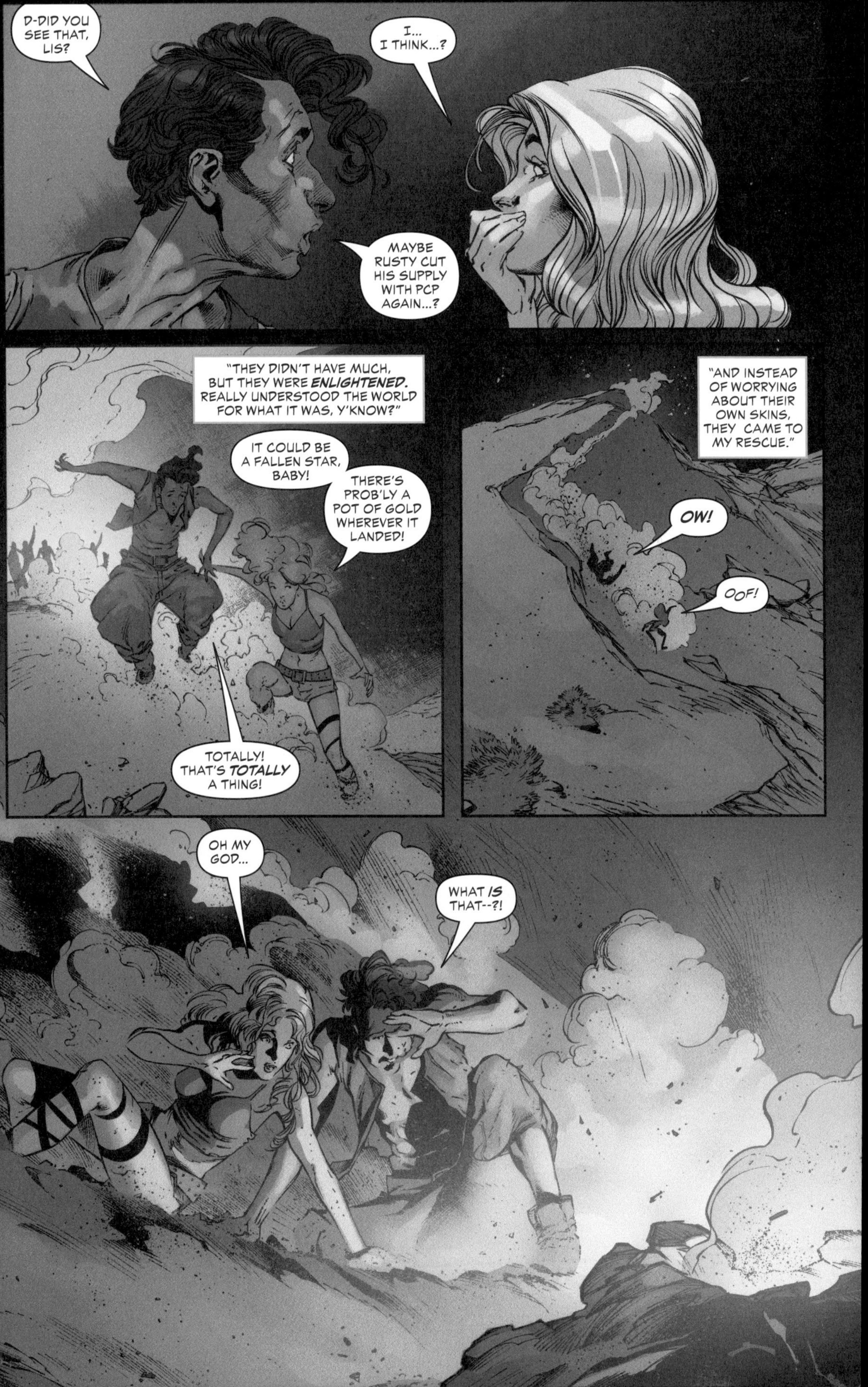
D-DID YOU SEE THAT, LIS?
I... I THINK...?
MAYBE RUSTY CUT HIS SUPPLY WITH PCP AGAIN...?
"THEY DIDN'T HAVE MUCH, BUT THEY WERE *ENLIGHTENED.* REALLY UNDERSTOOD THE WORLD FOR WHAT IT WAS, Y'KNOW?"
IT COULD BE A FALLEN STAR, BABY!
THERE'S PROB'LY A POT OF GOLD WHEREVER IT LANDED!
TOTALLY! THAT'S *TOTALLY* A THING!
"AND INSTEAD OF WORRYING ABOUT THEIR OWN SKINS, THEY CAME TO MY RESCUE."
OW!
OOF!
OH MY GOD...
WHAT *IS* THAT--?!

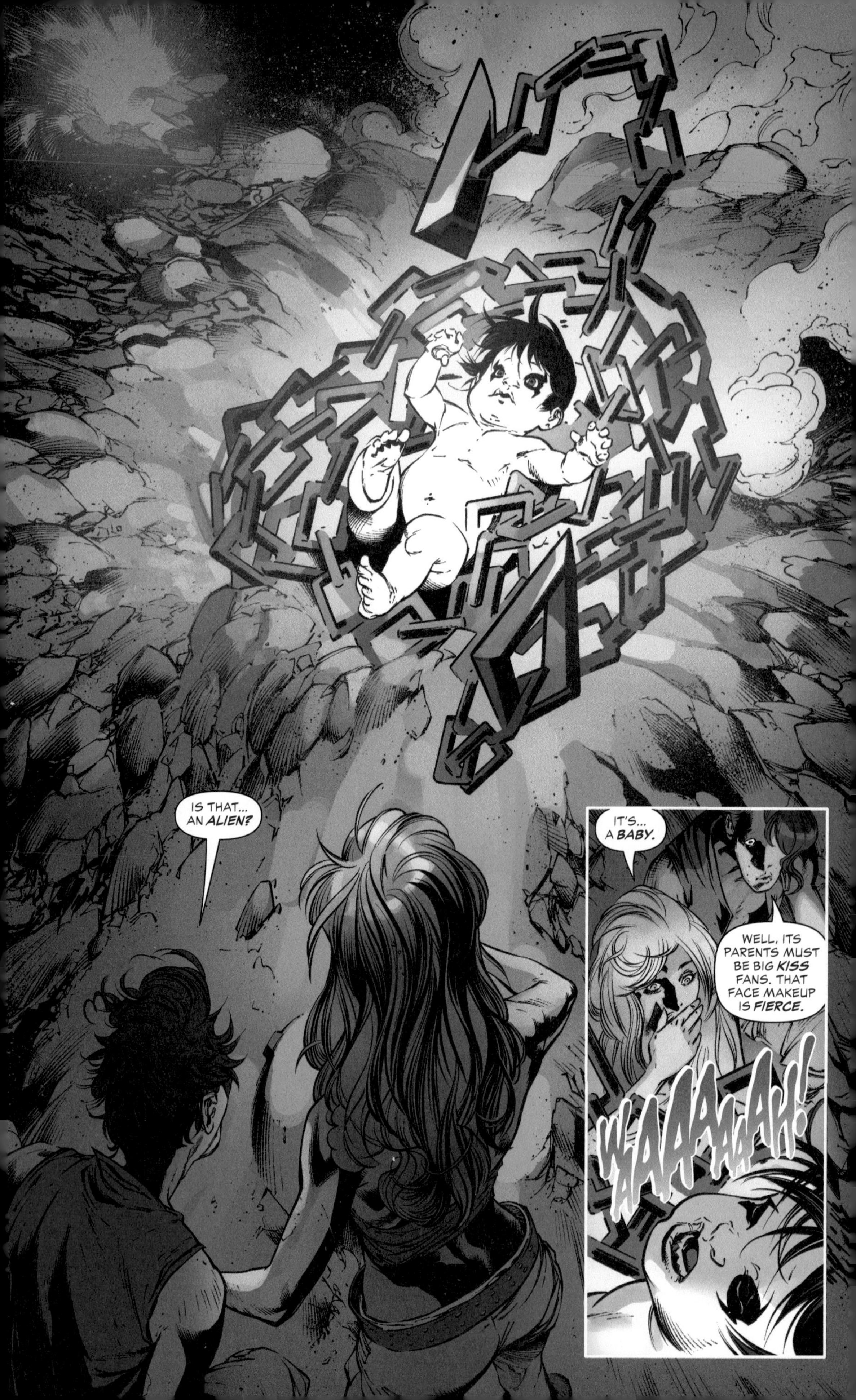
IS THAT... AN ALIEN?
IT'S... A BABY.
WELL, ITS PARENTS MUST BE BIG KISS FANS. THAT FACE MAKEUP IS FIERCE.
WAAAAAAAH!

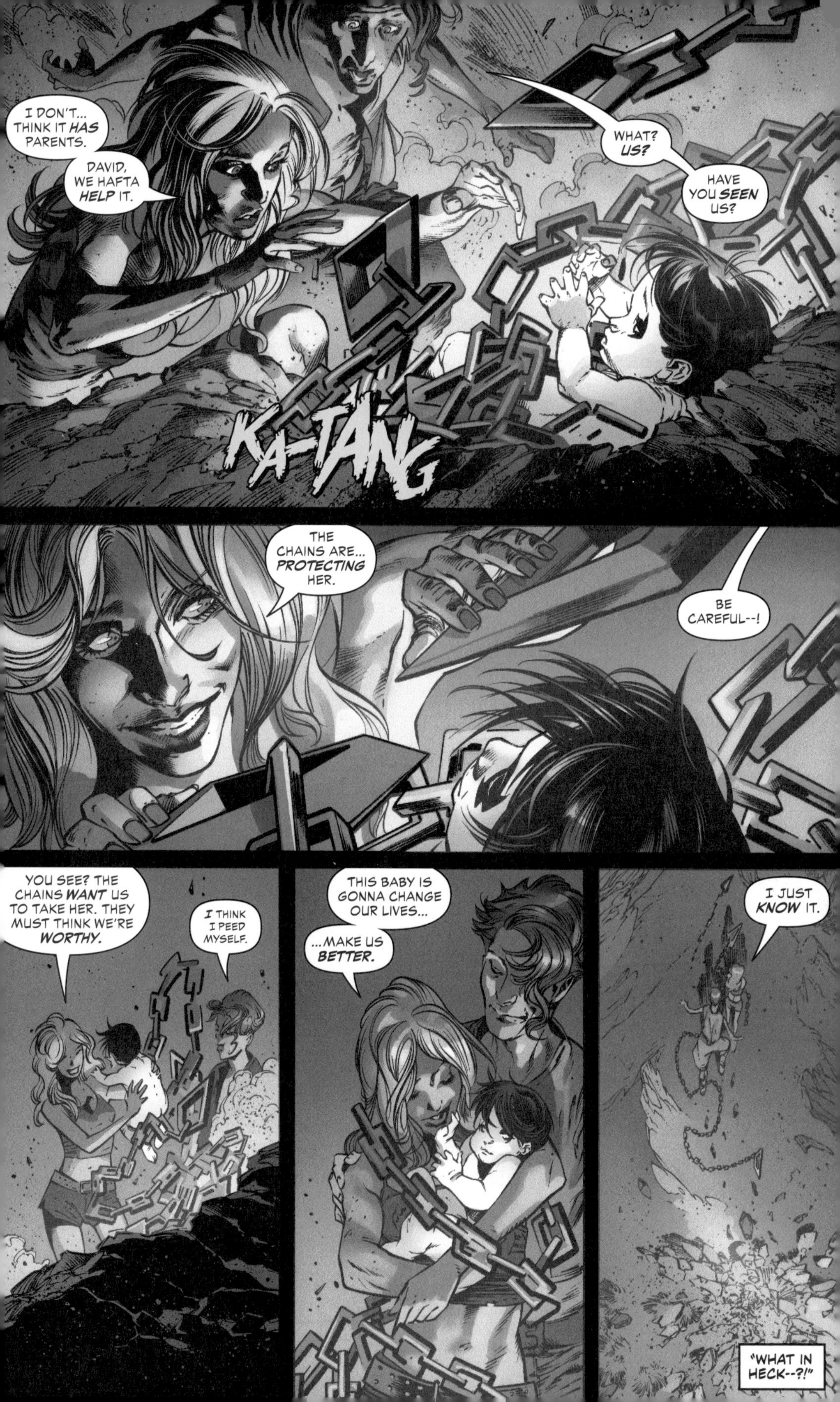
I DON'T... THINK IT HAS PARENTS.
DAVID, WE HAFTA HELP IT.
WHAT? US?
HAVE YOU SEEN US?
KA-TANG
THE CHAINS ARE... PROTECTING HER.
BE CAREFUL--!
YOU SEE? THE CHAINS WANT US TO TAKE HER. THEY MUST THINK WE'RE WORTHY.
I THINK I PEED MYSELF.
THIS BABY IS GONNA CHANGE OUR LIVES...
...MAKE US BETTER.
I JUST KNOW IT.
"WHAT IN HECK--?!"

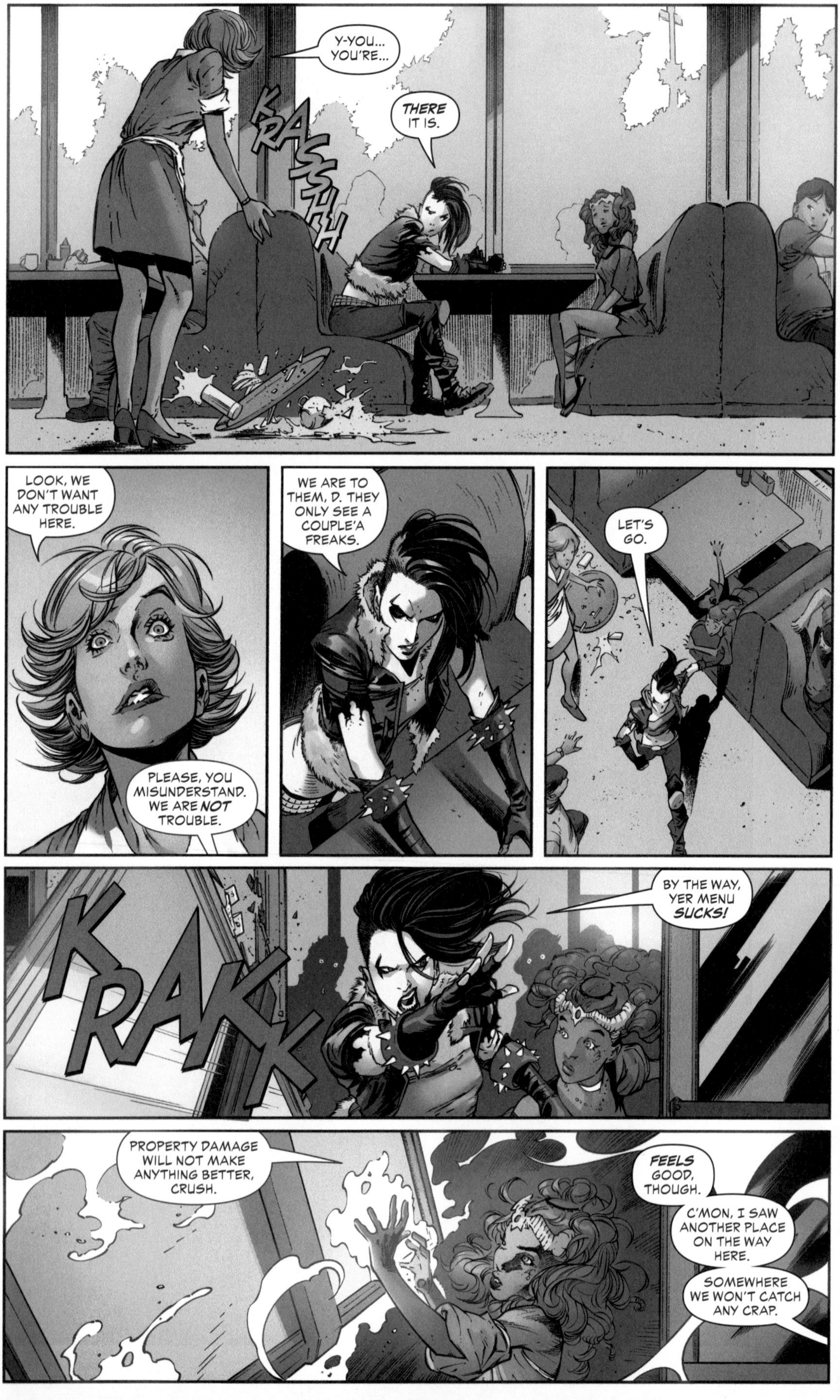
Y-YOU... YOU'RE...
KRASSHH
THERE IT IS.
LOOK, WE DON'T WANT ANY TROUBLE HERE.
PLEASE, YOU MISUNDERSTAND. WE ARE NOT TROUBLE.
WE ARE TO THEM, D. THEY ONLY SEE A COUPLE'A FREAKS.
LET'S GO.
KRAKK
BY THE WAY, YER MENU SUCKS!
PROPERTY DAMAGE WILL NOT MAKE ANYTHING BETTER, CRUSH.
FEELS GOOD, THOUGH.
C'MON, I SAW ANOTHER PLACE ON THE WAY HERE.
SOMEWHERE WE WON'T CATCH ANY CRAP.

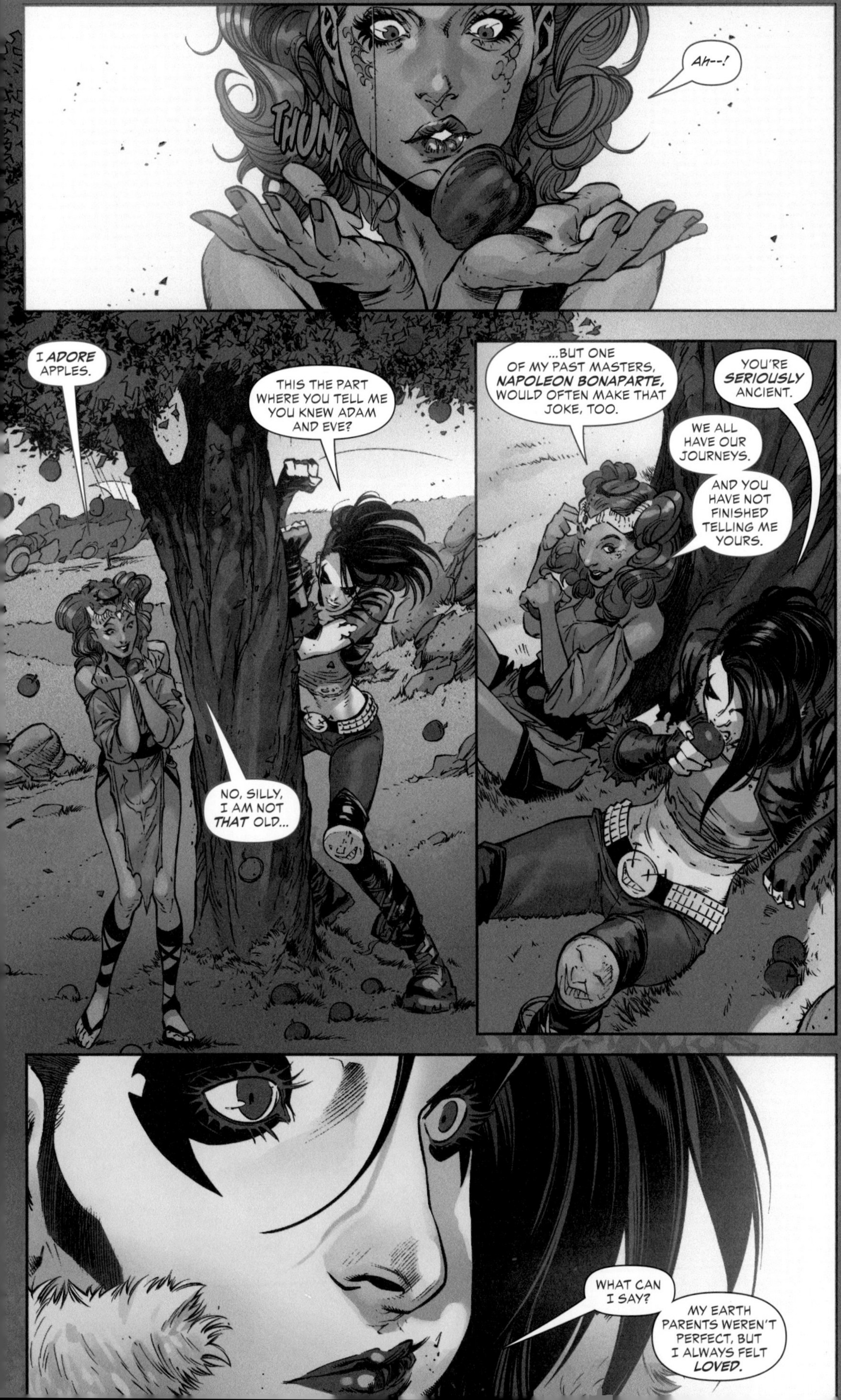

THUNK
Ah--!
I ADORE APPLES.
THIS THE PART WHERE YOU TELL ME YOU KNEW ADAM AND EVE?
NO, SILLY, I AM NOT THAT OLD...
...BUT ONE OF MY PAST MASTERS, NAPOLEON BONAPARTE, WOULD OFTEN MAKE THAT JOKE, TOO.
YOU'RE SERIOUSLY ANCIENT.
WE ALL HAVE OUR JOURNEYS.
AND YOU HAVE NOT FINISHED TELLING ME YOURS.
WHAT CAN I SAY?
MY EARTH PARENTS WEREN'T PERFECT, BUT I ALWAYS FELT LOVED.

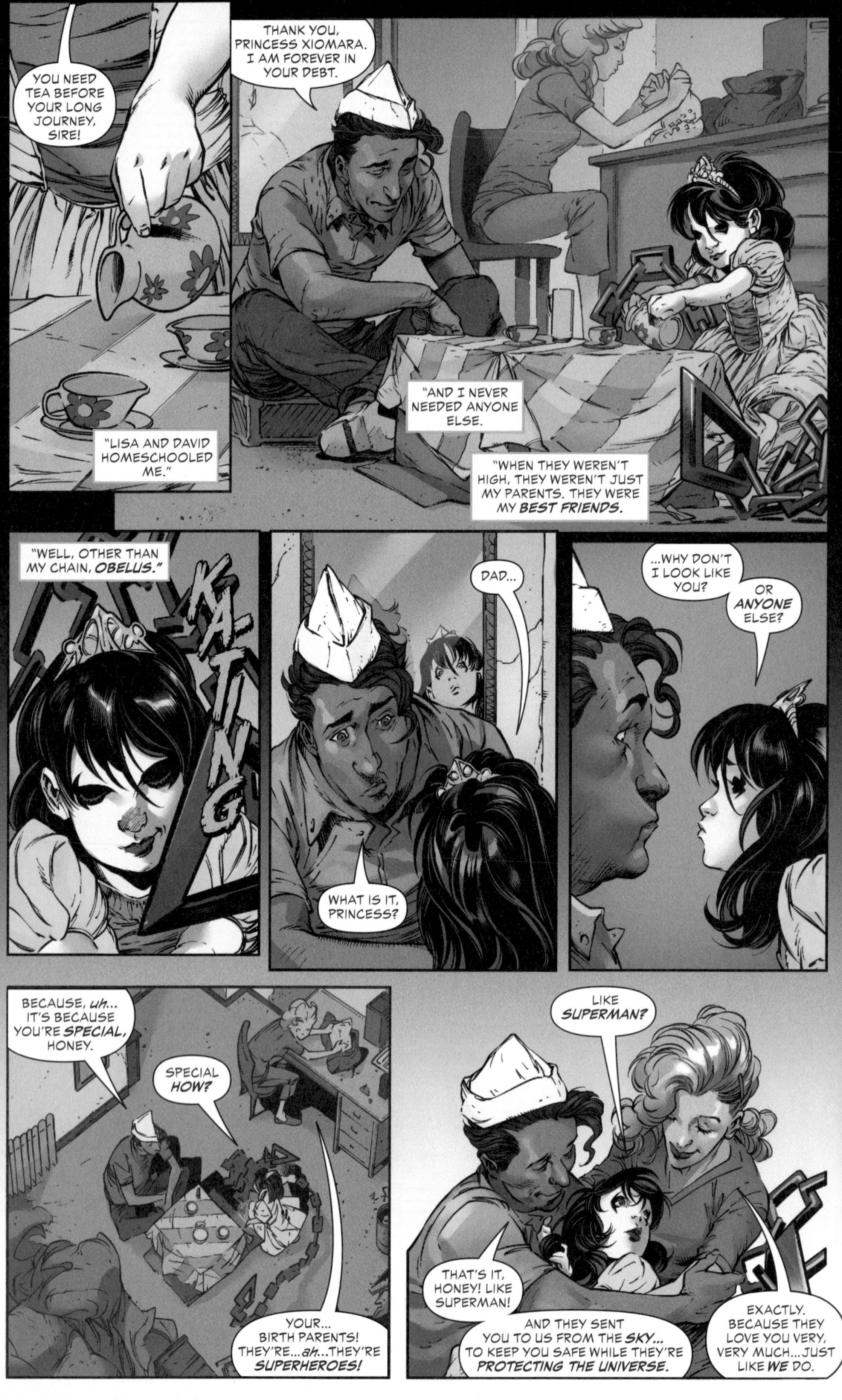
YOU NEED TEA BEFORE YOUR LONG JOURNEY, SIRE!
THANK YOU, PRINCESS XIOMARA. I AM FOREVER IN YOUR DEBT.
"LISA AND DAVID HOMESCHOOLED ME."
"AND I NEVER NEEDED ANYONE ELSE.
"WHEN THEY WEREN'T HIGH, THEY WEREN'T JUST MY PARENTS. THEY WERE MY BEST FRIENDS.
"WELL, OTHER THAN MY CHAIN, OBELUS."
KA-TING
DAD...
WHAT IS IT, PRINCESS?
...WHY DON'T I LOOK LIKE YOU?
OR ANYONE ELSE?
BECAUSE, uh... IT'S BECAUSE YOU'RE SPECIAL, HONEY.
SPECIAL HOW?
YOUR... BIRTH PARENTS! THEY'RE...ah...THEY'RE SUPERHEROES!
LIKE SUPERMAN?
THAT'S IT, HONEY! LIKE SUPERMAN!
AND THEY SENT YOU TO US FROM THE SKY... TO KEEP YOU SAFE WHILE THEY'RE PROTECTING THE UNIVERSE.
EXACTLY. BECAUSE THEY LOVE YOU VERY, VERY MUCH...JUST LIKE WE DO.

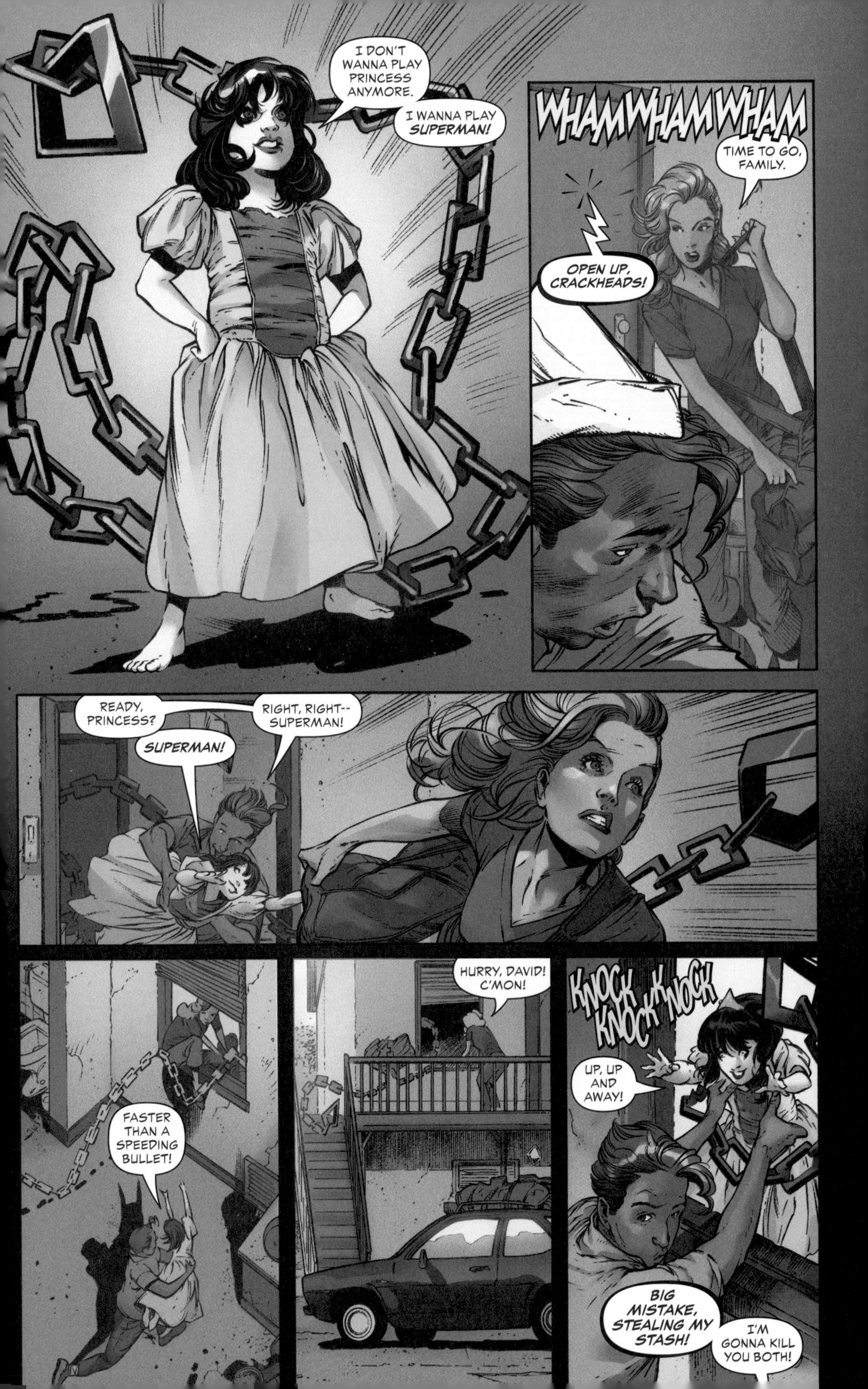
I DON'T WANNA PLAY PRINCESS ANYMORE.
I WANNA PLAY SUPERMAN!
WHAMWHAMWHAM
TIME TO GO, FAMILY.
OPEN UP, CRACKHEADS!
READY, PRINCESS?
RIGHT, RIGHT-- SUPERMAN!
SUPERMAN!
FASTER THAN A SPEEDING BULLET!
HURRY, DAVID! C'MON!
KNOCK KNOCK KNOCK
UP, UP AND AWAY!
BIG MISTAKE, STEALING MY STASH!
I'M GONNA KILL YOU BOTH!

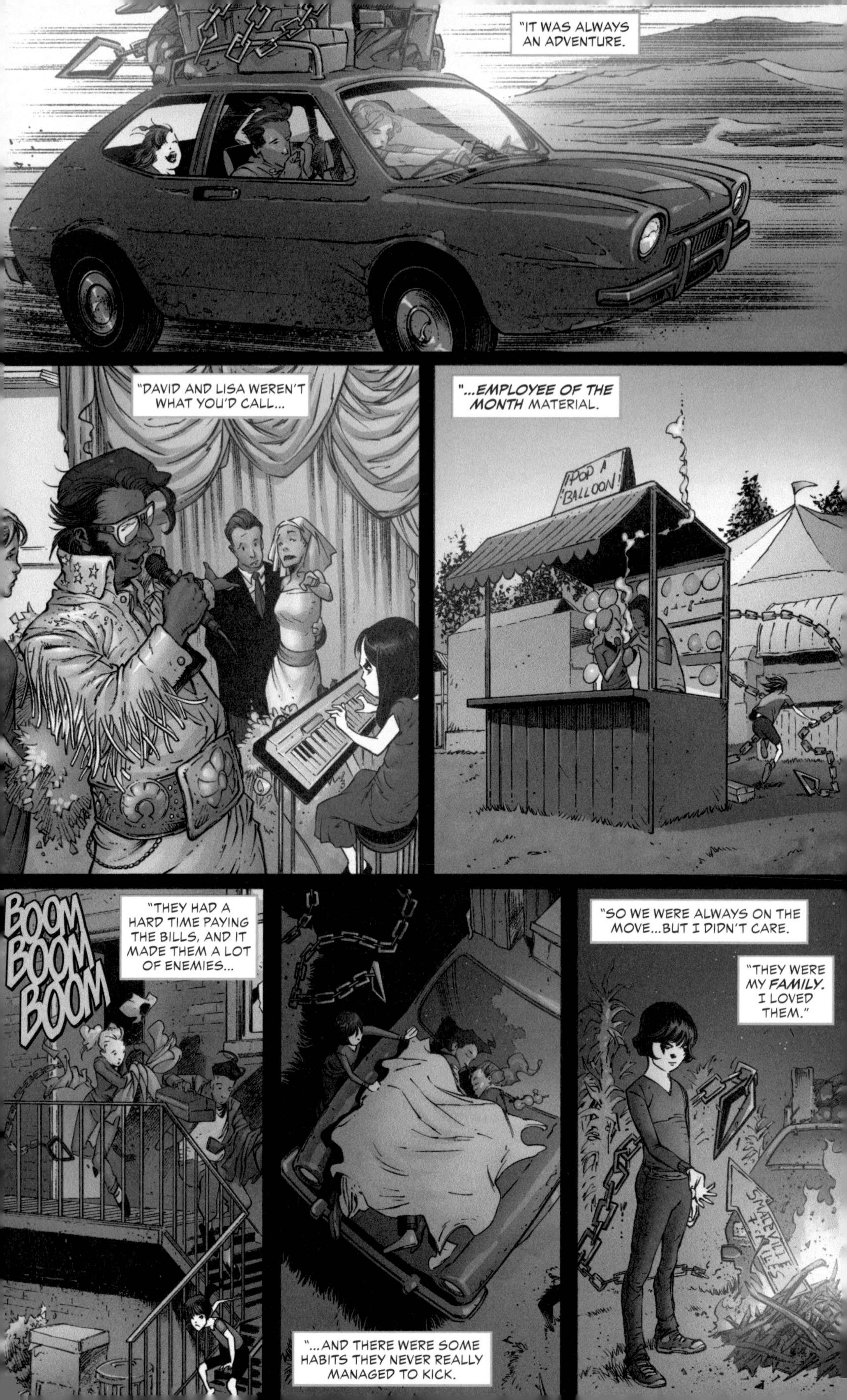
"IT WAS ALWAYS AN ADVENTURE.
"DAVID AND LISA WEREN'T WHAT YOU'D CALL...
"...*EMPLOYEE OF THE MONTH* MATERIAL.
POP A BALLOON!
BOOM BOOM BOOM
"THEY HAD A HARD TIME PAYING THE BILLS, AND IT MADE THEM A LOT OF ENEMIES...
"...AND THERE WERE SOME HABITS THEY NEVER REALLY MANAGED TO KICK.
"SO WE WERE ALWAYS ON THE MOVE...BUT I DIDN'T CARE.
"THEY WERE MY *FAMILY.* I LOVED THEM."
SMALLVILLE

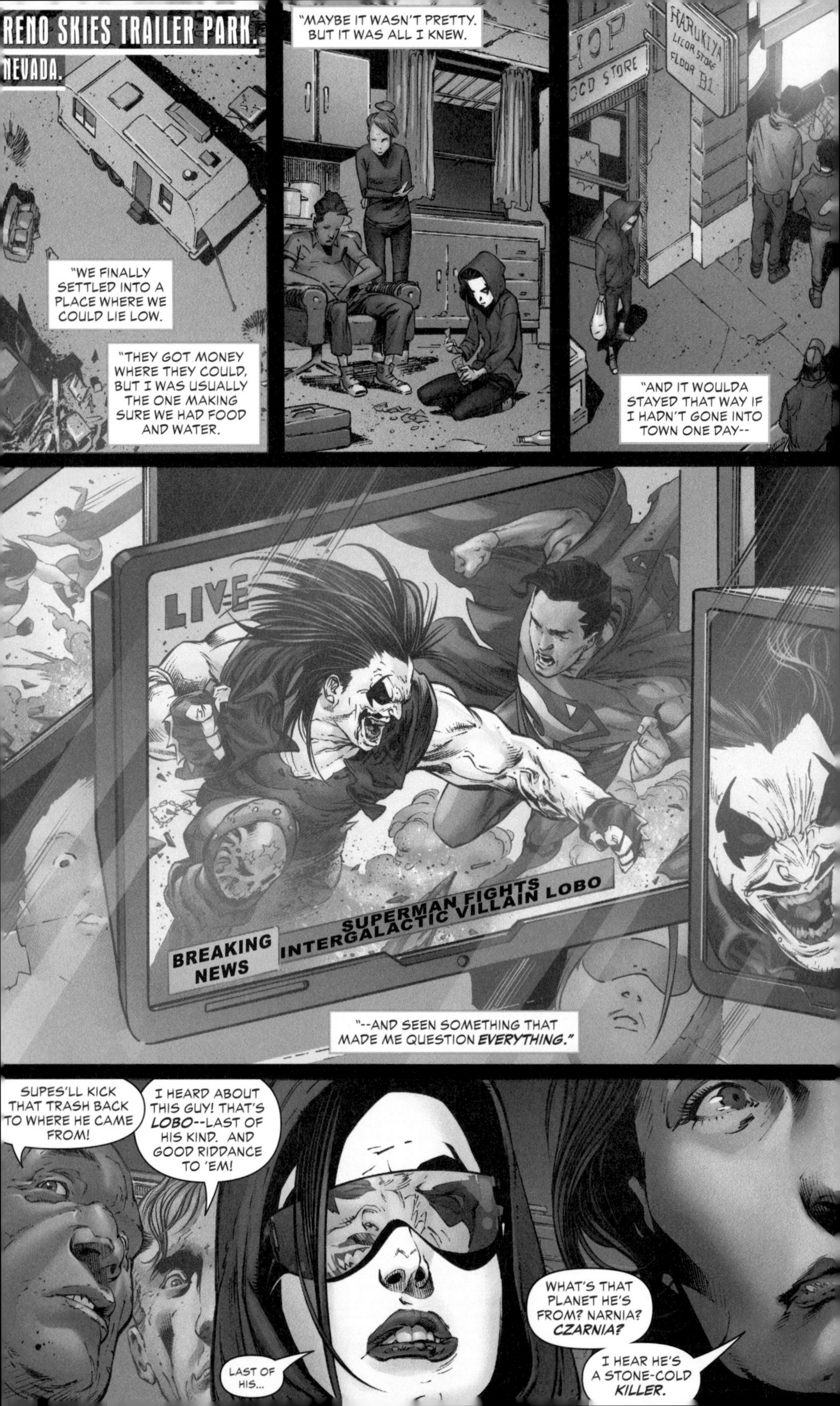

RENO SKIES TRAILER PARK.
NEVADA.
"WE FINALLY SETTLED INTO A PLACE WHERE WE COULD LIE LOW.
"THEY GOT MONEY WHERE THEY COULD, BUT I WAS USUALLY THE ONE MAKING SURE WE HAD FOOD AND WATER.
"MAYBE IT WASN'T PRETTY. BUT IT WAS ALL I KNEW.
HARUKIYA LICOR STORE FLOOR B1
"AND IT WOULDA STAYED THAT WAY IF I HADN'T GONE INTO TOWN ONE DAY--
LIVE
BREAKING NEWS
SUPERMAN FIGHTS INTERGALACTIC VILLAIN LOBO
"--AND SEEN SOMETHING THAT MADE ME QUESTION *EVERYTHING.*"
SUPES'LL KICK THAT TRASH BACK TO WHERE HE CAME FROM!
I HEARD ABOUT THIS GUY! THAT'S *LOBO*--LAST OF HIS KIND. AND GOOD RIDDANCE TO 'EM!
LAST OF HIS...
WHAT'S THAT PLANET HE'S FROM? NARNIA? *CZARNIA?*
I HEAR HE'S A STONE-COLD *KILLER.*

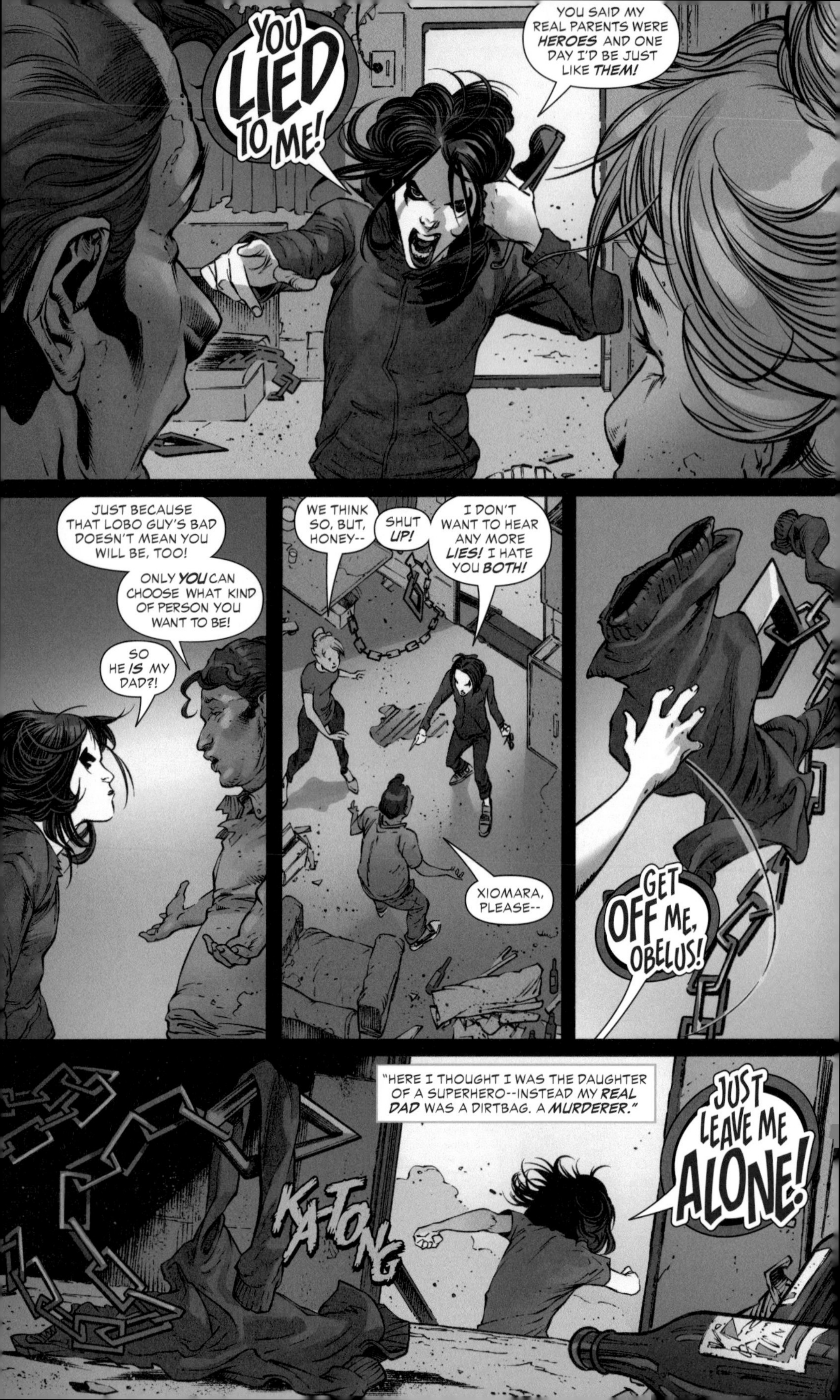
YOU LIED TO ME!
YOU SAID MY REAL PARENTS WERE HEROES AND ONE DAY I'D BE JUST LIKE THEM!
JUST BECAUSE THAT LOBO GUY'S BAD DOESN'T MEAN YOU WILL BE, TOO!
ONLY YOU CAN CHOOSE WHAT KIND OF PERSON YOU WANT TO BE!
SO HE IS MY DAD?!
WE THINK SO, BUT, HONEY--
SHUT UP!
I DON'T WANT TO HEAR ANY MORE LIES! I HATE YOU BOTH!
XIOMARA, PLEASE--
GET OFF ME, OBELUS!
"HERE I THOUGHT I WAS THE DAUGHTER OF A SUPERHERO--INSTEAD MY REAL DAD WAS A DIRTBAG. A MURDERER."
JUST LEAVE ME ALONE!
KA-TONG

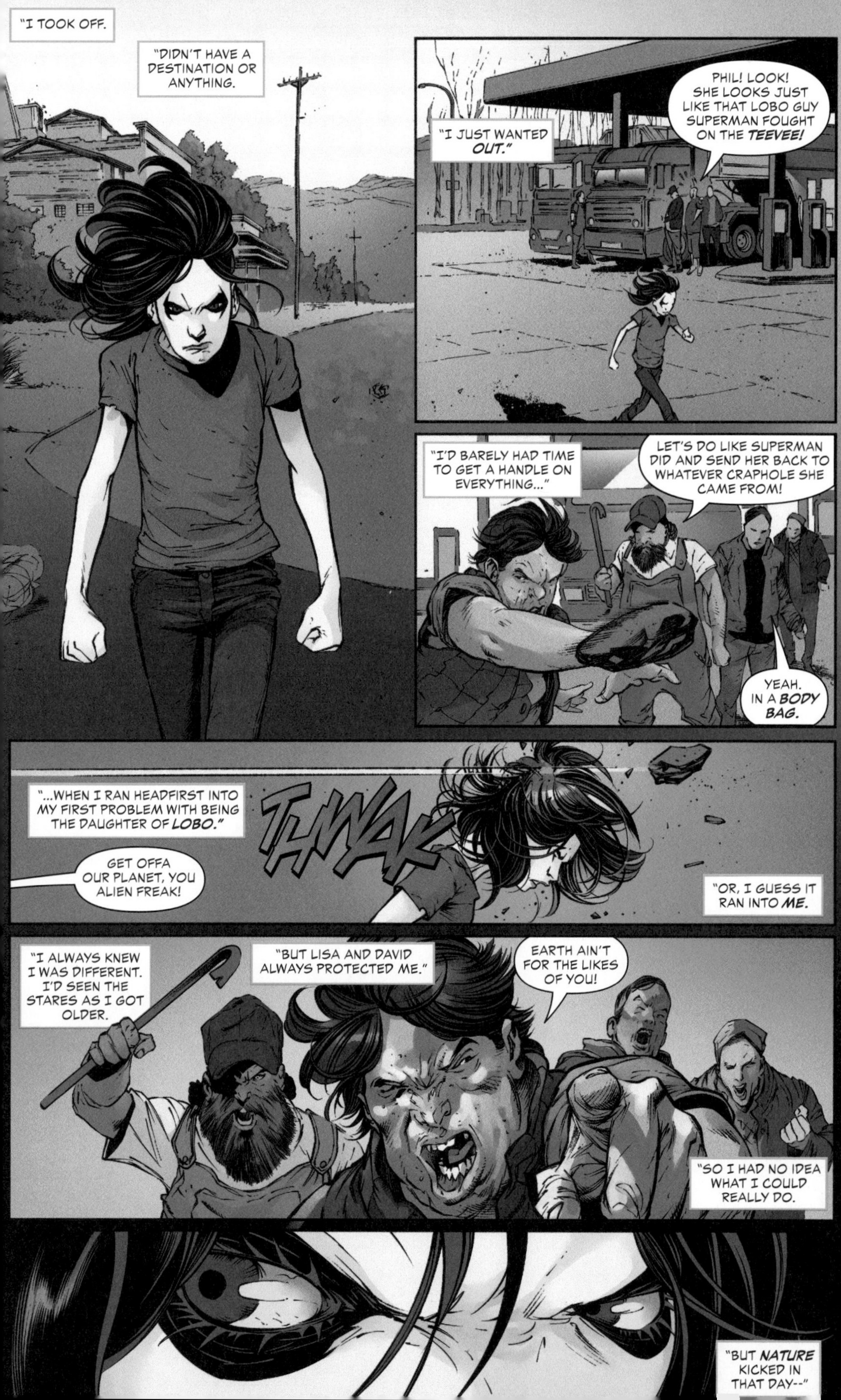
"I TOOK OFF.
"DIDN'T HAVE A DESTINATION OR ANYTHING.
"I JUST WANTED OUT."
PHIL! LOOK! SHE LOOKS JUST LIKE THAT LOBO GUY SUPERMAN FOUGHT ON THE TEEVEE!
"I'D BARELY HAD TIME TO GET A HANDLE ON EVERYTHING..."
LET'S DO LIKE SUPERMAN DID AND SEND HER BACK TO WHATEVER CRAPHOLE SHE CAME FROM!
YEAH. IN A BODY BAG.
"...WHEN I RAN HEADFIRST INTO MY FIRST PROBLEM WITH BEING THE DAUGHTER OF LOBO."
THWAK
GET OFFA OUR PLANET, YOU ALIEN FREAK!
"OR, I GUESS IT RAN INTO ME.
"I ALWAYS KNEW I WAS DIFFERENT. I'D SEEN THE STARES AS I GOT OLDER.
"BUT LISA AND DAVID ALWAYS PROTECTED ME."
EARTH AIN'T FOR THE LIKES OF YOU!
"SO I HAD NO IDEA WHAT I COULD REALLY DO.
"BUT NATURE KICKED IN THAT DAY--"

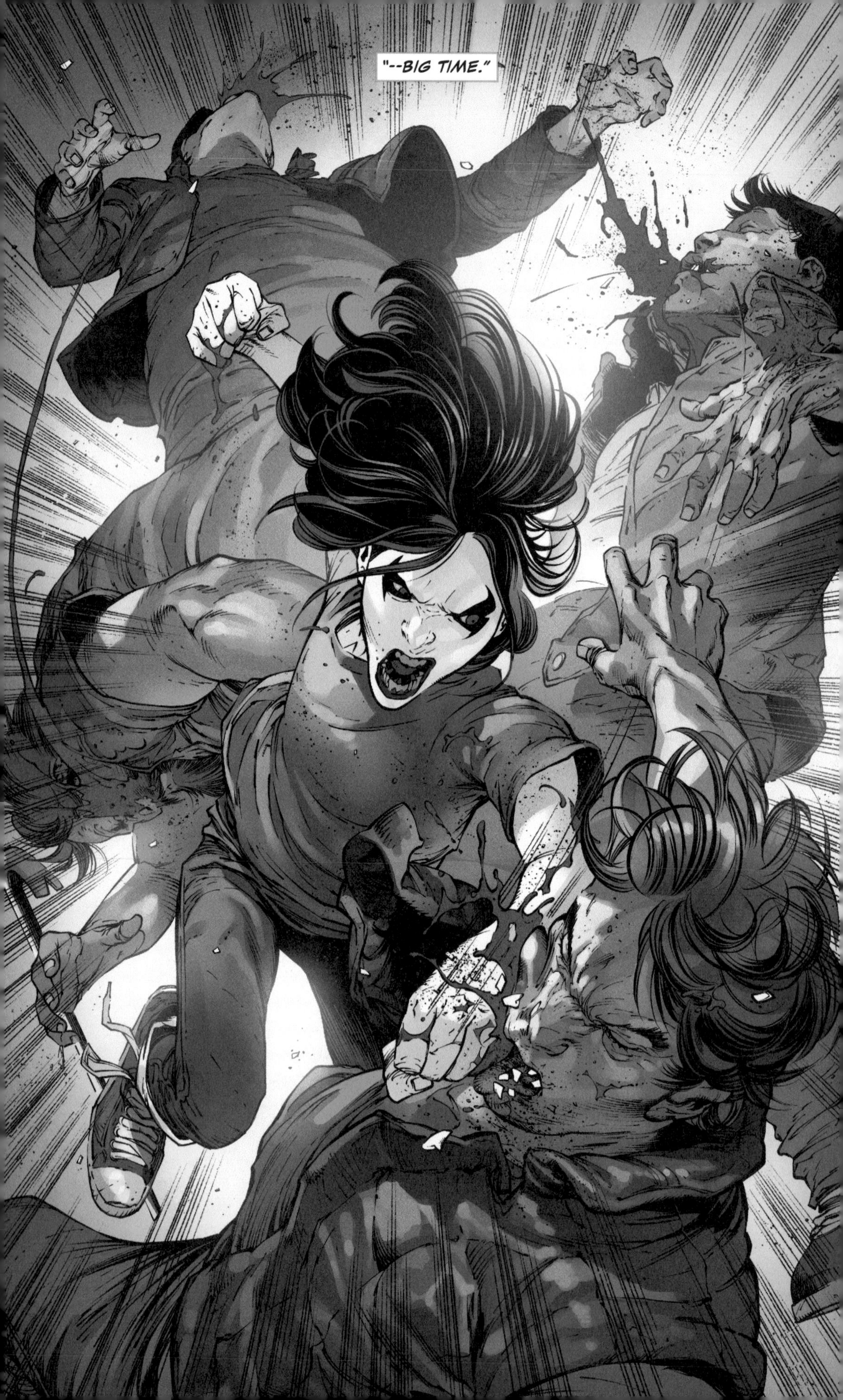
"--BIG TIME."

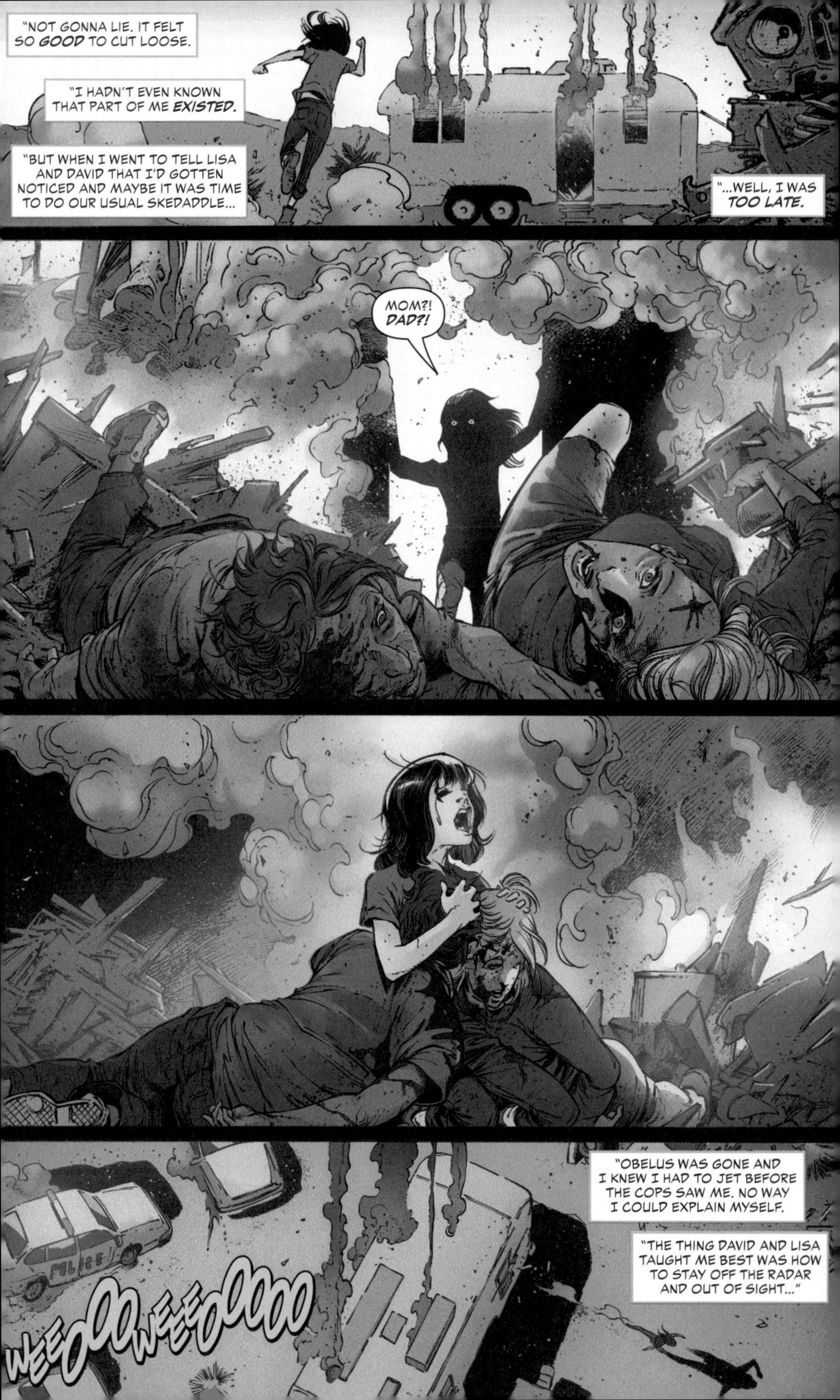
"NOT GONNA LIE. IT FELT SO *GOOD* TO CUT LOOSE.
"I HADN'T EVEN KNOWN THAT PART OF ME *EXISTED.*
"BUT WHEN I WENT TO TELL LISA AND DAVID THAT I'D GOTTEN NOTICED AND MAYBE IT WAS TIME TO DO OUR USUAL SKEDADDLE...
"...WELL, I WAS *TOO LATE.*
MOM?! *DAD?!*
"OBELUS WAS GONE AND I KNEW I HAD TO JET BEFORE THE COPS SAW ME. NO WAY I COULD EXPLAIN MYSELF.
"THE THING DAVID AND LISA TAUGHT ME BEST WAS HOW TO STAY OFF THE RADAR AND OUT OF SIGHT..."
WEEOOOWEEOOOOO

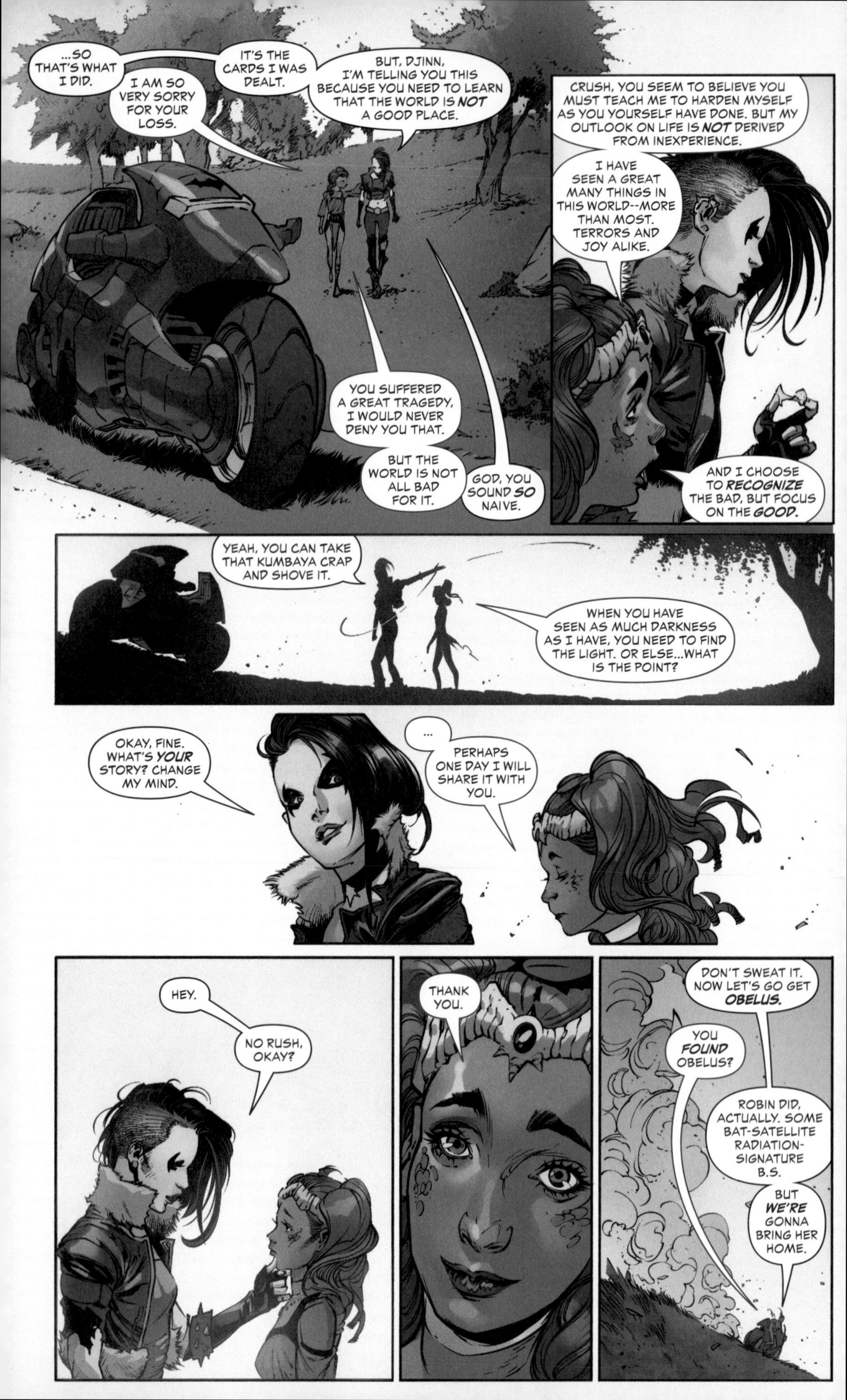

...SO THAT'S WHAT I DID.
IT'S THE CARDS I WAS DEALT.
I AM SO VERY SORRY FOR YOUR LOSS.
BUT, DJINN, I'M TELLING YOU THIS BECAUSE YOU NEED TO LEARN THAT THE WORLD IS NOT A GOOD PLACE.
YOU SUFFERED A GREAT TRAGEDY, I WOULD NEVER DENY YOU THAT.
BUT THE WORLD IS NOT ALL BAD FOR IT.
GOD, YOU SOUND SO NAIVE.
CRUSH, YOU SEEM TO BELIEVE YOU MUST TEACH ME TO HARDEN MYSELF AS YOU YOURSELF HAVE DONE. BUT MY OUTLOOK ON LIFE IS NOT DERIVED FROM INEXPERIENCE.
I HAVE SEEN A GREAT MANY THINGS IN THIS WORLD--MORE THAN MOST. TERRORS AND JOY ALIKE.
AND I CHOOSE TO RECOGNIZE THE BAD, BUT FOCUS ON THE GOOD.
YEAH, YOU CAN TAKE THAT KUMBAYA CRAP AND SHOVE IT.
WHEN YOU HAVE SEEN AS MUCH DARKNESS AS I HAVE, YOU NEED TO FIND THE LIGHT. OR ELSE...WHAT IS THE POINT?
OKAY, FINE. WHAT'S YOUR STORY? CHANGE MY MIND.
...
PERHAPS ONE DAY I WILL SHARE IT WITH YOU.
HEY.
NO RUSH, OKAY?
THANK YOU.
DON'T SWEAT IT. NOW LET'S GO GET OBELUS.
YOU FOUND OBELUS?
ROBIN DID, ACTUALLY. SOME BAT-SATELLITE RADIATION-SIGNATURE B.S.
BUT WE'RE GONNA BRING HER HOME.

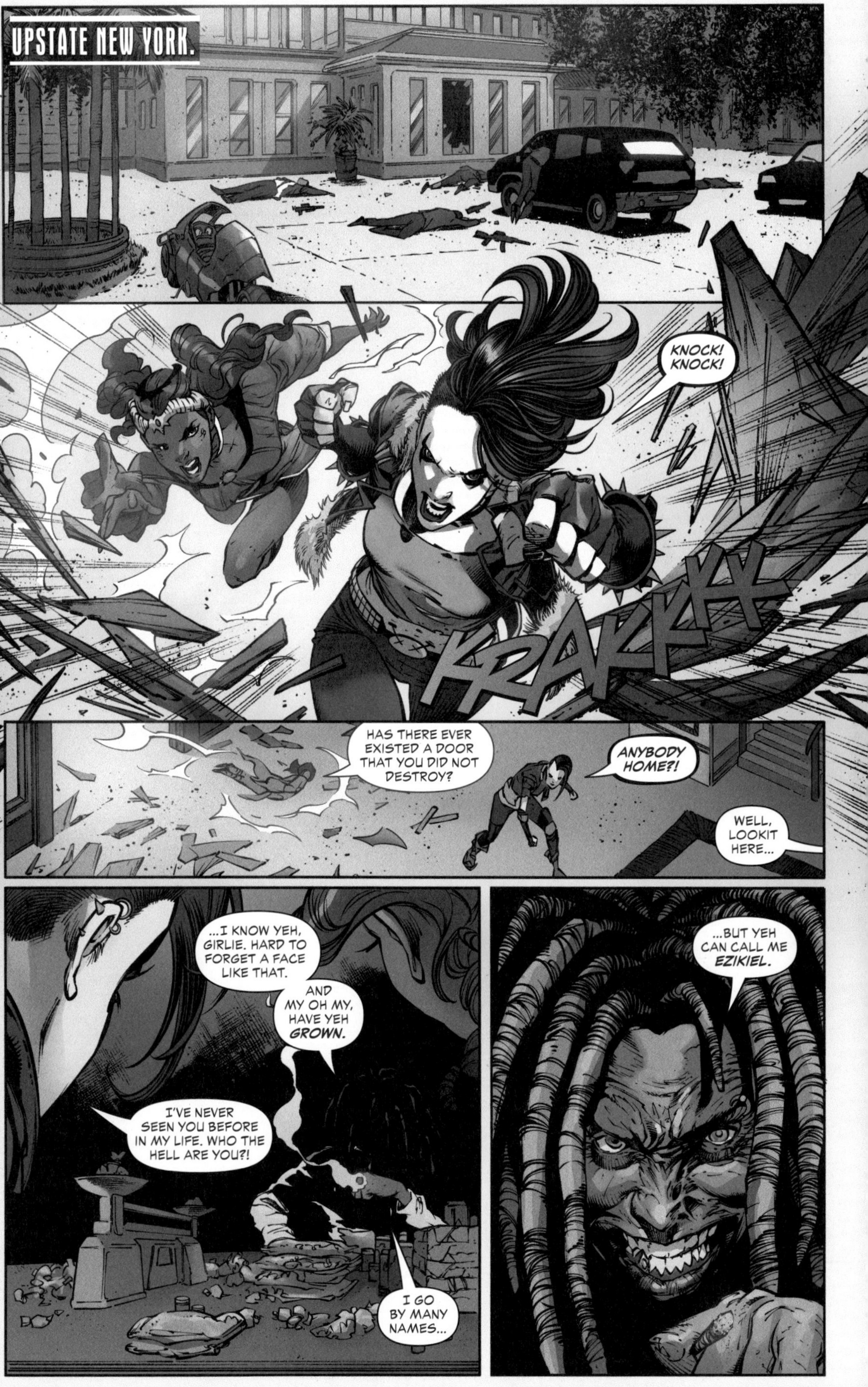
UPSTATE NEW YORK.
KNOCK! KNOCK!
KRAKKK
HAS THERE EVER EXISTED A DOOR THAT YOU DID NOT DESTROY?
ANYBODY HOME?!
WELL, LOOKIT HERE...
...I KNOW YEH, GIRLIE. HARD TO FORGET A FACE LIKE THAT.
AND MY OH MY, HAVE YEH GROWN.
I'VE NEVER SEEN YOU BEFORE IN MY LIFE. WHO THE HELL ARE YOU?!
I GO BY MANY NAMES...
...BUT YEH CAN CALL ME EZIKIEL.

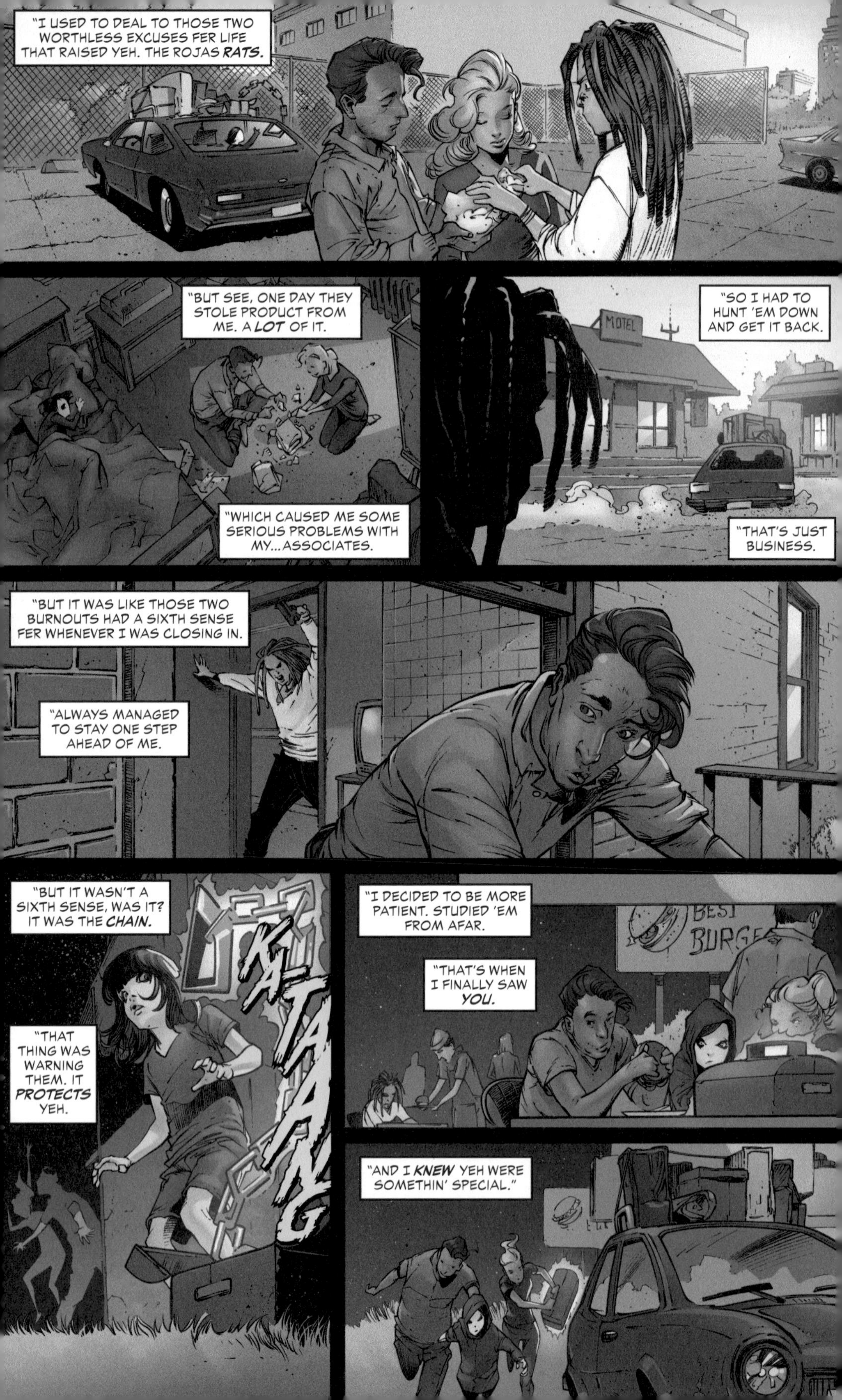
"I USED TO DEAL TO THOSE TWO WORTHLESS EXCUSES FER LIFE THAT RAISED YEH. THE ROJAS RATS.
"BUT SEE, ONE DAY THEY STOLE PRODUCT FROM ME. A LOT OF IT.
"WHICH CAUSED ME SOME SERIOUS PROBLEMS WITH MY...ASSOCIATES.
"SO I HAD TO HUNT 'EM DOWN AND GET IT BACK.
MOTEL
"THAT'S JUST BUSINESS.
"BUT IT WAS LIKE THOSE TWO BURNOUTS HAD A SIXTH SENSE FER WHENEVER I WAS CLOSING IN.
"ALWAYS MANAGED TO STAY ONE STEP AHEAD OF ME.
"BUT IT WASN'T A SIXTH SENSE, WAS IT? IT WAS THE CHAIN.
KA-TANG
"THAT THING WAS WARNING THEM. IT PROTECTS YEH.
"I DECIDED TO BE MORE PATIENT. STUDIED 'EM FROM AFAR.
BEST BURG
"THAT'S WHEN I FINALLY SAW YOU.
"AND I KNEW YEH WERE SOMETHIN' SPECIAL."

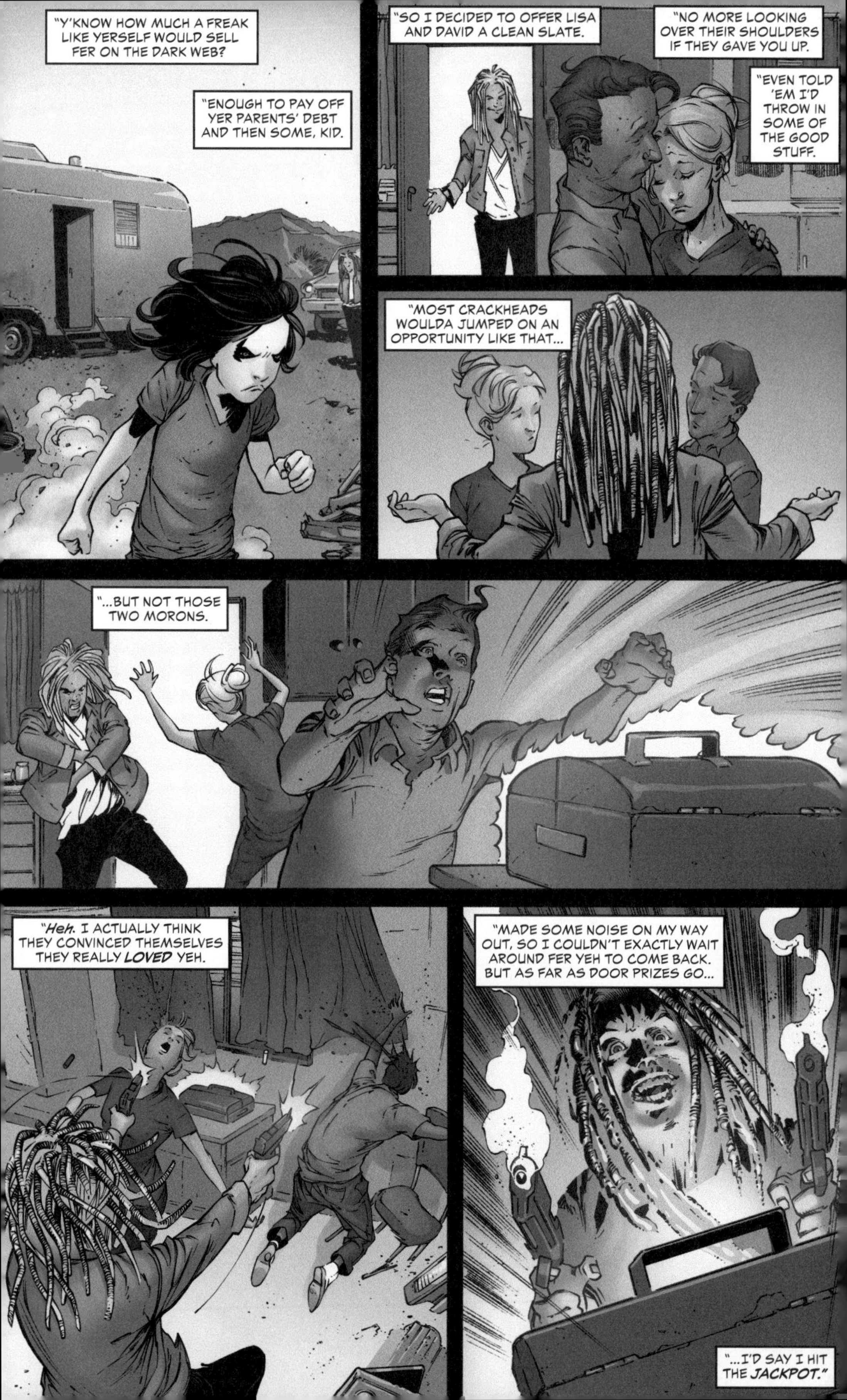
"Y'KNOW HOW MUCH A FREAK LIKE YERSELF WOULD SELL FER ON THE DARK WEB?
"ENOUGH TO PAY OFF YER PARENTS' DEBT AND THEN SOME, KID.
"SO I DECIDED TO OFFER LISA AND DAVID A CLEAN SLATE.
"NO MORE LOOKING OVER THEIR SHOULDERS IF THEY GAVE YOU UP.
"EVEN TOLD 'EM I'D THROW IN SOME OF THE GOOD STUFF.
"MOST CRACKHEADS WOULDA JUMPED ON AN OPPORTUNITY LIKE THAT...
"...BUT NOT THOSE TWO MORONS.
"*Heh.* I ACTUALLY THINK THEY CONVINCED THEMSELVES THEY REALLY ***LOVED*** YEH.
"MADE SOME NOISE ON MY WAY OUT, SO I COULDN'T EXACTLY WAIT AROUND FER YEH TO COME BACK. BUT AS FAR AS DOOR PRIZES GO...
"...I'D SAY I HIT THE ***JACKPOT.***"

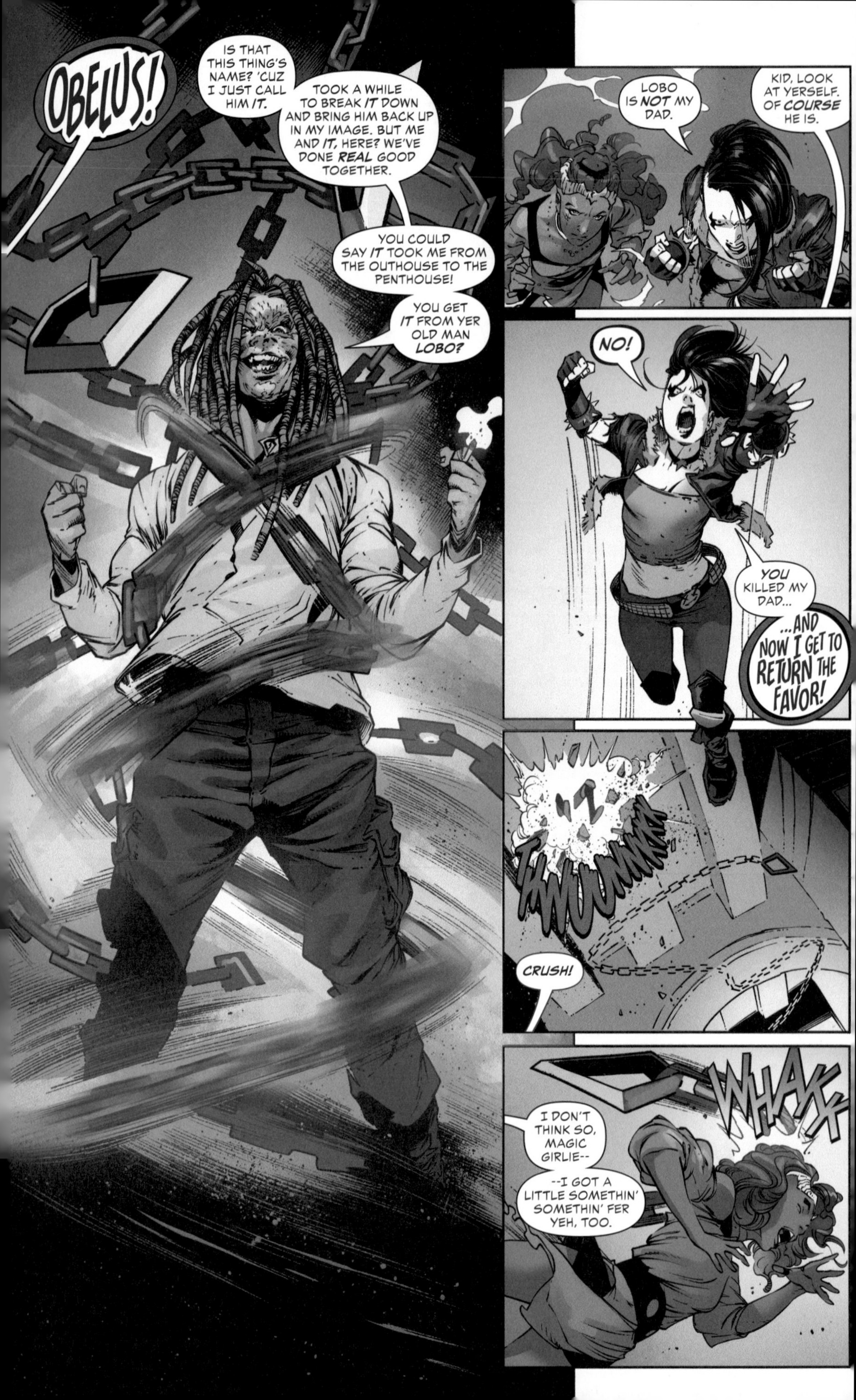
OBELUS!
IS THAT THIS THING'S NAME? 'CUZ I JUST CALL HIM IT.
TOOK A WHILE TO BREAK IT DOWN AND BRING HIM BACK UP IN MY IMAGE. BUT ME AND IT, HERE? WE'VE DONE REAL GOOD TOGETHER.
YOU COULD SAY IT TOOK ME FROM THE OUTHOUSE TO THE PENTHOUSE!
YOU GET IT FROM YER OLD MAN LOBO?
LOBO IS NOT MY DAD.
KID, LOOK AT YERSELF. OF COURSE HE IS.
NO!
YOU KILLED MY DAD...
...AND NOW I GET TO RETURN THE FAVOR!
THWOOMMM
CRUSH!
WHAKK
I DON'T THINK SO, MAGIC GIRLIE--
--I GOT A LITTLE SOMETHIN' SOMETHIN' FER YEH, TOO.

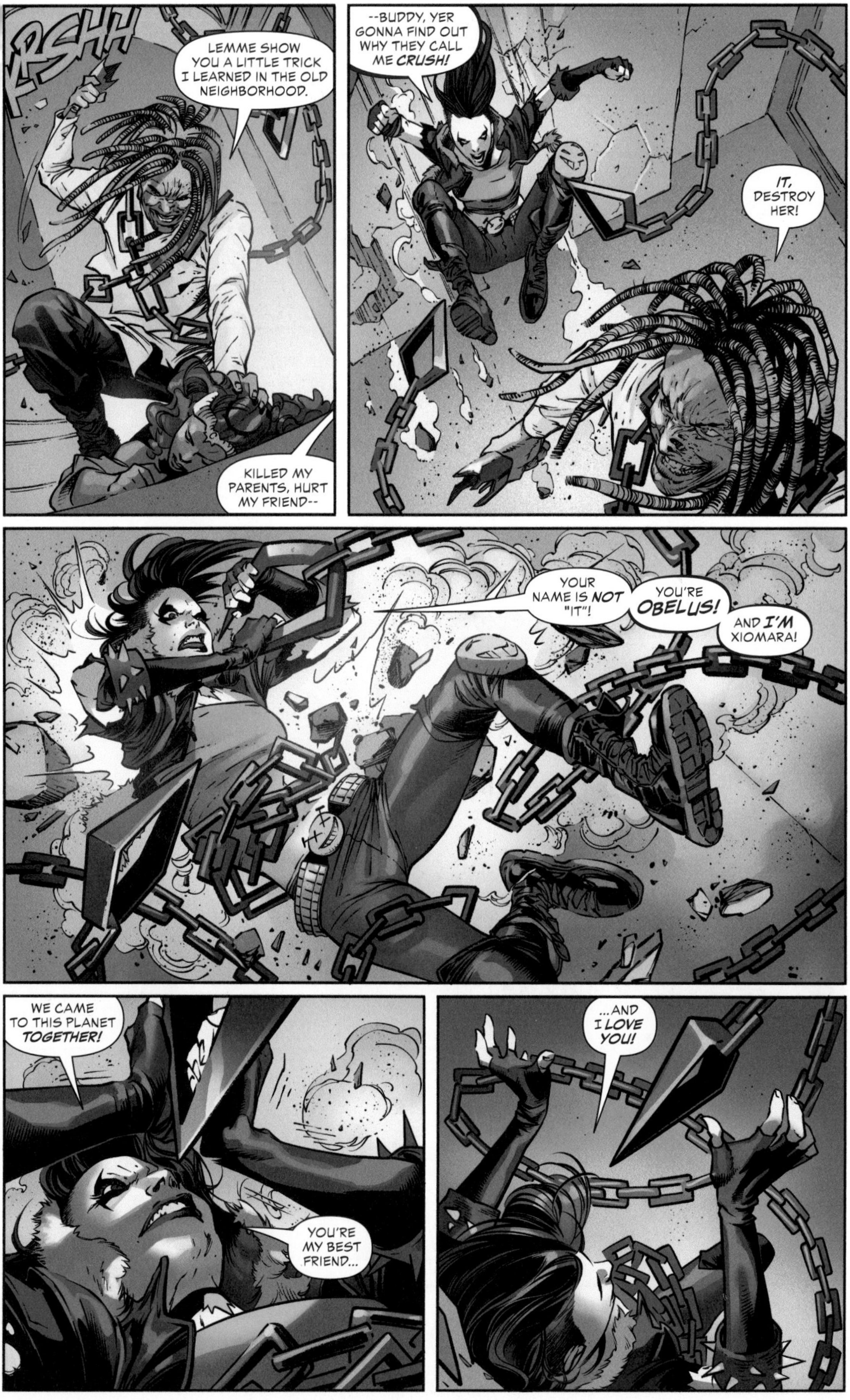
KRSHH
LEMME SHOW YOU A LITTLE TRICK I LEARNED IN THE OLD NEIGHBORHOOD.
KILLED MY PARENTS, HURT MY FRIEND--
--BUDDY, YER GONNA FIND OUT WHY THEY CALL ME CRUSH!
IT, DESTROY HER!
YOUR NAME IS NOT "IT"!
YOU'RE OBELUS!
AND I'M XIOMARA!
WE CAME TO THIS PLANET TOGETHER!
YOU'RE MY BEST FRIEND...
...AND I LOVE YOU!

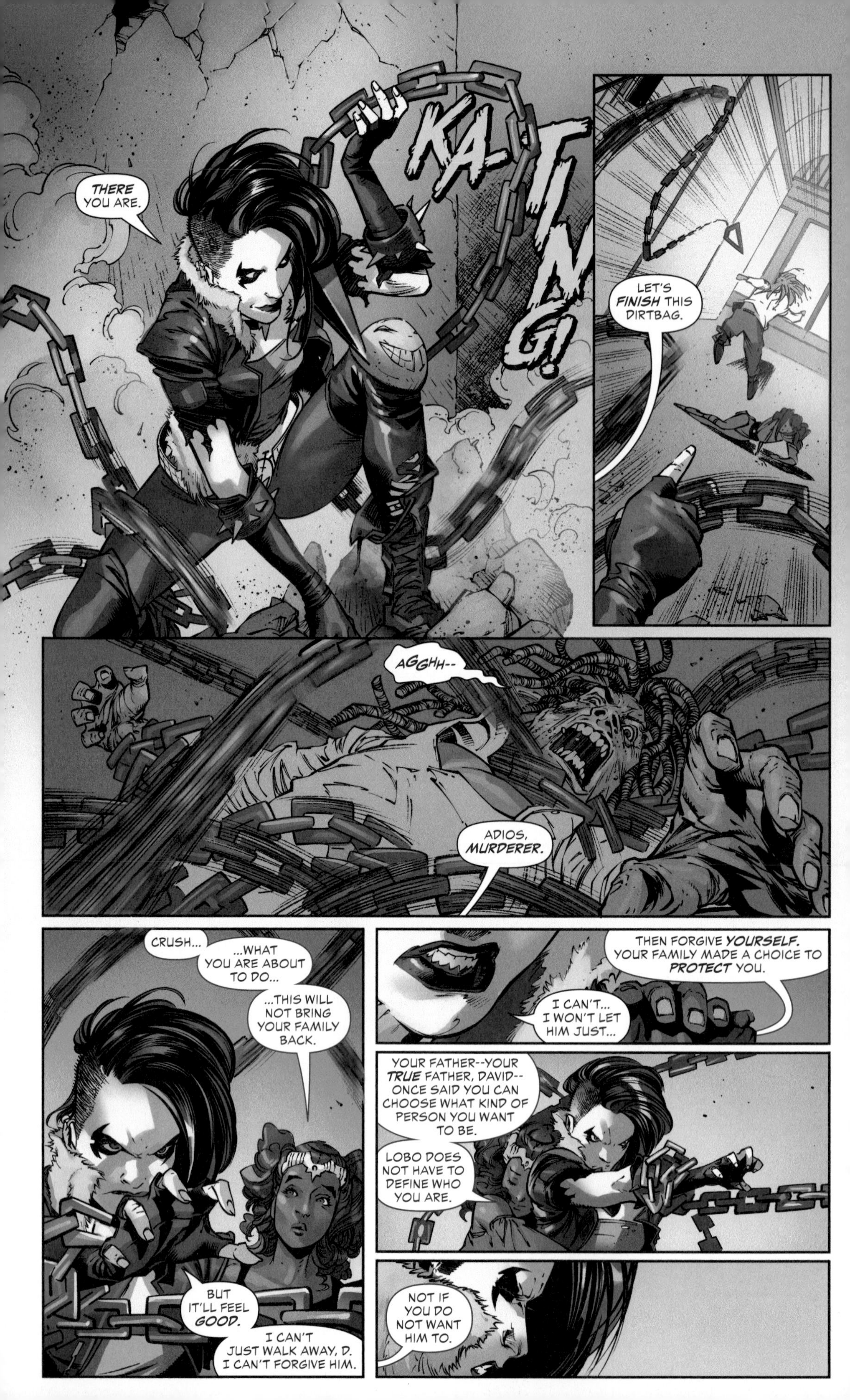
THERE YOU ARE.
KA-TING!
LET'S FINISH THIS DIRTBAG.
AGGHH--
ADIOS, MURDERER.
CRUSH...
...WHAT YOU ARE ABOUT TO DO...
...THIS WILL NOT BRING YOUR FAMILY BACK.
BUT IT'LL FEEL GOOD.
I CAN'T JUST WALK AWAY, D. I CAN'T FORGIVE HIM.
THEN FORGIVE YOURSELF. YOUR FAMILY MADE A CHOICE TO PROTECT YOU.
I CAN'T... I WON'T LET HIM JUST...
YOUR FATHER--YOUR TRUE FATHER, DAVID--ONCE SAID YOU CAN CHOOSE WHAT KIND OF PERSON YOU WANT TO BE.
LOBO DOES NOT HAVE TO DEFINE WHO YOU ARE.
NOT IF YOU DO NOT WANT HIM TO.

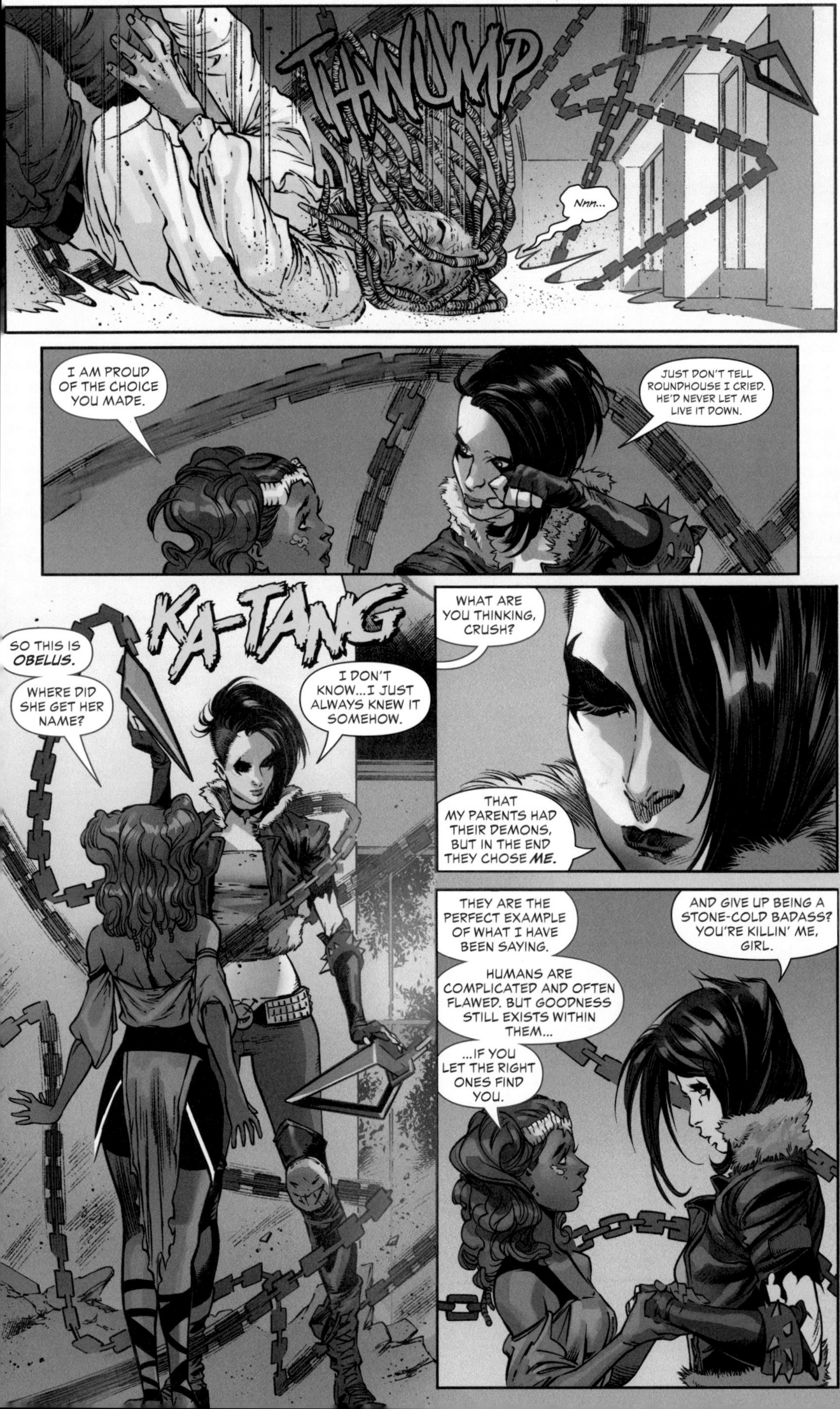
THWUMP
Nnn...
I AM PROUD OF THE CHOICE YOU MADE.
JUST DON'T TELL ROUNDHOUSE I CRIED. HE'D NEVER LET ME LIVE IT DOWN.
KA-TANG
SO THIS IS *OBELUS*.
WHERE DID SHE GET HER NAME?
I DON'T KNOW...I JUST ALWAYS KNEW IT SOMEHOW.
WHAT ARE YOU THINKING, CRUSH?
THAT MY PARENTS HAD THEIR DEMONS, BUT IN THE END THEY CHOSE *ME*.
THEY ARE THE PERFECT EXAMPLE OF WHAT I HAVE BEEN SAYING.
HUMANS ARE COMPLICATED AND OFTEN FLAWED. BUT GOODNESS STILL EXISTS WITHIN THEM...
...IF YOU LET THE RIGHT ONES FIND YOU.
AND GIVE UP BEING A STONE-COLD BADASS? YOU'RE KILLIN' ME, GIRL.

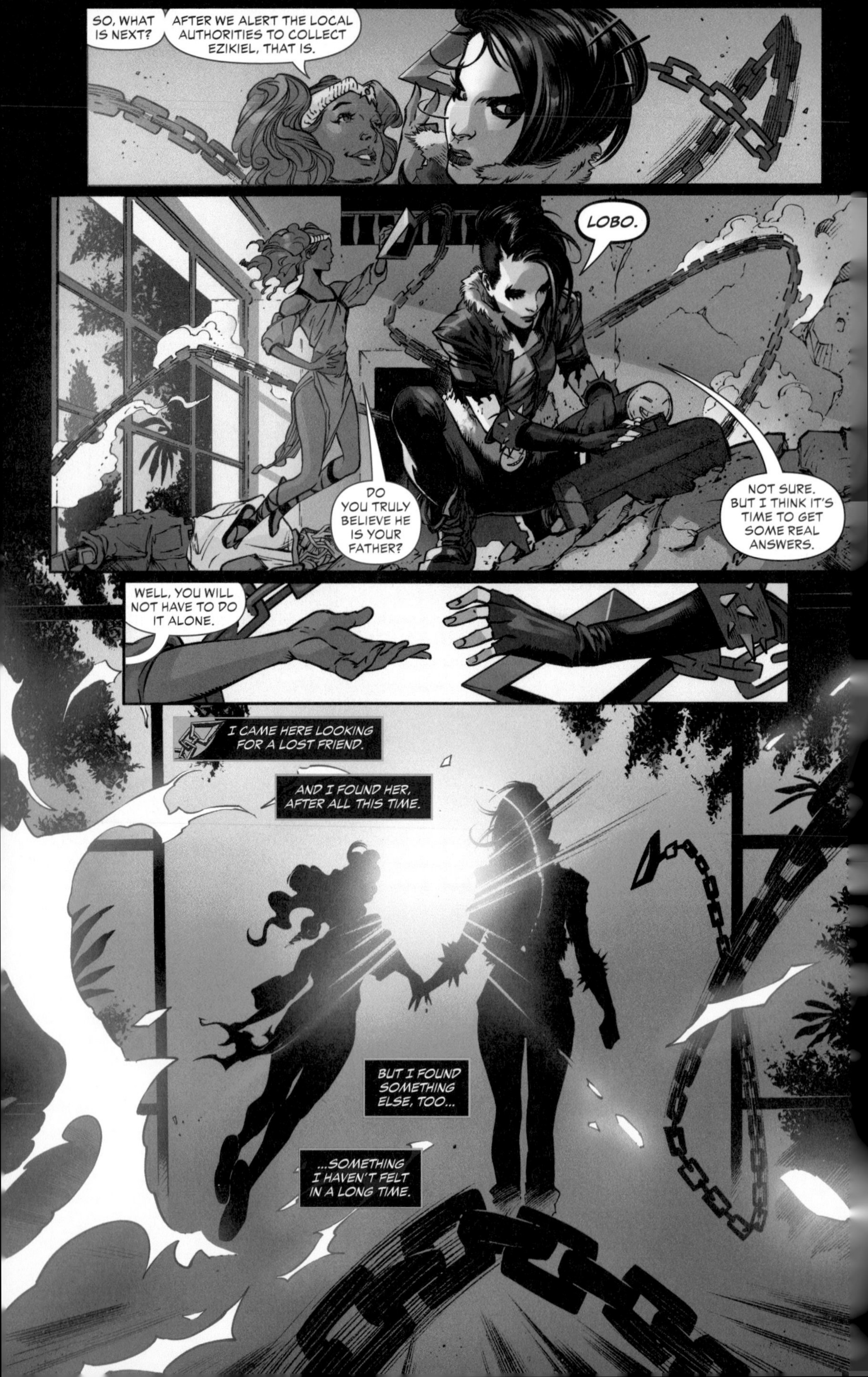
SO, WHAT IS NEXT?
AFTER WE ALERT THE LOCAL AUTHORITIES TO COLLECT EZIKIEL, THAT IS.
LOBO.
DO YOU TRULY BELIEVE HE IS YOUR FATHER?
NOT SURE. BUT I THINK IT'S TIME TO GET SOME REAL ANSWERS.
WELL, YOU WILL NOT HAVE TO DO IT ALONE.
I CAME HERE LOOKING FOR A LOST FRIEND.
AND I FOUND HER, AFTER ALL THIS TIME.
BUT I FOUND SOMETHING ELSE, TOO...
...SOMETHING I HAVEN'T FELT IN A LONG TIME.

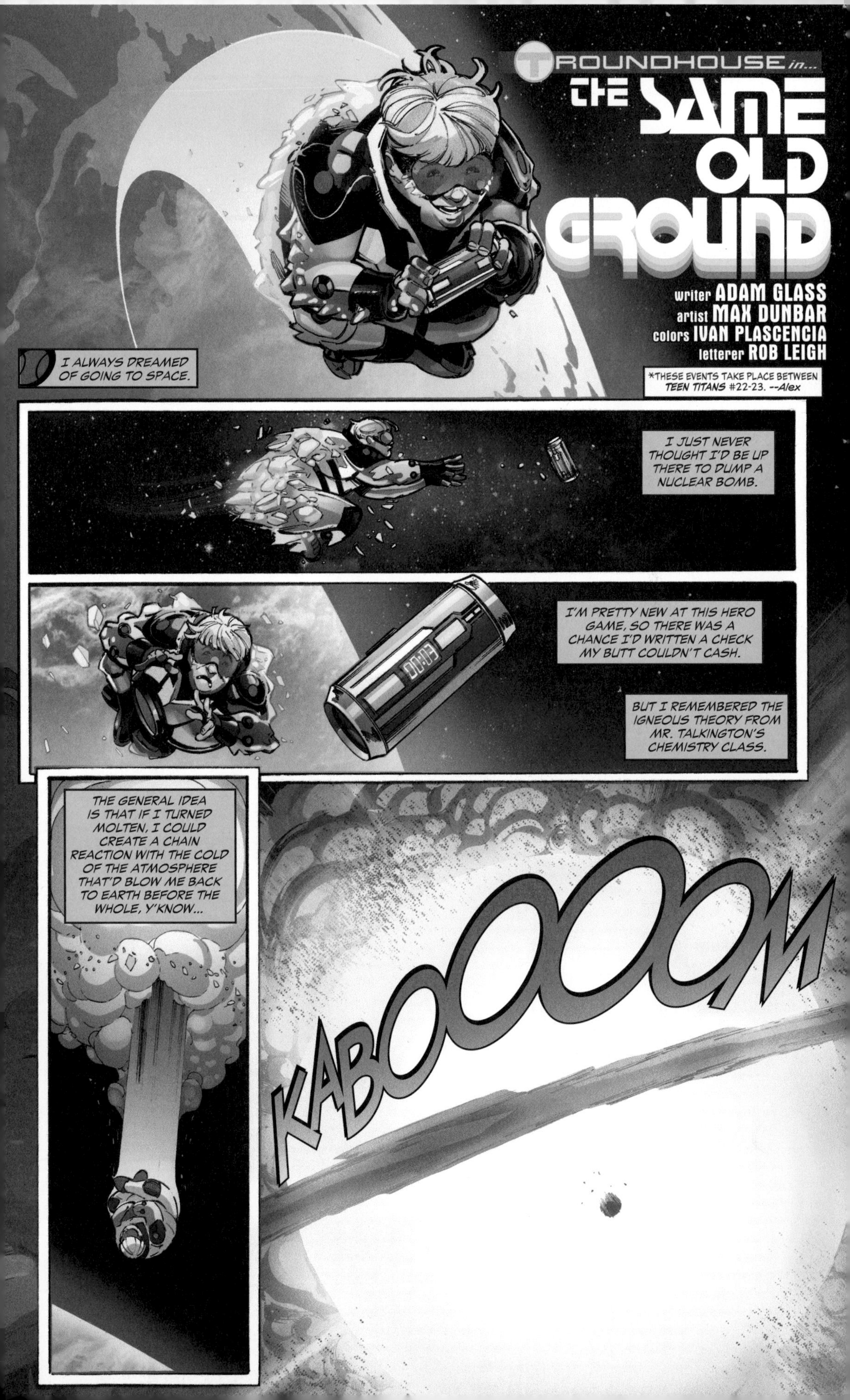
ROUNDHOUSE in...
THE SAME OLD GROUND
writer ADAM GLASS
artist MAX DUNBAR
colors IVAN PLASCENCIA
letterer ROB LEIGH
I ALWAYS DREAMED OF GOING TO SPACE.
*THESE EVENTS TAKE PLACE BETWEEN TEEN TITANS #22-23. --Alex
I JUST NEVER THOUGHT I'D BE UP THERE TO DUMP A NUCLEAR BOMB.
I'M PRETTY NEW AT THIS HERO GAME, SO THERE WAS A CHANCE I'D WRITTEN A CHECK MY BUTT COULDN'T CASH.
BUT I REMEMBERED THE IGNEOUS THEORY FROM MR. TALKINGTON'S CHEMISTRY CLASS.
THE GENERAL IDEA IS THAT IF I TURNED MOLTEN, I COULD CREATE A CHAIN REACTION WITH THE COLD OF THE ATMOSPHERE THAT'D BLOW ME BACK TO EARTH BEFORE THE WHOLE, Y'KNOW...
KABOOOOM

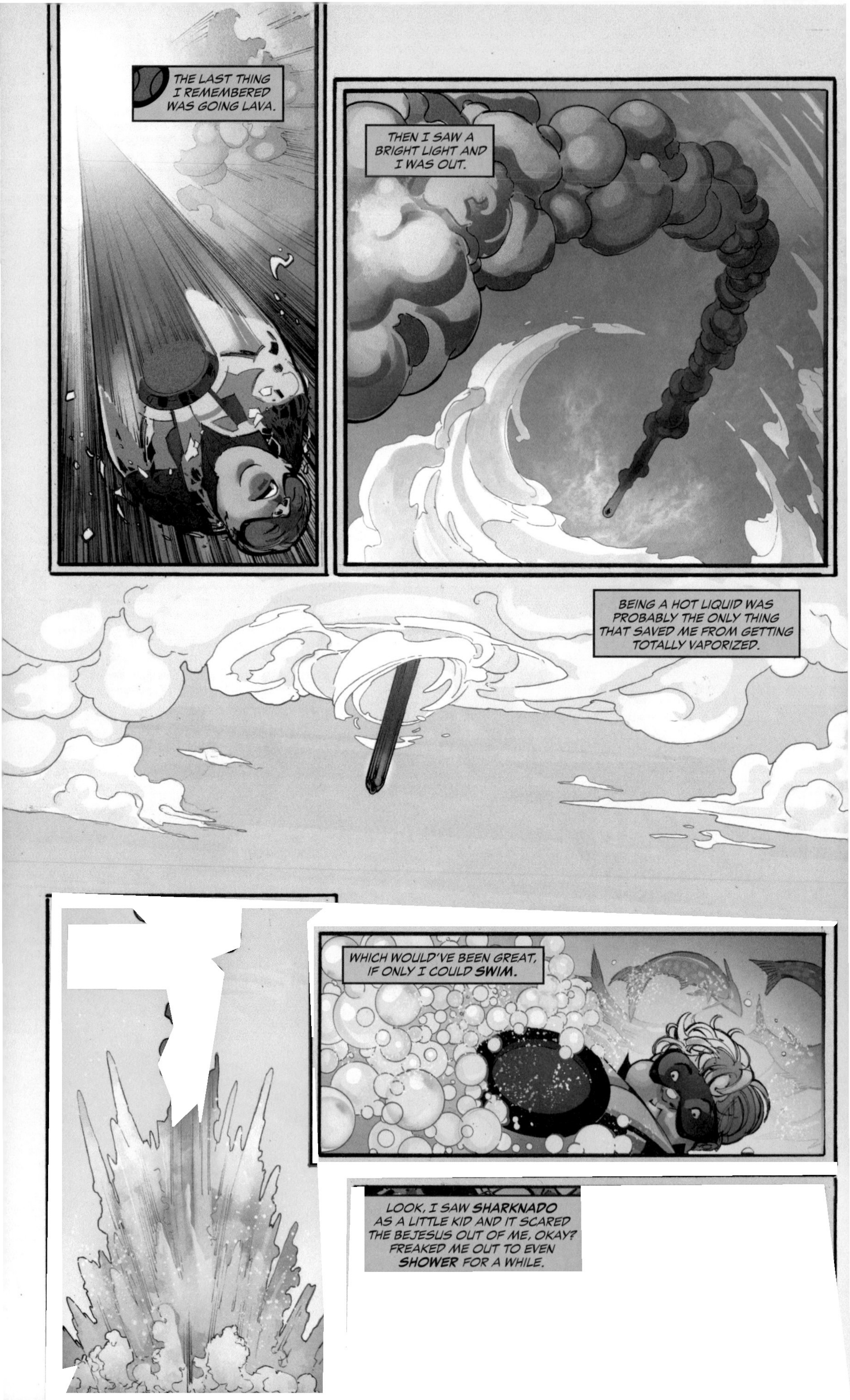
THE LAST THING I REMEMBERED WAS GOING LAVA.
THEN I SAW A BRIGHT LIGHT AND I WAS OUT.
BEING A HOT LIQUID WAS PROBABLY THE ONLY THING THAT SAVED ME FROM GETTING TOTALLY VAPORIZED.
WHICH WOULD'VE BEEN GREAT, IF ONLY I COULD SWIM.
LOOK, I SAW SHARKNADO AS A LITTLE KID AND IT SCARED THE BEJESUS OUT OF ME, OKAY? FREAKED ME OUT TO EVEN SHOWER FOR A WHILE.

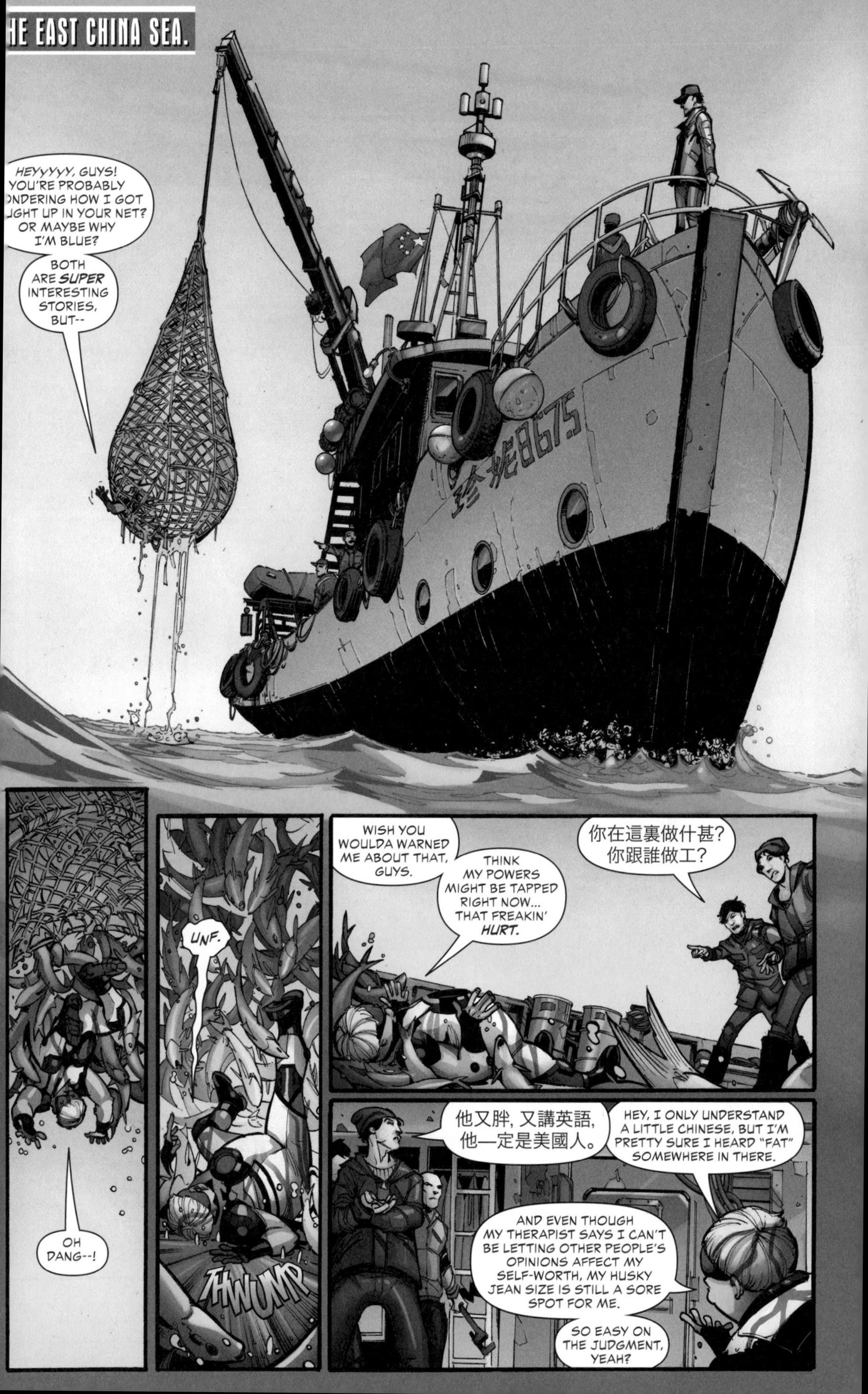
HE EAST CHINA SEA.
HEYYYYY, GUYS! YOU'RE PROBABLY ONDERING HOW I GOT UGHT UP IN YOUR NET? OR MAYBE WHY I'M BLUE?
BOTH ARE SUPER INTERESTING STORIES, BUT--
珍妮8675
OH DANG--!
UNF.
THWUMP
WISH YOU WOULDA WARNED ME ABOUT THAT, GUYS.
THINK MY POWERS MIGHT BE TAPPED RIGHT NOW... THAT FREAKIN' HURT.
你在這裏做什甚?
你跟誰做工?
他又胖, 又講英語,
他一定是美國人。
HEY, I ONLY UNDERSTAND A LITTLE CHINESE, BUT I'M PRETTY SURE I HEARD "FAT" SOMEWHERE IN THERE.
AND EVEN THOUGH MY THERAPIST SAYS I CAN'T BE LETTING OTHER PEOPLE'S OPINIONS AFFECT MY SELF-WORTH, MY HUSKY JEAN SIZE IS STILL A SORE SPOT FOR ME.
SO EASY ON THE JUDGMENT, YEAH?

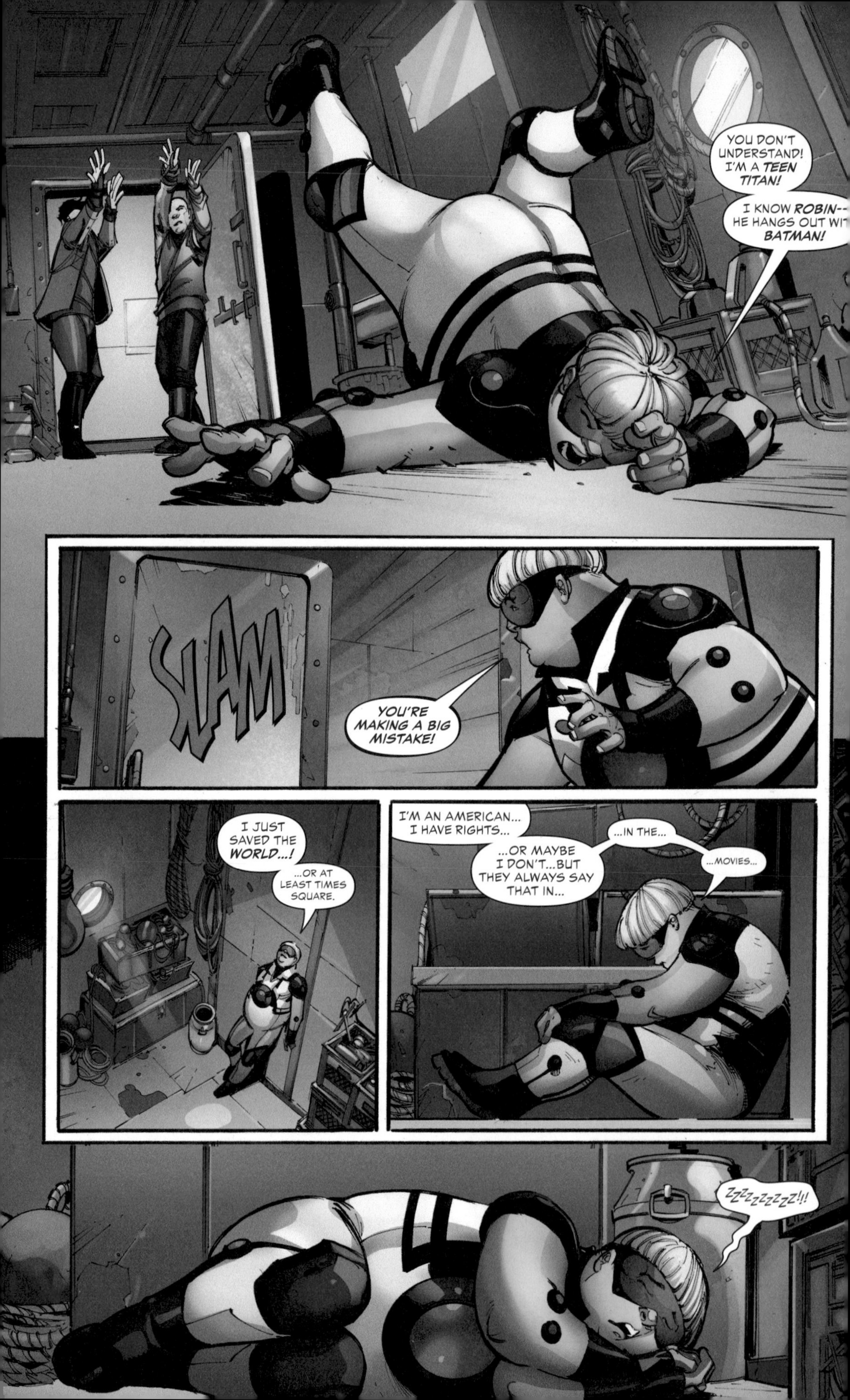
YOU DON'T UNDERSTAND! I'M A TEEN TITAN!
I KNOW ROBIN-- HE HANGS OUT WIT BATMAN!
SLAM
YOU'RE MAKING A BIG MISTAKE!
I JUST SAVED THE WORLD...!
...OR AT LEAST TIMES SQUARE.
I'M AN AMERICAN... I HAVE RIGHTS...
...OR MAYBE I DON'T...BUT THEY ALWAYS SAY THAT IN...
...IN THE...
...MOVIES...
ZZZZZZZZZZ!!!

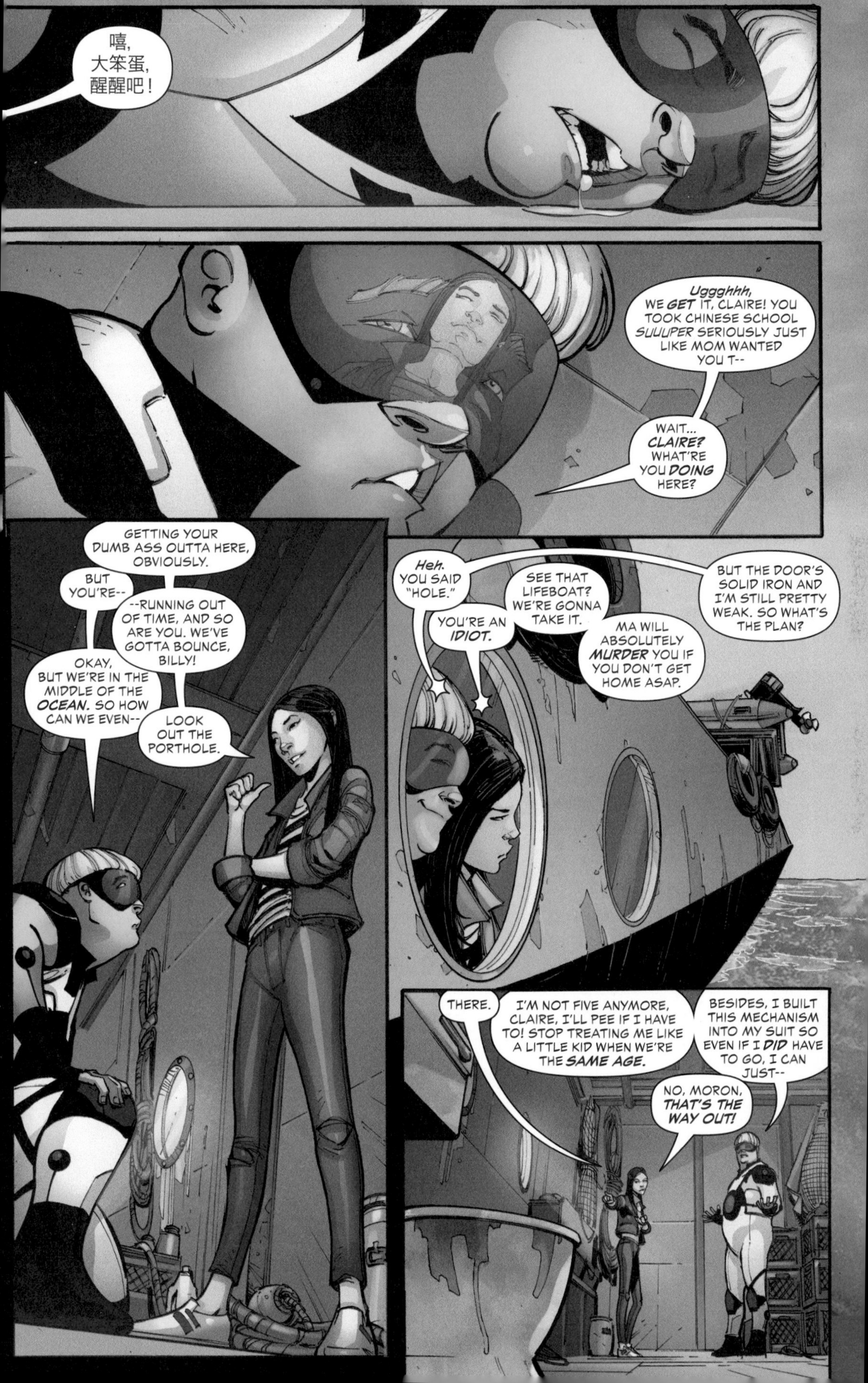

嘻,
大笨蛋,
醒醒吧!
Uggghhh, WE GET IT, CLAIRE! YOU TOOK CHINESE SCHOOL SUUUPER SERIOUSLY JUST LIKE MOM WANTED YOU T--
WAIT... CLAIRE? WHAT'RE YOU DOING HERE?
GETTING YOUR DUMB ASS OUTTA HERE, OBVIOUSLY.
BUT YOU'RE--
--RUNNING OUT OF TIME, AND SO ARE YOU. WE'VE GOTTA BOUNCE, BILLY!
OKAY, BUT WE'RE IN THE MIDDLE OF THE OCEAN. SO HOW CAN WE EVEN--
LOOK OUT THE PORTHOLE.
SEE THAT LIFEBOAT? WE'RE GONNA TAKE IT.
MA WILL ABSOLUTELY MURDER YOU IF YOU DON'T GET HOME ASAP.
BUT THE DOOR'S SOLID IRON AND I'M STILL PRETTY WEAK. SO WHAT'S THE PLAN?
Heh. YOU SAID "HOLE."
YOU'RE AN IDIOT.
THERE.
I'M NOT FIVE ANYMORE, CLAIRE, I'LL PEE IF I HAVE TO! STOP TREATING ME LIKE A LITTLE KID WHEN WE'RE THE SAME AGE.
BESIDES, I BUILT THIS MECHANISM INTO MY SUIT SO EVEN IF I DID HAVE TO GO, I CAN JUST--
NO, MORON, THAT'S THE WAY OUT!

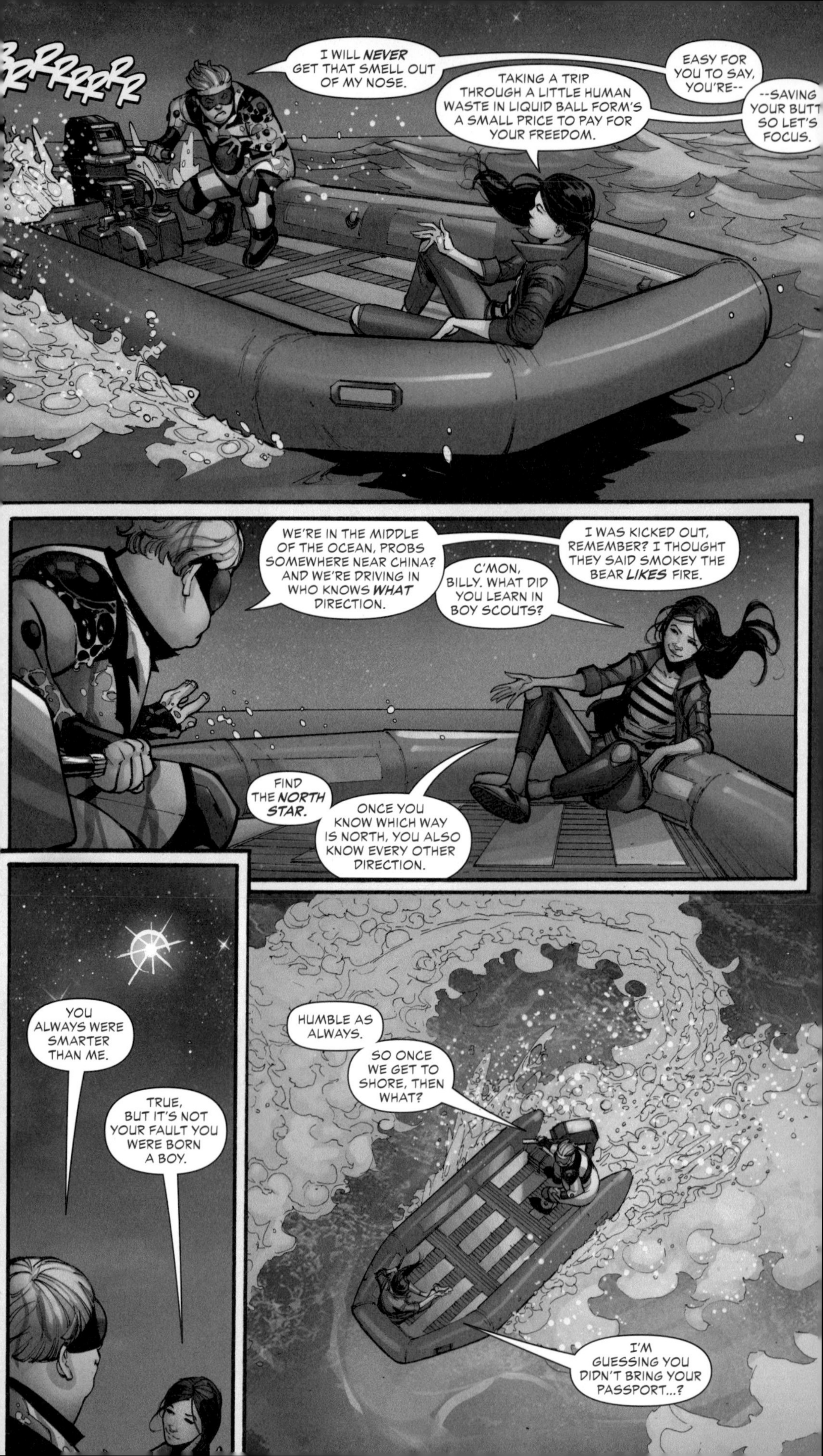
RRRRRRRR
I WILL NEVER GET THAT SMELL OUT OF MY NOSE.
TAKING A TRIP THROUGH A LITTLE HUMAN WASTE IN LIQUID BALL FORM'S A SMALL PRICE TO PAY FOR YOUR FREEDOM.
EASY FOR YOU TO SAY, YOU'RE--
--SAVING YOUR BUTT SO LET'S FOCUS.
WE'RE IN THE MIDDLE OF THE OCEAN, PROBS SOMEWHERE NEAR CHINA? AND WE'RE DRIVING IN WHO KNOWS WHAT DIRECTION.
C'MON, BILLY. WHAT DID YOU LEARN IN BOY SCOUTS?
I WAS KICKED OUT, REMEMBER? I THOUGHT THEY SAID SMOKEY THE BEAR LIKES FIRE.
FIND THE NORTH STAR.
ONCE YOU KNOW WHICH WAY IS NORTH, YOU ALSO KNOW EVERY OTHER DIRECTION.
YOU ALWAYS WERE SMARTER THAN ME.
TRUE, BUT IT'S NOT YOUR FAULT YOU WERE BORN A BOY.
HUMBLE AS ALWAYS.
SO ONCE WE GET TO SHORE, THEN WHAT?
I'M GUESSING YOU DIDN'T BRING YOUR PASSPORT...?

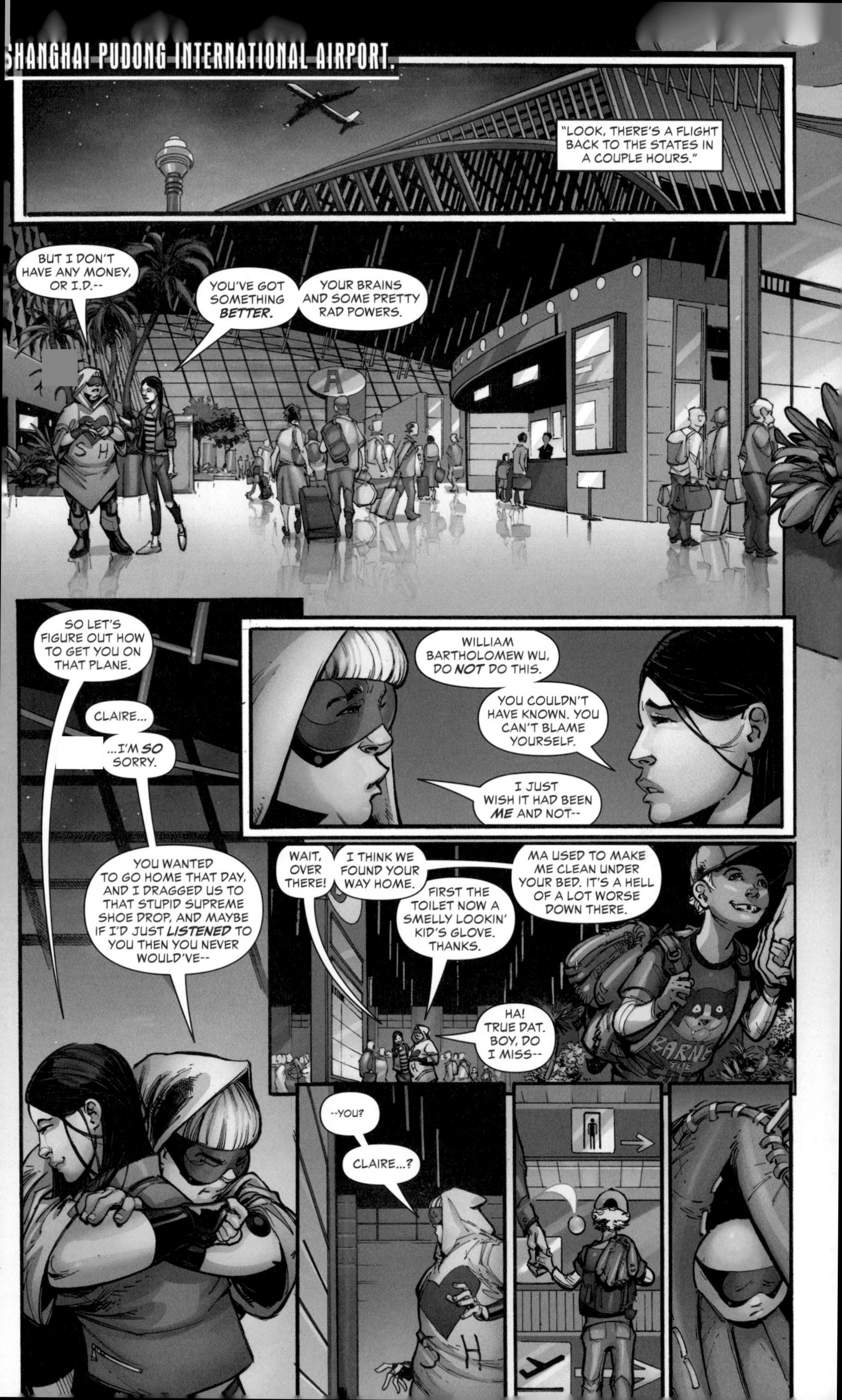
SHANGHAI PUDONG INTERNATIONAL AIRPORT.
"LOOK, THERE'S A FLIGHT BACK TO THE STATES IN A COUPLE HOURS."
BUT I DON'T HAVE ANY MONEY, OR I.D.--
YOU'VE GOT SOMETHING BETTER.
YOUR BRAINS AND SOME PRETTY RAD POWERS.
SO LET'S FIGURE OUT HOW TO GET YOU ON THAT PLANE.
WILLIAM BARTHOLOMEW WU, DO NOT DO THIS.
YOU COULDN'T HAVE KNOWN. YOU CAN'T BLAME YOURSELF.
I JUST WISH IT HAD BEEN ME AND NOT--
CLAIRE...
...I'M SO SORRY.
YOU WANTED TO GO HOME THAT DAY, AND I DRAGGED US TO THAT STUPID SUPREME SHOE DROP, AND MAYBE IF I'D JUST LISTENED TO YOU THEN YOU NEVER WOULD'VE--
WAIT, OVER THERE!
I THINK WE FOUND YOUR WAY HOME.
MA USED TO MAKE ME CLEAN UNDER YOUR BED. IT'S A HELL OF A LOT WORSE DOWN THERE.
FIRST THE TOILET NOW A SMELLY LOOKIN' KID'S GLOVE. THANKS.
HA! TRUE DAT. BOY, DO I MISS--
--YOU?
CLAIRE...?

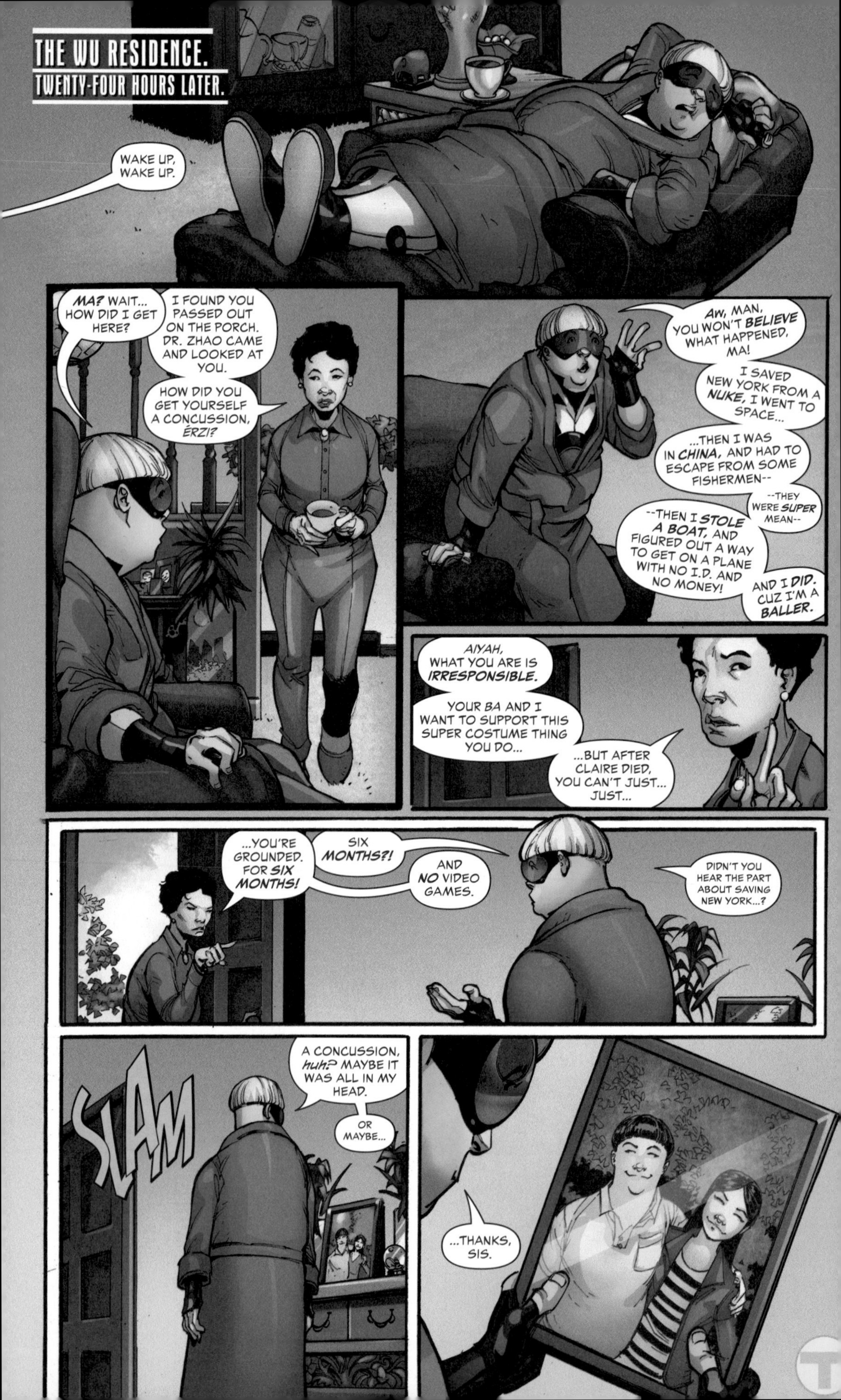
THE WU RESIDENCE.
TWENTY-FOUR HOURS LATER.
WAKE UP, WAKE UP.
MA? WAIT... HOW DID I GET HERE?
I FOUND YOU PASSED OUT ON THE PORCH. DR. ZHAO CAME AND LOOKED AT YOU.
HOW DID YOU GET YOURSELF A CONCUSSION, ÉRZI?
AW, MAN, YOU WON'T BELIEVE WHAT HAPPENED, MA!
I SAVED NEW YORK FROM A NUKE, I WENT TO SPACE...
...THEN I WAS IN CHINA, AND HAD TO ESCAPE FROM SOME FISHERMEN--
--THEY WERE SUPER MEAN--
--THEN I STOLE A BOAT, AND FIGURED OUT A WAY TO GET ON A PLANE WITH NO I.D. AND NO MONEY!
AND I DID. CUZ I'M A BALLER.
AIYAH, WHAT YOU ARE IS IRRESPONSIBLE.
YOUR BA AND I WANT TO SUPPORT THIS SUPER COSTUME THING YOU DO...
...BUT AFTER CLAIRE DIED, YOU CAN'T JUST... JUST...
...YOU'RE GROUNDED. FOR SIX MONTHS!
SIX MONTHS?!
AND NO VIDEO GAMES.
DIDN'T YOU HEAR THE PART ABOUT SAVING NEW YORK...?
SLAM
A CONCUSSION, huh? MAYBE IT WAS ALL IN MY HEAD.
OR MAYBE...
...THANKS, SIS.

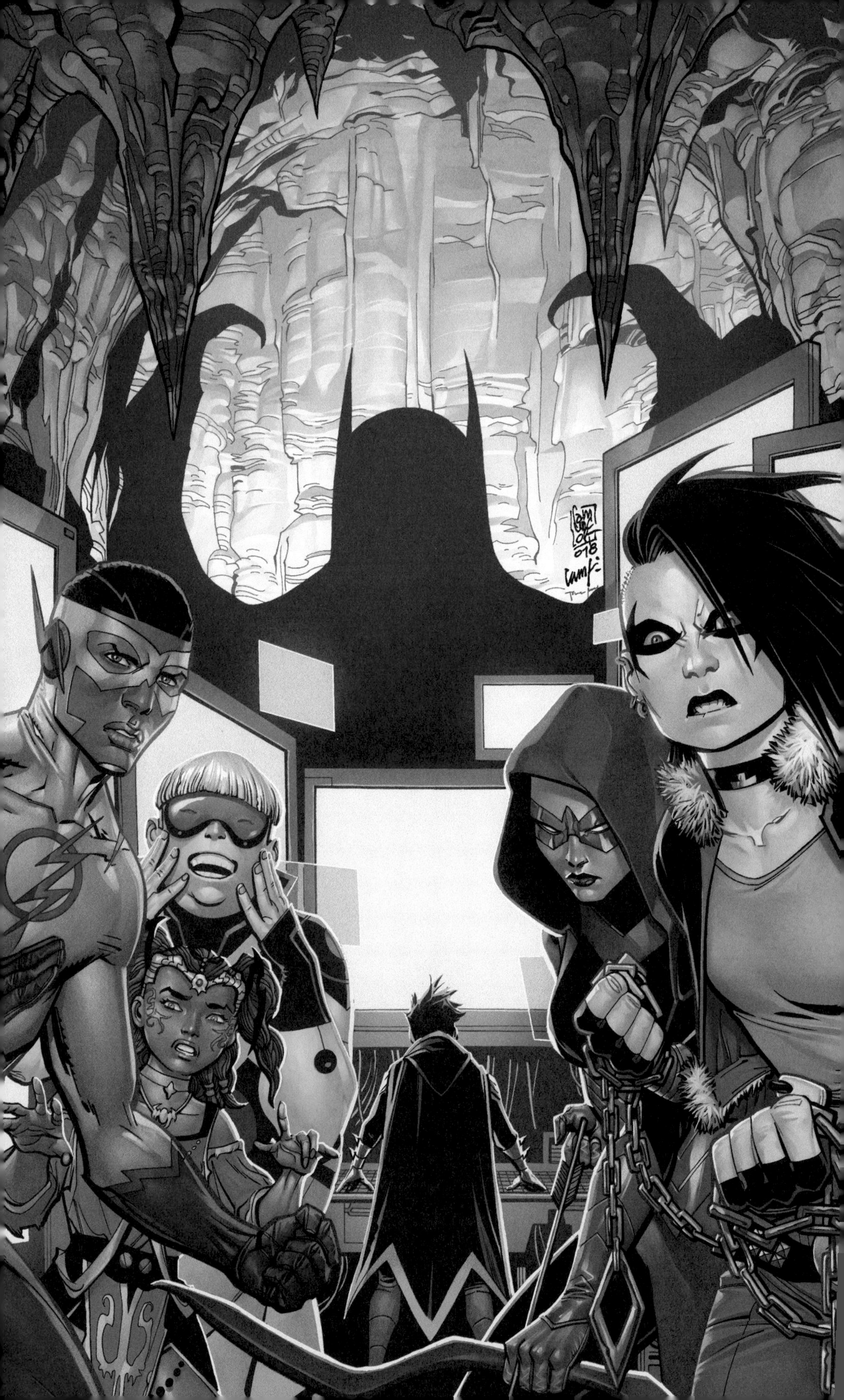

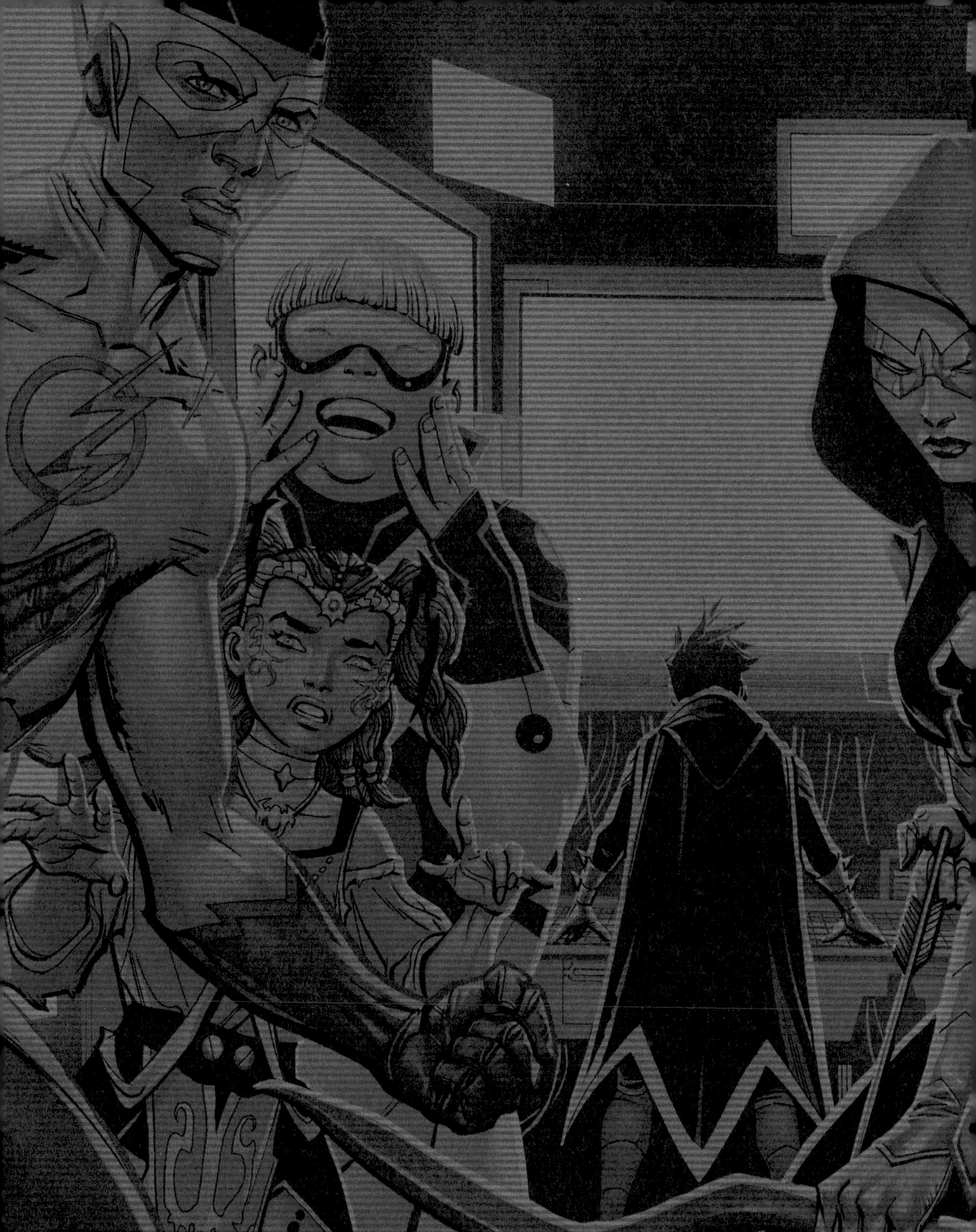

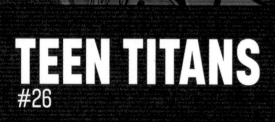

TEEN TITANS

#26

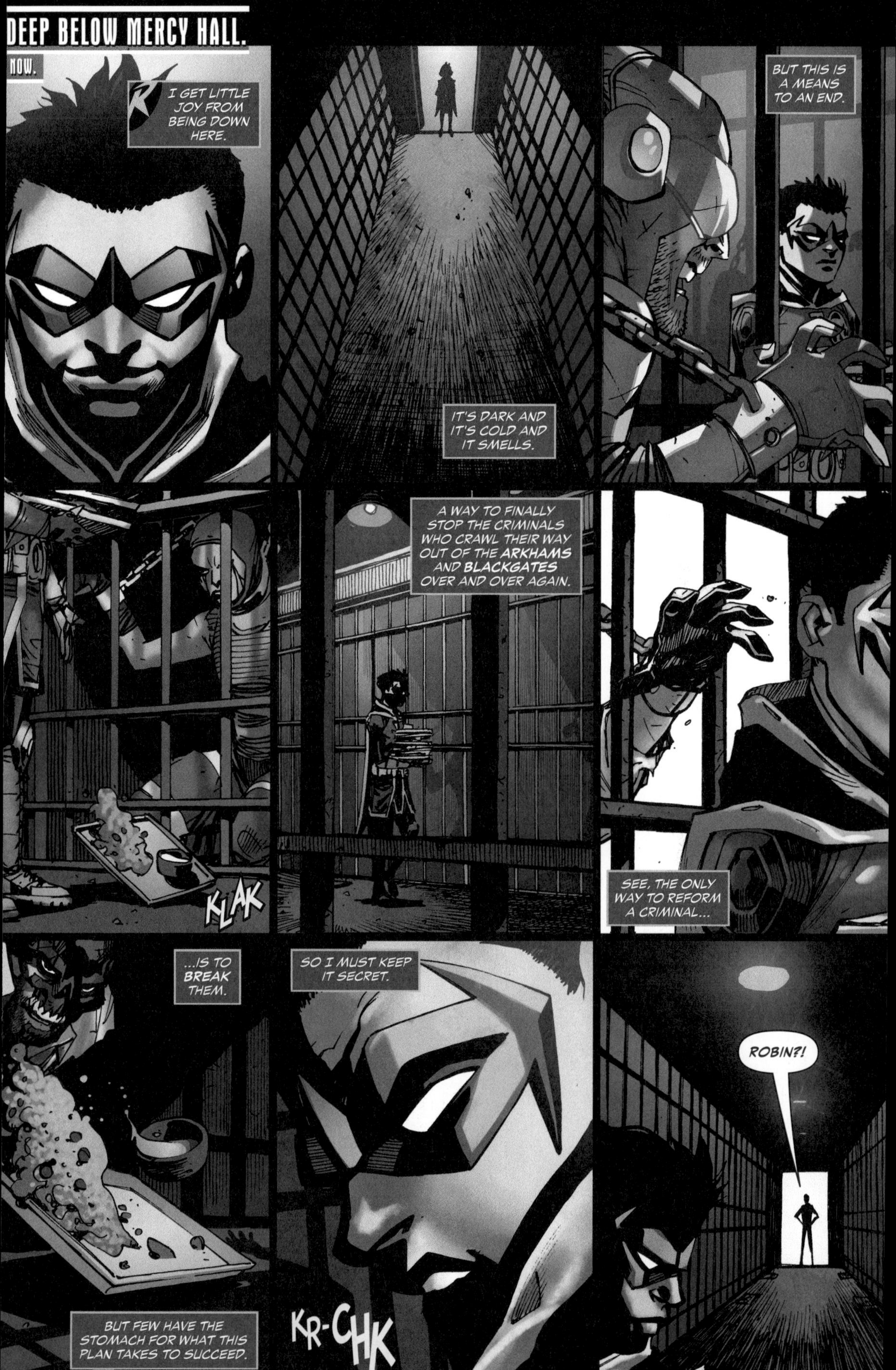
DEEP BELOW MERCY HALL.
NOW.
I GET LITTLE JOY FROM BEING DOWN HERE.
IT'S DARK AND IT'S COLD AND IT SMELLS.
BUT THIS IS A MEANS TO AN END.
KLAK
A WAY TO FINALLY STOP THE CRIMINALS WHO CRAWL THEIR WAY OUT OF THE **ARKHAMS** AND **BLACKGATES** OVER AND OVER AGAIN.
SEE, THE ONLY WAY TO REFORM A CRIMINAL...
...IS TO **BREAK** THEM.
BUT FEW HAVE THE STOMACH FOR WHAT THIS PLAN TAKES TO SUCCEED.
SO I MUST KEEP IT SECRET.
KR-CHK
ROBIN?!

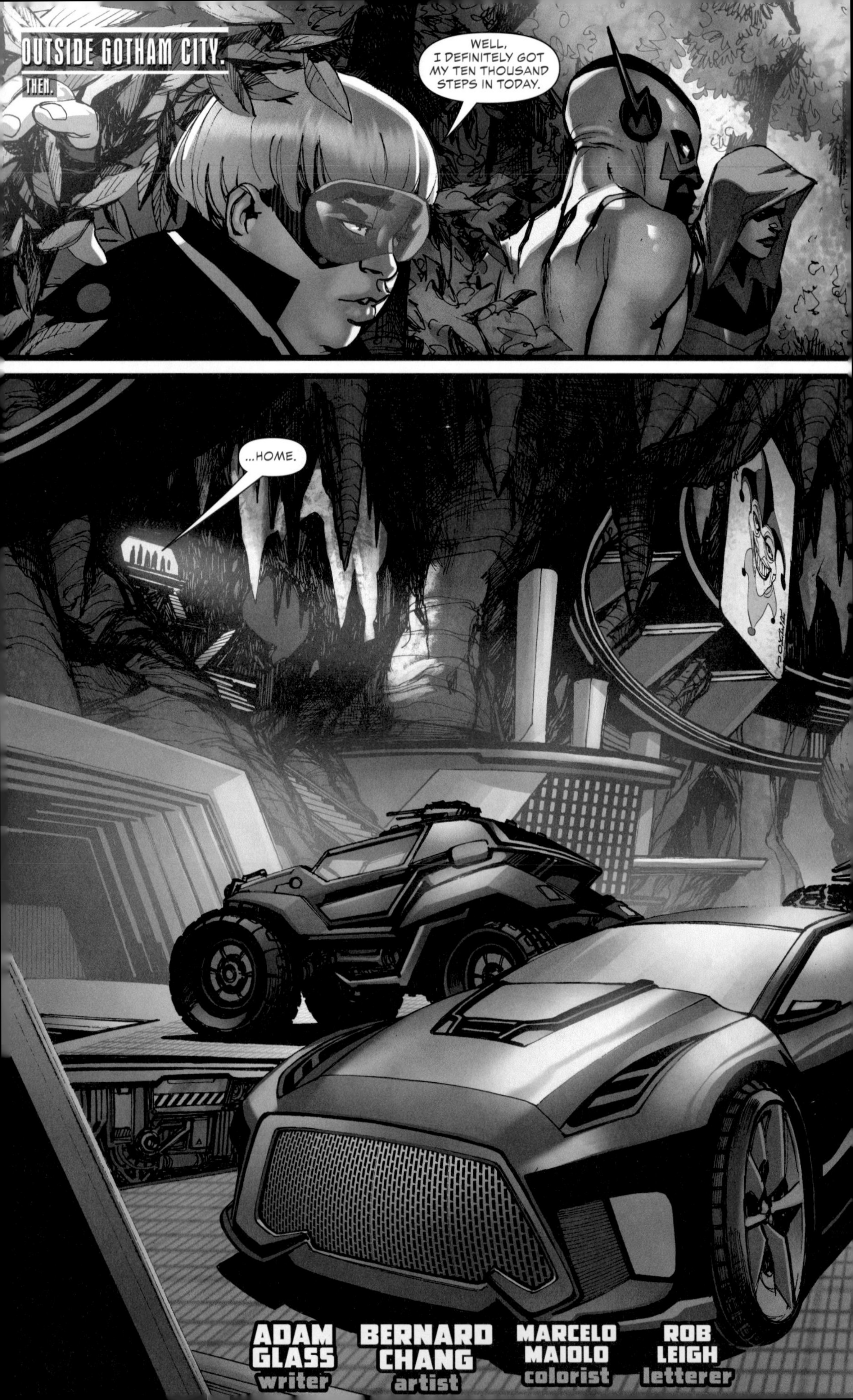
OUTSIDE GOTHAM CITY.
THEN.
WELL, I DEFINITELY GOT MY TEN THOUSAND STEPS IN TODAY.
...HOME.
ADAM GLASS writer
BERNARD CHANG artist
MARCELO MAIOLO colorist
ROB LEIGH letterer

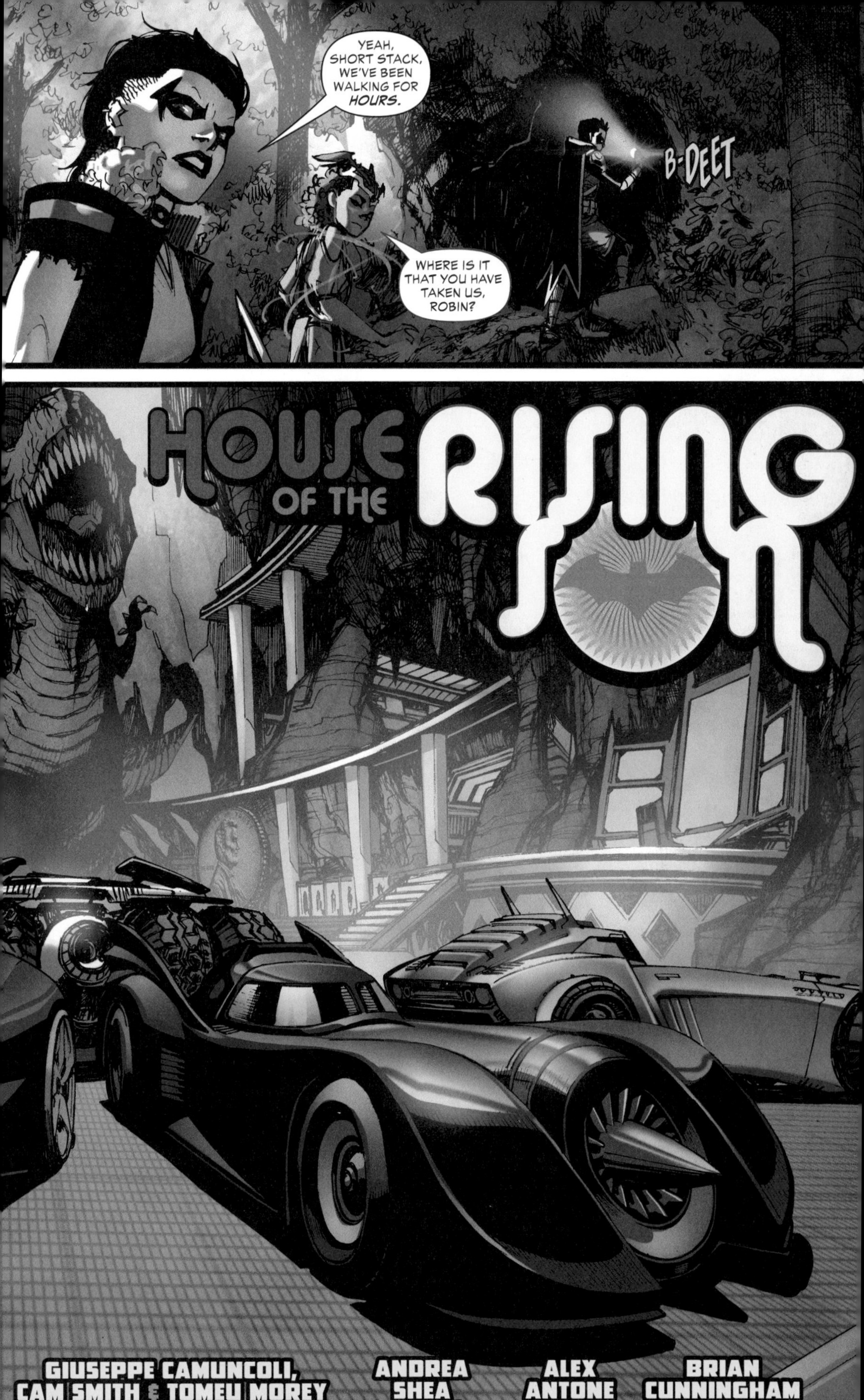
YEAH, SHORT STACK, WE'VE BEEN WALKING FOR HOURS.
B-DEET
WHERE IS IT THAT YOU HAVE TAKEN US, ROBIN?
HOUSE OF THE RISING SON

GIUSEPPE CAMUNCOLI, CAM SMITH & TOMEU MOREY cover
ANDREA SHEA asst. editor
ALEX ANTONE editor
BRIAN CUNNINGHAM group editor

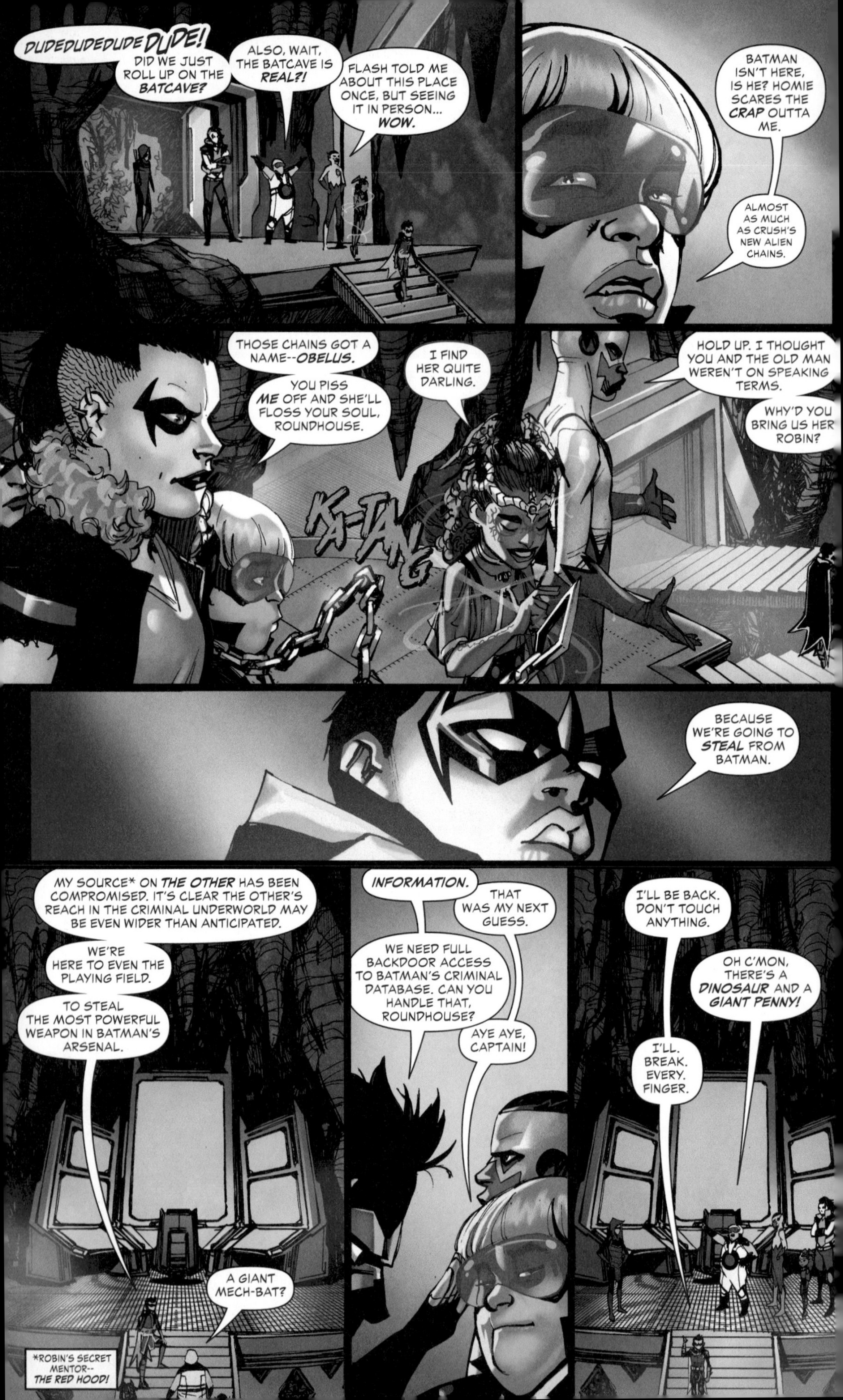
DUDEDUDEDUDE DUDE!
DID WE JUST ROLL UP ON THE BATCAVE?
ALSO, WAIT, THE BATCAVE IS REAL?!
FLASH TOLD ME ABOUT THIS PLACE ONCE, BUT SEEING IT IN PERSON... WOW.
BATMAN ISN'T HERE, IS HE? HOMIE SCARES THE CRAP OUTTA ME.
ALMOST AS MUCH AS CRUSH'S NEW ALIEN CHAINS.
THOSE CHAINS GOT A NAME--OBELUS.
YOU PISS ME OFF AND SHE'LL FLOSS YOUR SOUL, ROUNDHOUSE.
I FIND HER QUITE DARLING.
KA-TANG
HOLD UP. I THOUGHT YOU AND THE OLD MAN WEREN'T ON SPEAKING TERMS.
WHY'D YOU BRING US HER ROBIN?
BECAUSE WE'RE GOING TO STEAL FROM BATMAN.
MY SOURCE* ON THE OTHER HAS BEEN COMPROMISED. IT'S CLEAR THE OTHER'S REACH IN THE CRIMINAL UNDERWORLD MAY BE EVEN WIDER THAN ANTICIPATED.
WE'RE HERE TO EVEN THE PLAYING FIELD.
TO STEAL THE MOST POWERFUL WEAPON IN BATMAN'S ARSENAL.
A GIANT MECH-BAT?
*ROBIN'S SECRET MENTOR-- THE RED HOOD!
INFORMATION.
THAT WAS MY NEXT GUESS.
WE NEED FULL BACKDOOR ACCESS TO BATMAN'S CRIMINAL DATABASE. CAN YOU HANDLE THAT, ROUNDHOUSE?
AYE AYE, CAPTAIN!
I'LL BE BACK. DON'T TOUCH ANYTHING.
OH C'MON, THERE'S A DINOSAUR AND A GIANT PENNY!
I'LL. BREAK. EVERY. FINGER.

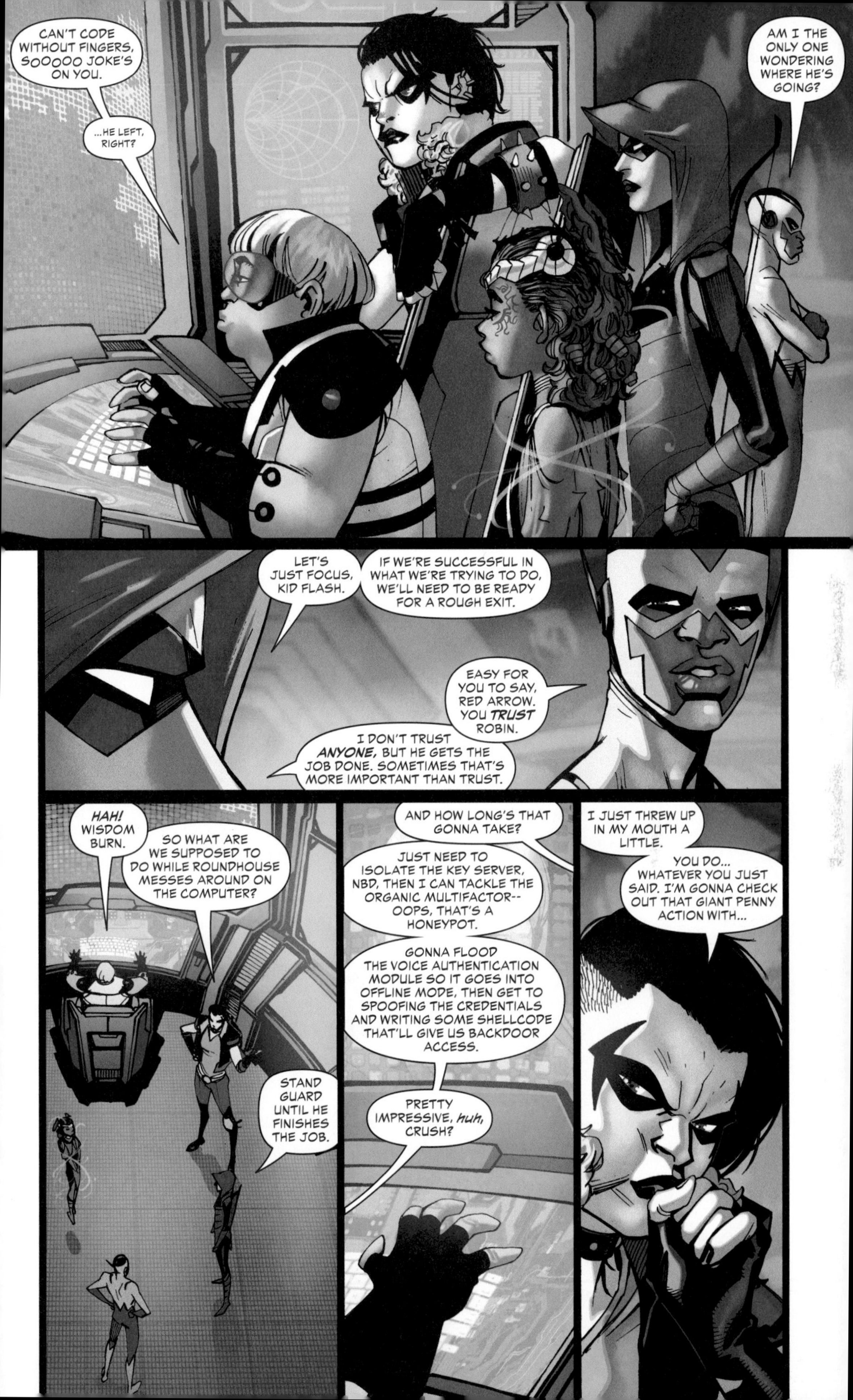
CAN'T CODE WITHOUT FINGERS, SOOOOO JOKE'S ON YOU.
...HE LEFT, RIGHT?
AM I THE ONLY ONE WONDERING WHERE HE'S GOING?
LET'S JUST FOCUS, KID FLASH.
IF WE'RE SUCCESSFUL IN WHAT WE'RE TRYING TO DO, WE'LL NEED TO BE READY FOR A ROUGH EXIT.
EASY FOR YOU TO SAY, RED ARROW. YOU TRUST ROBIN.
I DON'T TRUST ANYONE, BUT HE GETS THE JOB DONE. SOMETIMES THAT'S MORE IMPORTANT THAN TRUST.
HAH! WISDOM BURN.
SO WHAT ARE WE SUPPOSED TO DO WHILE ROUNDHOUSE MESSES AROUND ON THE COMPUTER?
STAND GUARD UNTIL HE FINISHES THE JOB.
AND HOW LONG'S THAT GONNA TAKE?
JUST NEED TO ISOLATE THE KEY SERVER, NBD, THEN I CAN TACKLE THE ORGANIC MULTIFACTOR-- OOPS, THAT'S A HONEYPOT.
GONNA FLOOD THE VOICE AUTHENTICATION MODULE SO IT GOES INTO OFFLINE MODE, THEN GET TO SPOOFING THE CREDENTIALS AND WRITING SOME SHELLCODE THAT'LL GIVE US BACKDOOR ACCESS.
PRETTY IMPRESSIVE, huh, CRUSH?
I JUST THREW UP IN MY MOUTH A LITTLE.
YOU DO... WHATEVER YOU JUST SAID. I'M GONNA CHECK OUT THAT GIANT PENNY ACTION WITH...

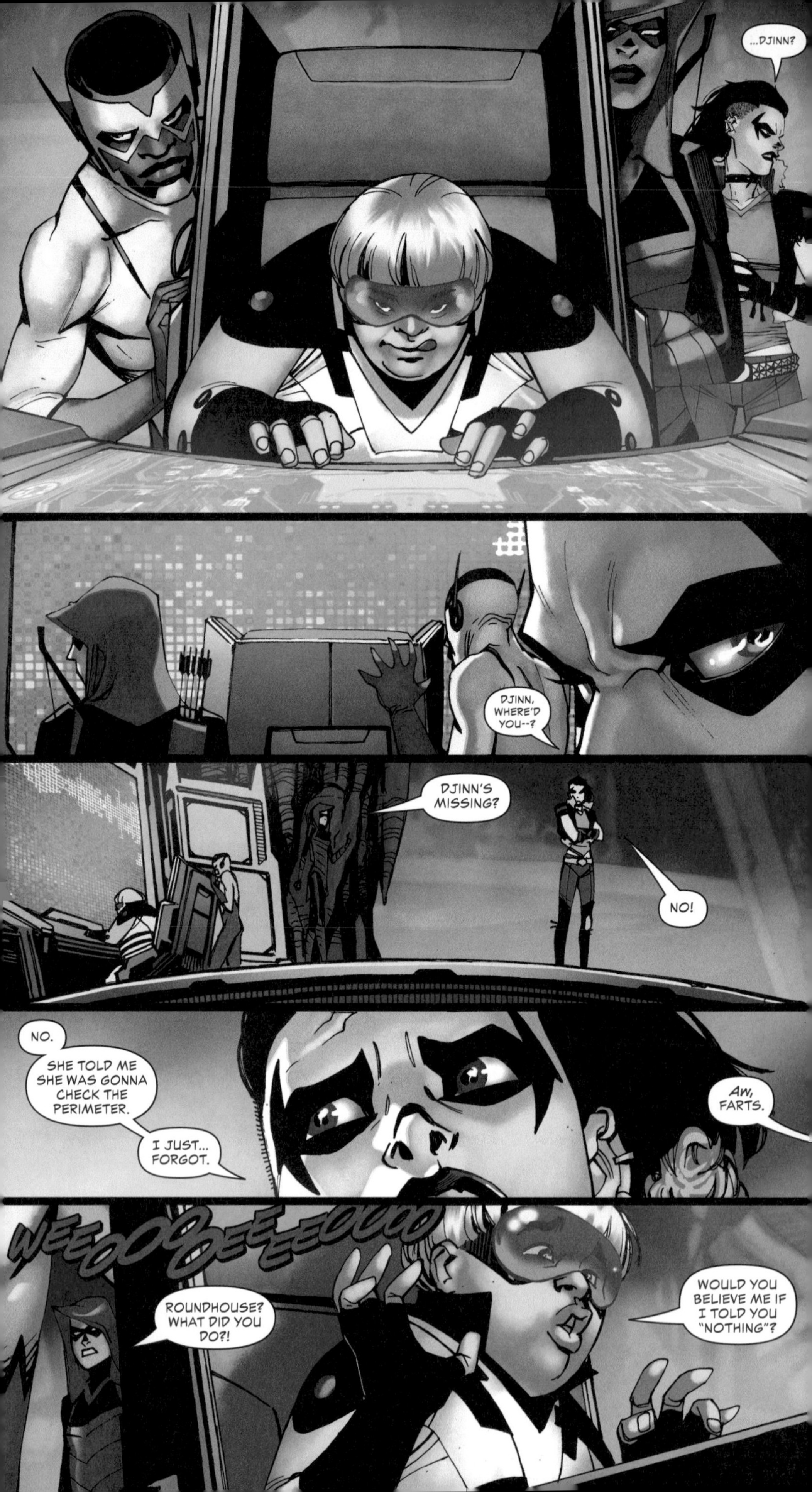
...DJINN?
DJINN, WHERE'D YOU--?
DJINN'S MISSING?
NO!
NO.
SHE TOLD ME SHE WAS GONNA CHECK THE PERIMETER.
I JUST... FORGOT.
AW, FARTS.
WEEOOOOEEEEEOOOO
ROUNDHOUSE? WHAT DID YOU DO?!
WOULD YOU BELIEVE ME IF I TOLD YOU "NOTHING"?

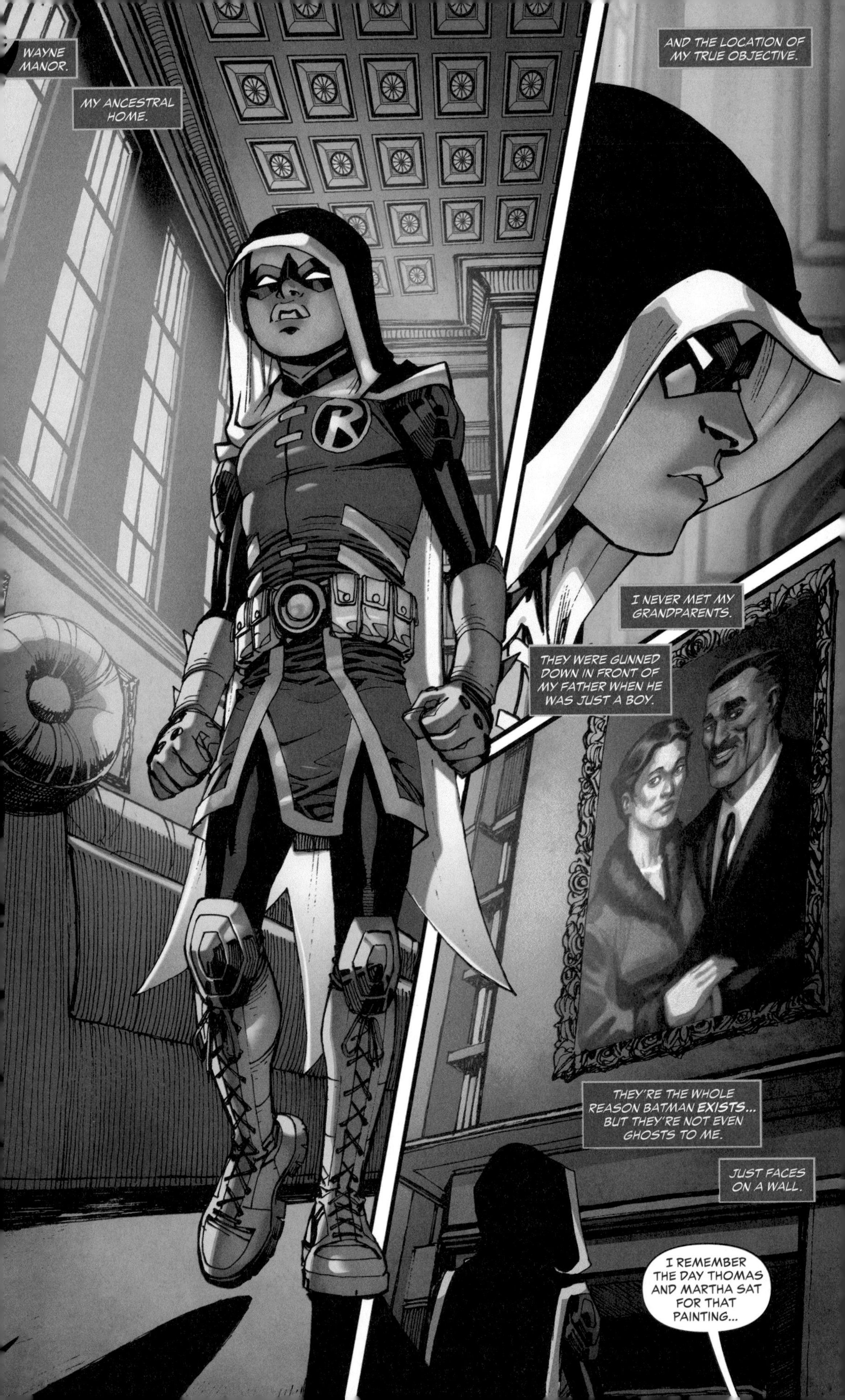
WAYNE MANOR.
MY ANCESTRAL HOME.
AND THE LOCATION OF MY TRUE OBJECTIVE.
I NEVER MET MY GRANDPARENTS.
THEY WERE GUNNED DOWN IN FRONT OF MY FATHER WHEN HE WAS JUST A BOY.
THEY'RE THE WHOLE REASON BATMAN EXISTS... BUT THEY'RE NOT EVEN GHOSTS TO ME.
JUST FACES ON A WALL.
I REMEMBER THE DAY THOMAS AND MARTHA SAT FOR THAT PAINTING...

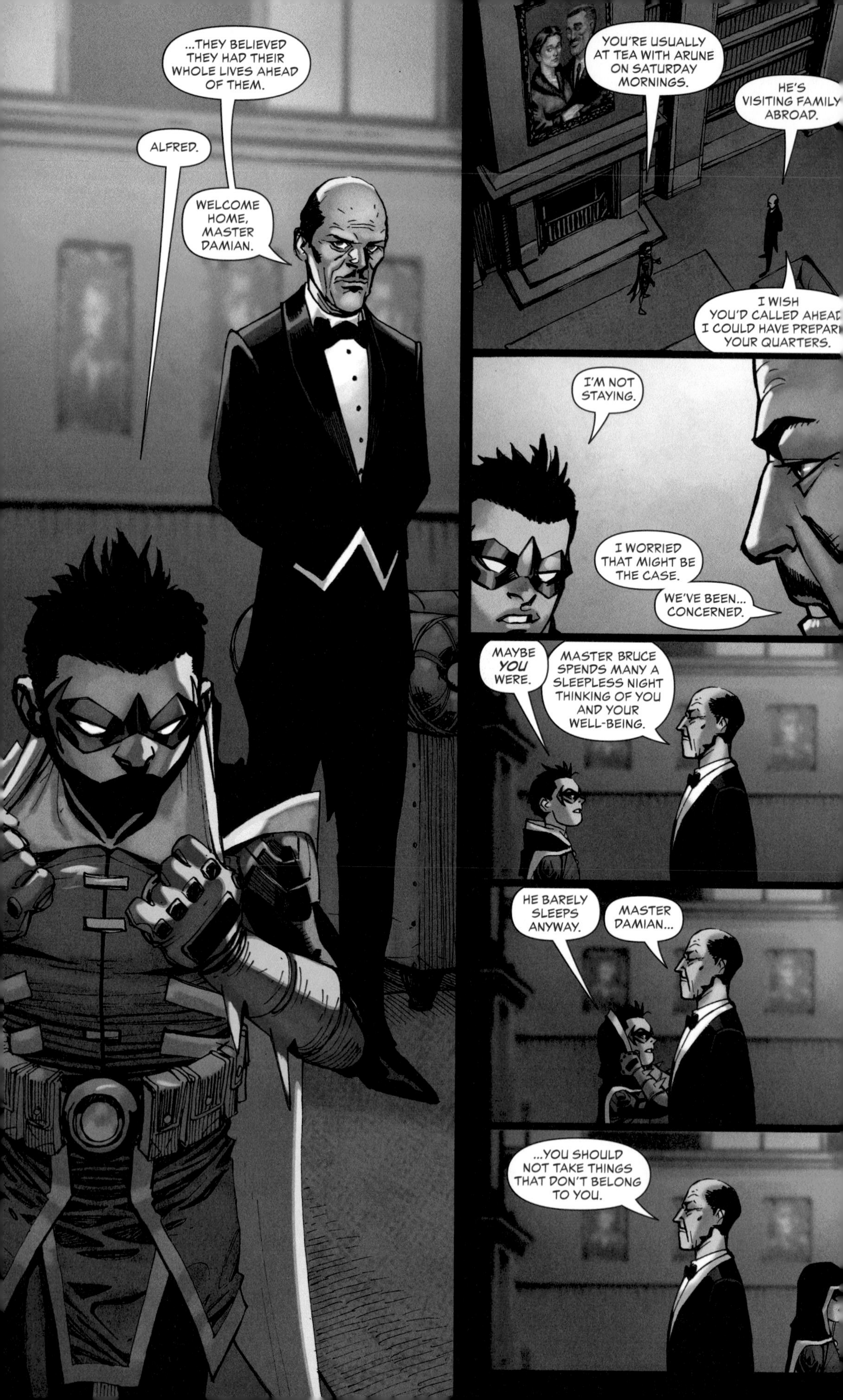
...THEY BELIEVED THEY HAD THEIR WHOLE LIVES AHEAD OF THEM.
ALFRED.
WELCOME HOME, MASTER DAMIAN.
YOU'RE USUALLY AT TEA WITH ARUNE ON SATURDAY MORNINGS.
HE'S VISITING FAMILY ABROAD.
I WISH YOU'D CALLED AHEAD I COULD HAVE PREPAR YOUR QUARTERS.
I'M NOT STAYING.
I WORRIED THAT MIGHT BE THE CASE.
WE'VE BEEN... CONCERNED.
MAYBE *YOU* WERE.
MASTER BRUCE SPENDS MANY A SLEEPLESS NIGHT THINKING OF YOU AND YOUR WELL-BEING.
HE BARELY SLEEPS ANYWAY.
MASTER DAMIAN...
...YOU SHOULD NOT TAKE THINGS THAT DON'T BELONG TO YOU.

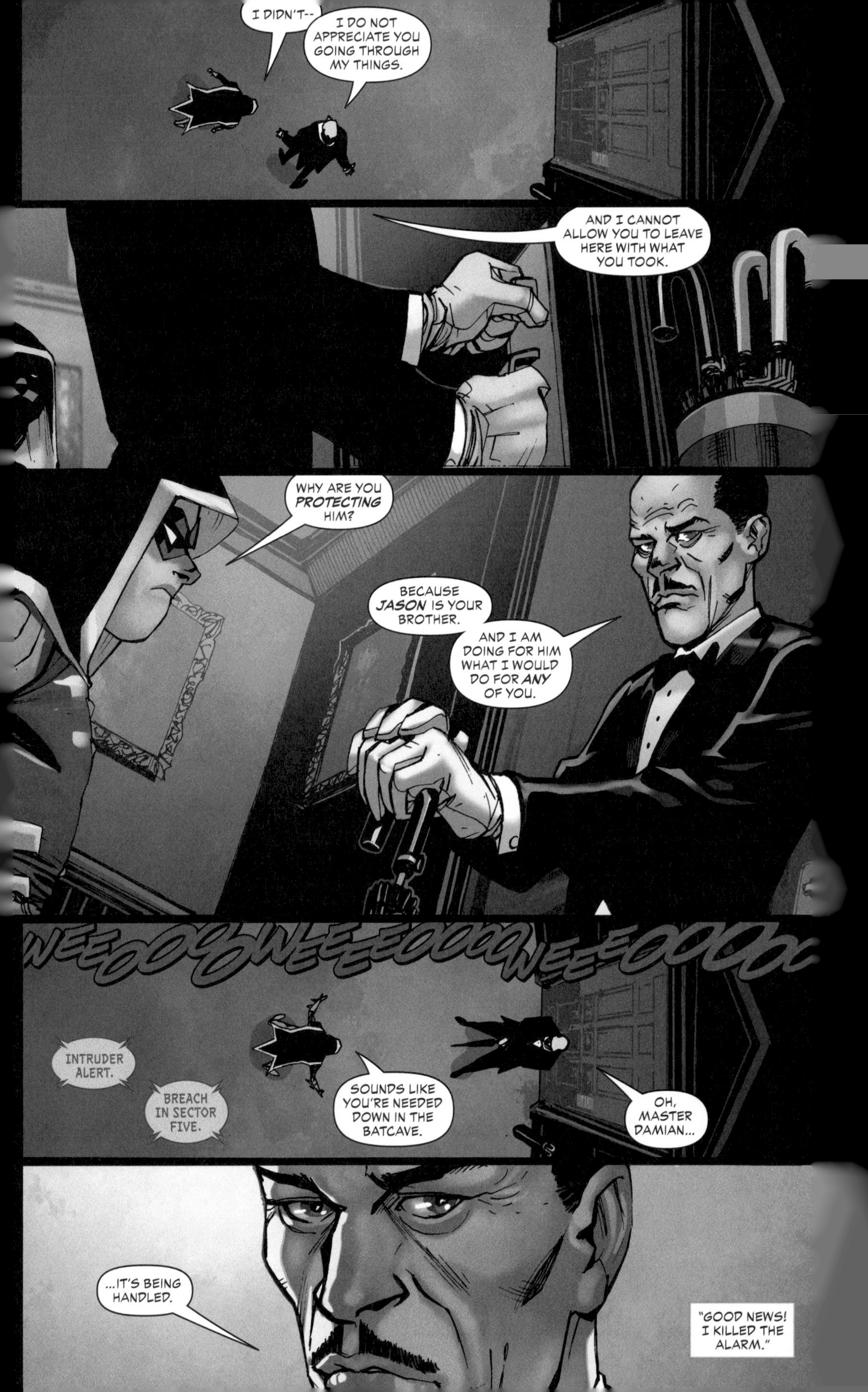
I DIDN'T--
I DO NOT APPRECIATE YOU GOING THROUGH MY THINGS.
AND I CANNOT ALLOW YOU TO LEAVE HERE WITH WHAT YOU TOOK.
WHY ARE YOU PROTECTING HIM?
BECAUSE JASON IS YOUR BROTHER.
AND I AM DOING FOR HIM WHAT I WOULD DO FOR ANY OF YOU.
WEEOOOOWEEEEOOOOWEEEEOOOOO
INTRUDER ALERT.
BREACH IN SECTOR FIVE.
SOUNDS LIKE YOU'RE NEEDED DOWN IN THE BATCAVE.
OH, MASTER DAMIAN...
...IT'S BEING HANDLED.
"GOOD NEWS! I KILLED THE ALARM."

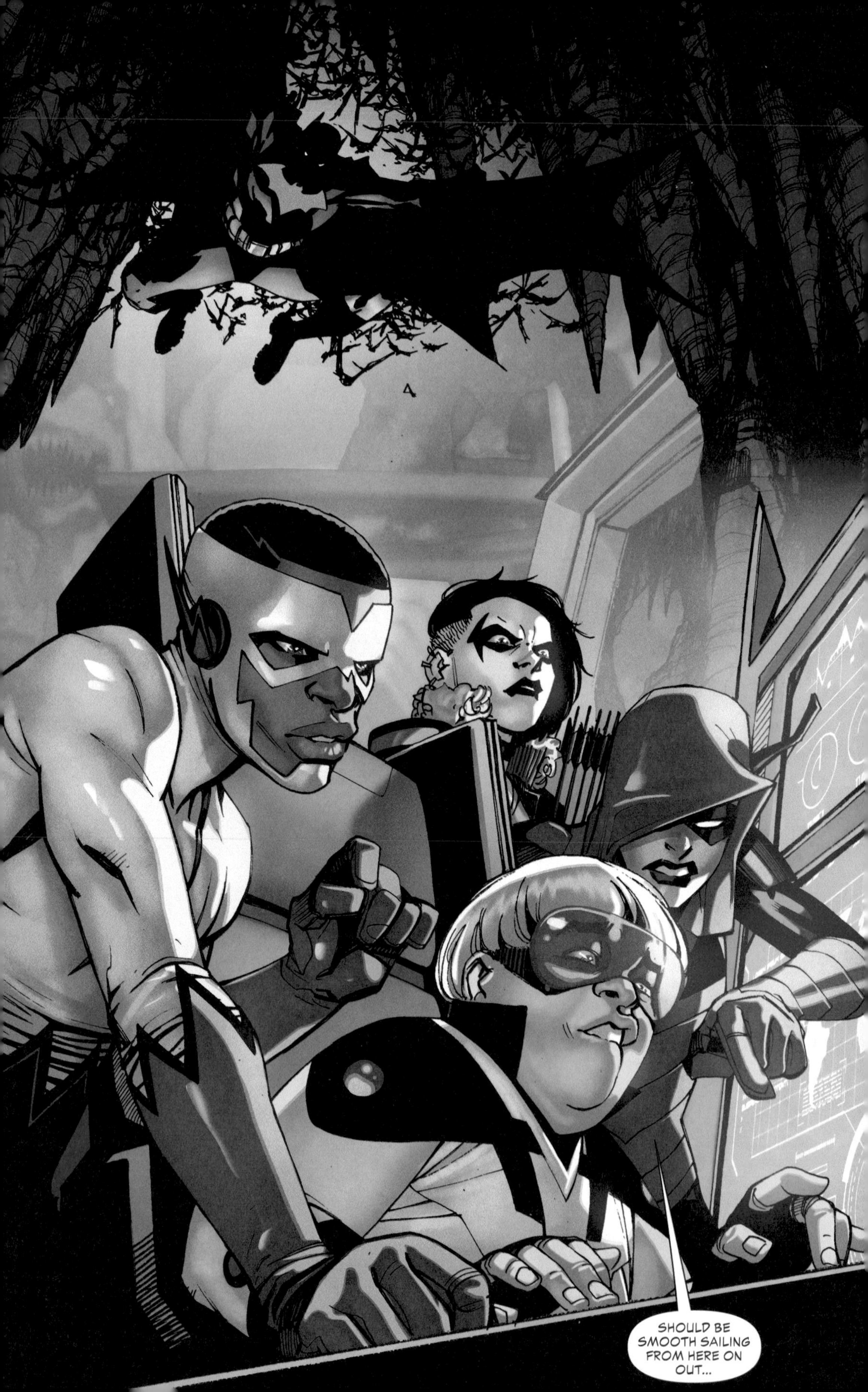
SHOULD BE SMOOTH SAILING FROM HERE ON OUT...

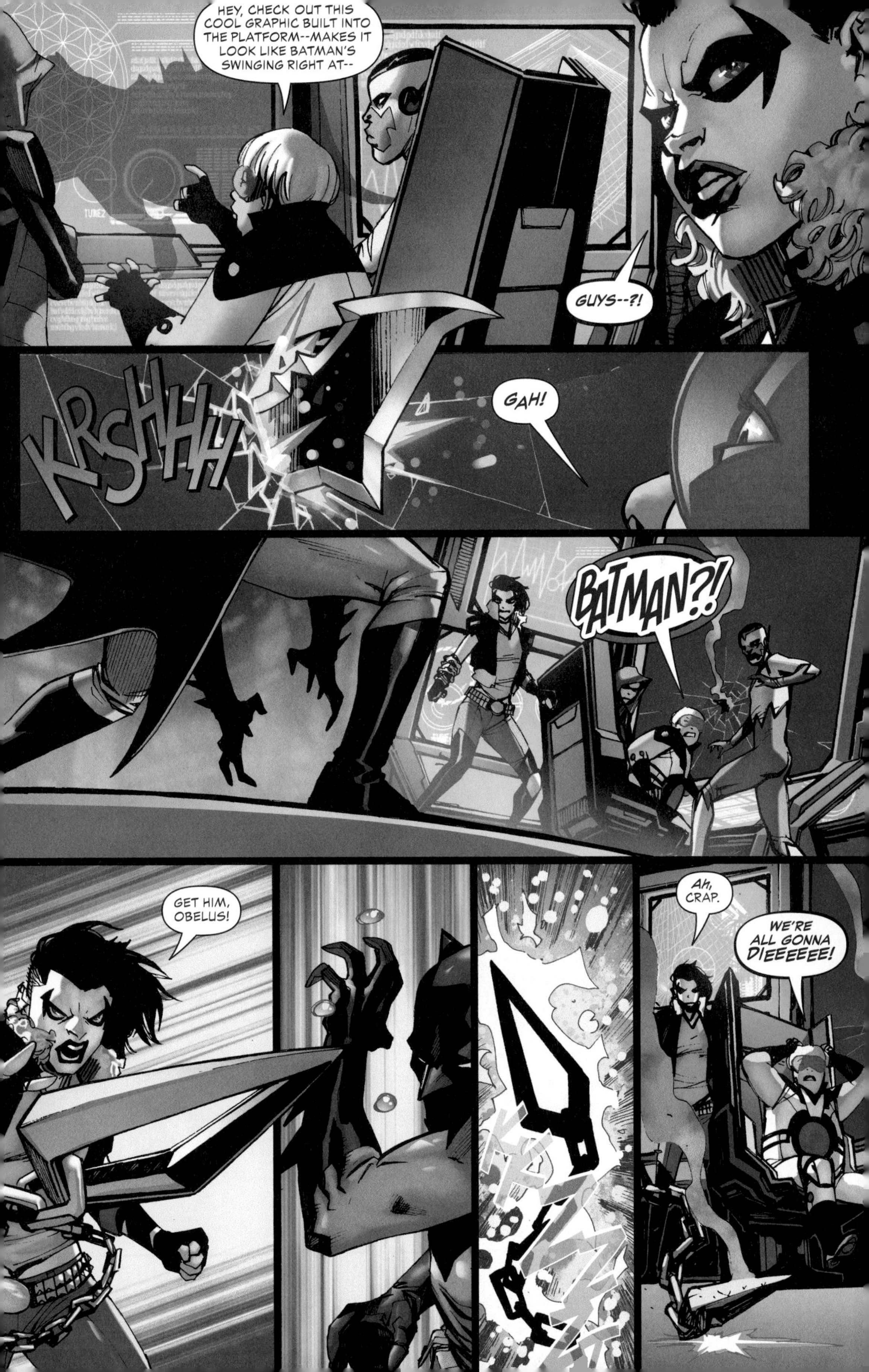
HEY, CHECK OUT THIS COOL GRAPHIC BUILT INTO THE PLATFORM--MAKES IT LOOK LIKE BATMAN'S SWINGING RIGHT AT--
GUYS--?!
KRSHHH
GAH!
BATMAN?!
GET HIM, OBELUS!
Ah, CRAP.
WE'RE ALL GONNA DIEEEEEE!

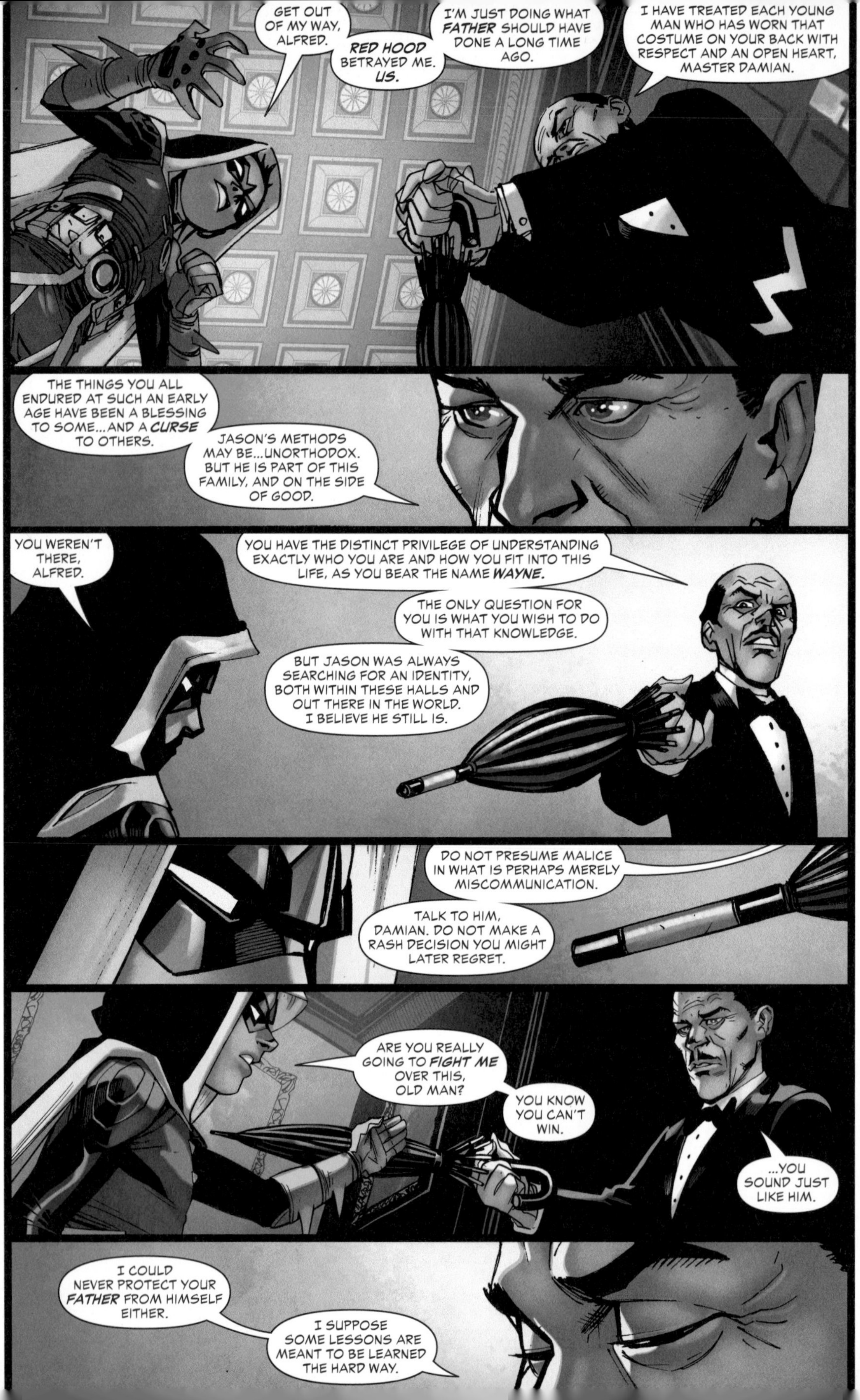
GET OUT OF MY WAY, ALFRED.
I'M JUST DOING WHAT FATHER SHOULD HAVE DONE A LONG TIME AGO.
RED HOOD BETRAYED ME. US.
I HAVE TREATED EACH YOUNG MAN WHO HAS WORN THAT COSTUME ON YOUR BACK WITH RESPECT AND AN OPEN HEART, MASTER DAMIAN.
THE THINGS YOU ALL ENDURED AT SUCH AN EARLY AGE HAVE BEEN A BLESSING TO SOME...AND A CURSE TO OTHERS.
JASON'S METHODS MAY BE...UNORTHODOX. BUT HE IS PART OF THIS FAMILY, AND ON THE SIDE OF GOOD.
YOU WEREN'T THERE, ALFRED.
YOU HAVE THE DISTINCT PRIVILEGE OF UNDERSTANDING EXACTLY WHO YOU ARE AND HOW YOU FIT INTO THIS LIFE, AS YOU BEAR THE NAME WAYNE.
THE ONLY QUESTION FOR YOU IS WHAT YOU WISH TO DO WITH THAT KNOWLEDGE.
BUT JASON WAS ALWAYS SEARCHING FOR AN IDENTITY, BOTH WITHIN THESE HALLS AND OUT THERE IN THE WORLD. I BELIEVE HE STILL IS.
DO NOT PRESUME MALICE IN WHAT IS PERHAPS MERELY MISCOMMUNICATION.
TALK TO HIM, DAMIAN. DO NOT MAKE A RASH DECISION YOU MIGHT LATER REGRET.
ARE YOU REALLY GOING TO FIGHT ME OVER THIS, OLD MAN?
YOU KNOW YOU CAN'T WIN.
...YOU SOUND JUST LIKE HIM.
I COULD NEVER PROTECT YOUR FATHER FROM HIMSELF EITHER.
I SUPPOSE SOME LESSONS ARE MEANT TO BE LEARNED THE HARD WAY.

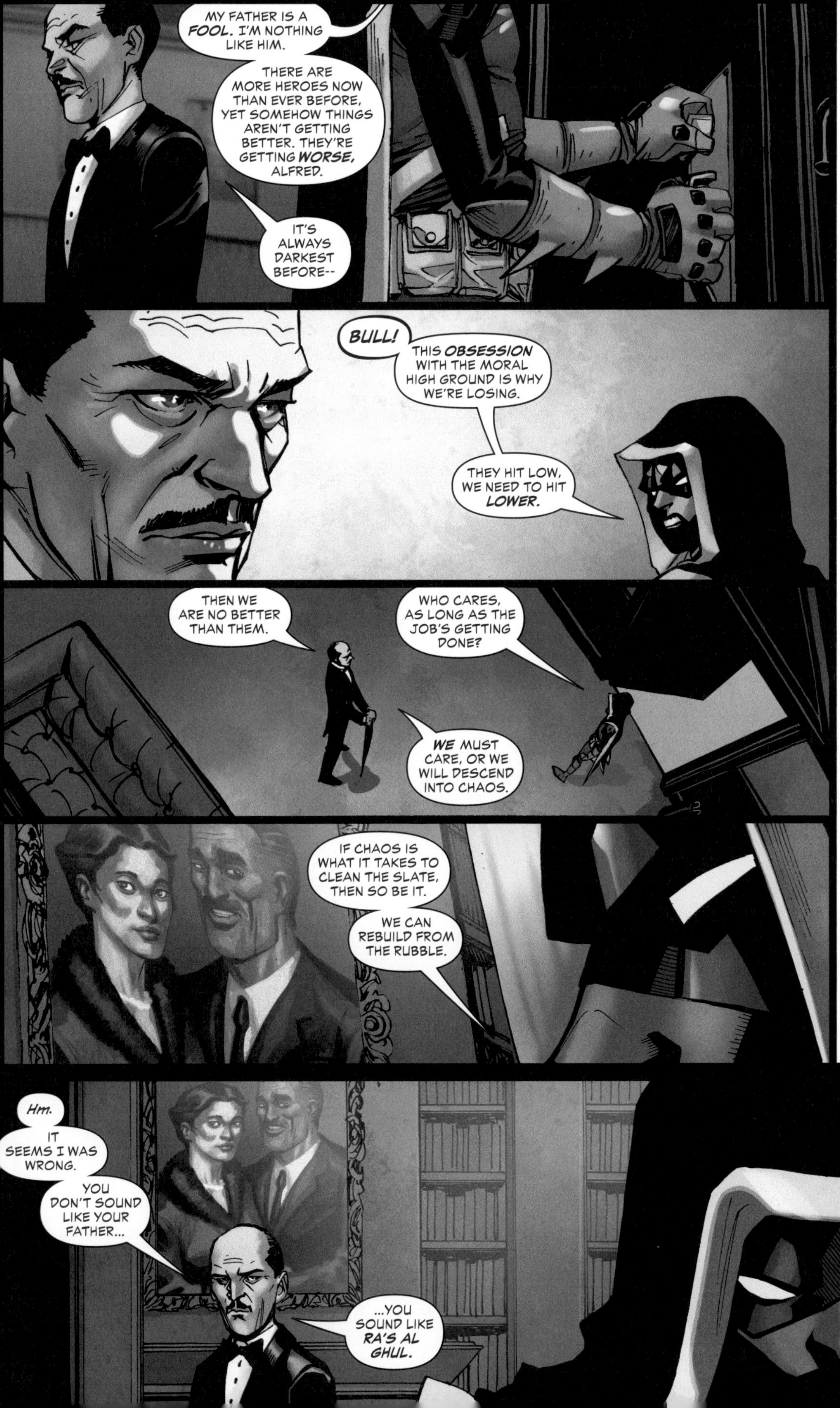

MY FATHER IS A *FOOL.* I'M NOTHING LIKE HIM.
THERE ARE MORE HEROES NOW THAN EVER BEFORE, YET SOMEHOW THINGS AREN'T GETTING BETTER. THEY'RE GETTING *WORSE,* ALFRED.
IT'S ALWAYS DARKEST BEFORE--
BULL!
THIS *OBSESSION* WITH THE MORAL HIGH GROUND IS WHY WE'RE LOSING.
THEY HIT LOW, WE NEED TO HIT *LOWER.*
THEN WE ARE NO BETTER THAN THEM.
WHO CARES, AS LONG AS THE JOB'S GETTING DONE?
WE MUST CARE, OR WE WILL DESCEND INTO CHAOS.
IF CHAOS IS WHAT IT TAKES TO CLEAN THE SLATE, THEN SO BE IT.
WE CAN REBUILD FROM THE RUBBLE.
Hm.
IT SEEMS I WAS WRONG.
YOU DON'T SOUND LIKE YOUR FATHER...
...YOU SOUND LIKE *RA'S AL GHUL.*

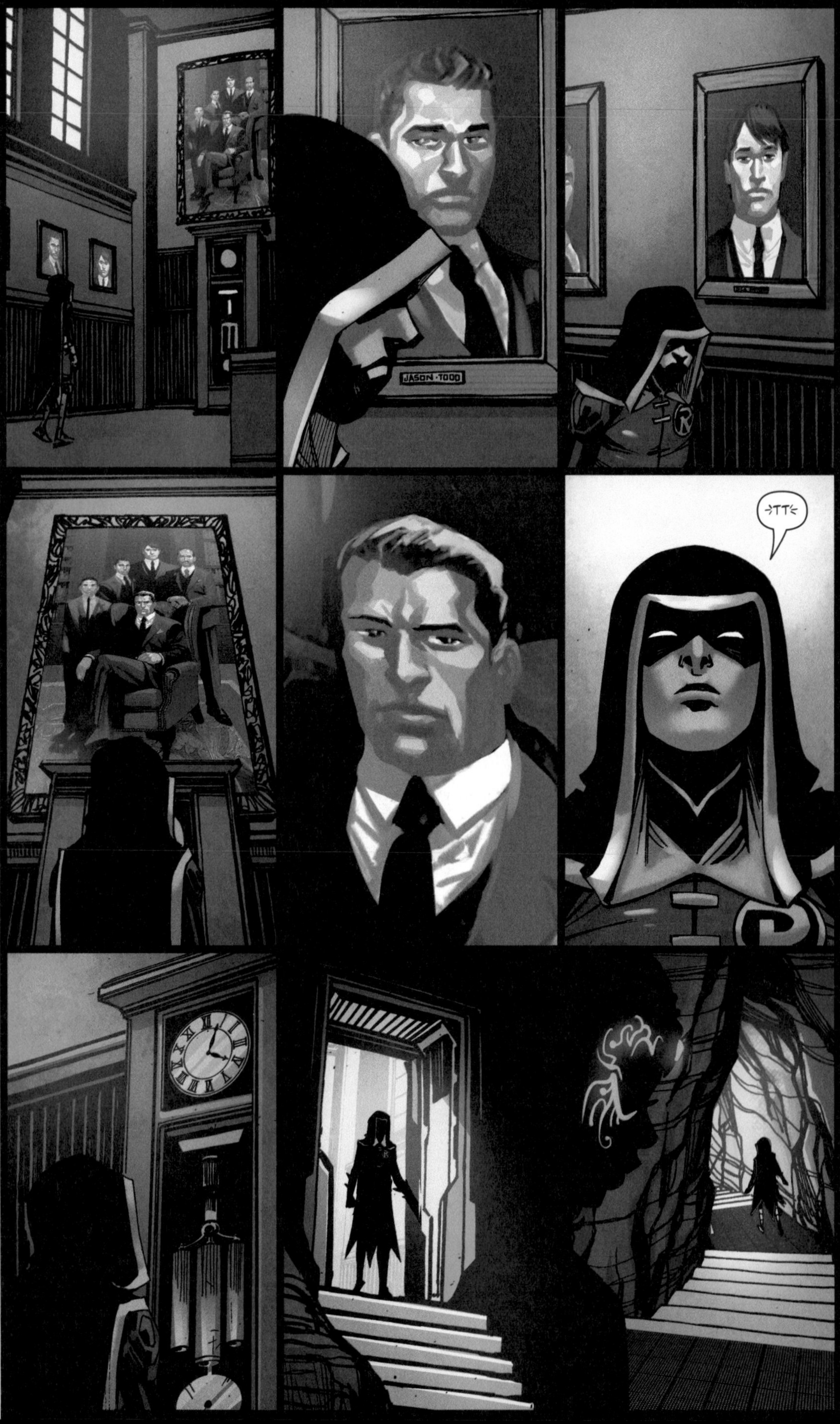
JASON · TODD
TT

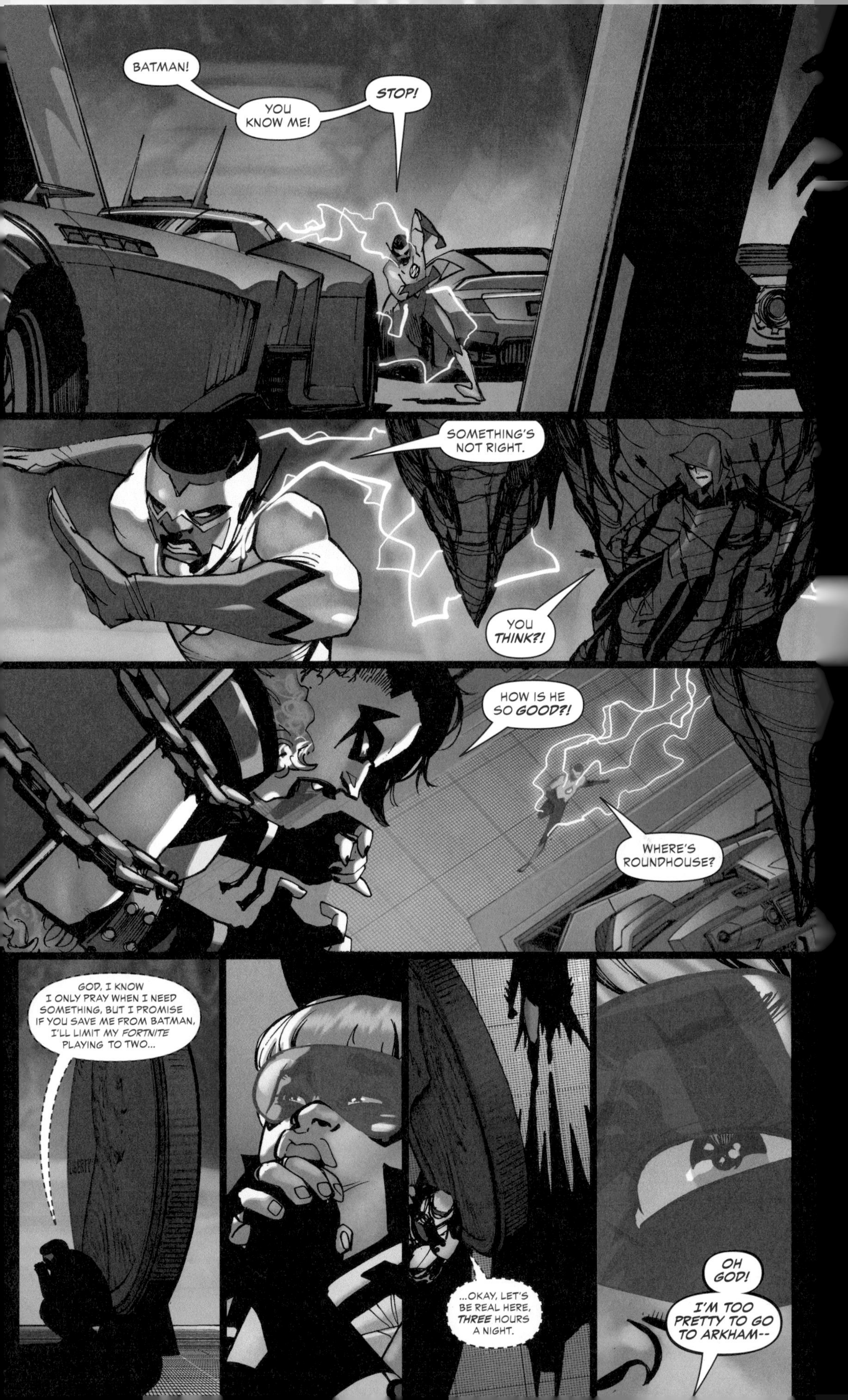
BATMAN!
YOU KNOW ME!
STOP!
SOMETHING'S NOT RIGHT.
YOU THINK?!
HOW IS HE SO GOOD?!
WHERE'S ROUNDHOUSE?
GOD, I KNOW I ONLY PRAY WHEN I NEED SOMETHING, BUT I PROMISE IF YOU SAVE ME FROM BATMAN, I'LL LIMIT MY FORTNITE PLAYING TO TWO...
...OKAY, LET'S BE REAL HERE, THREE HOURS A NIGHT.
OH GOD!
I'M TOO PRETTY TO GO TO ARKHAM--

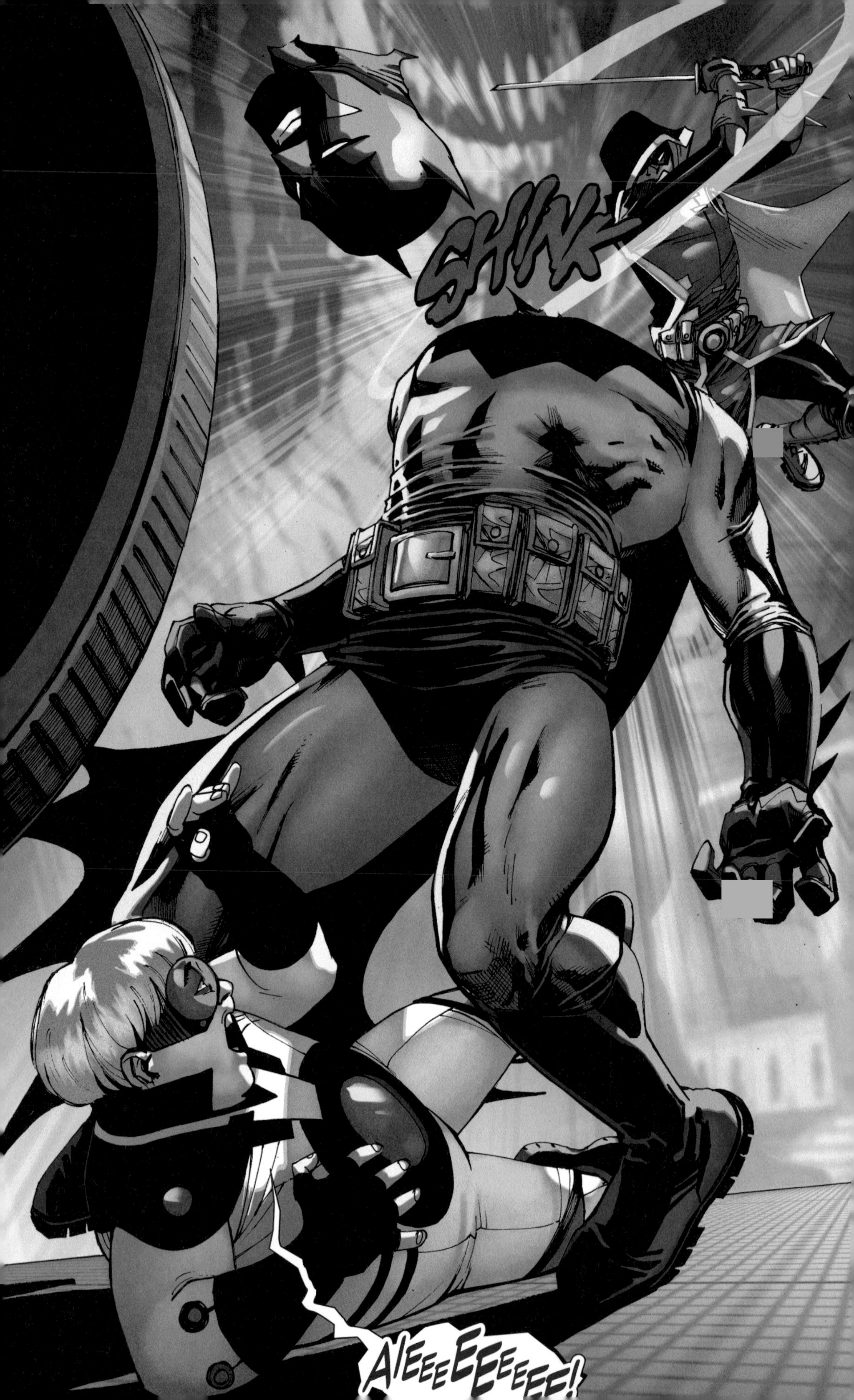
SHINK
AIEEEEEEEEE!

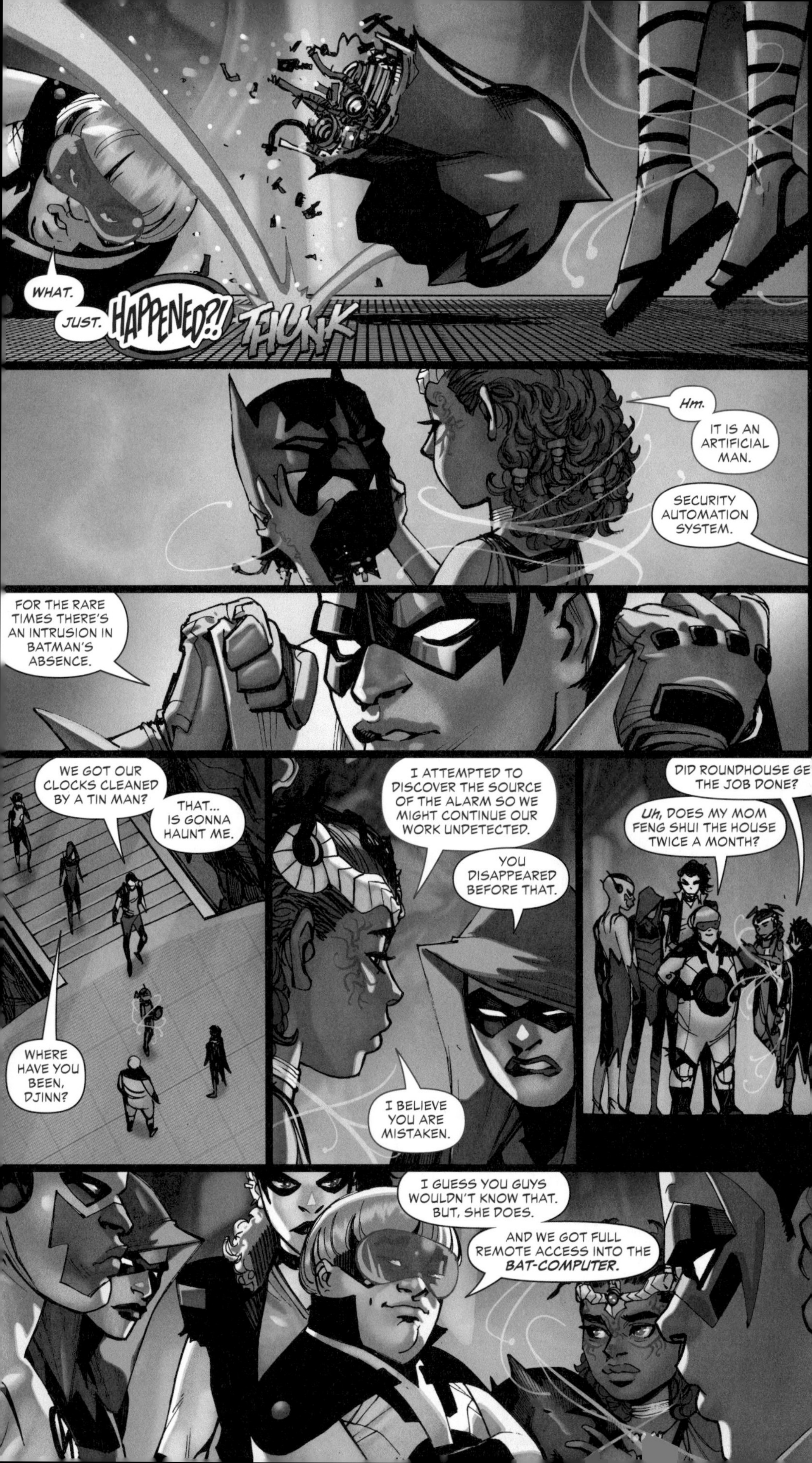
WHAT.
JUST.
HAPPENED?!
THUNK
Hm.
IT IS AN ARTIFICIAL MAN.
SECURITY AUTOMATION SYSTEM.
FOR THE RARE TIMES THERE'S AN INTRUSION IN BATMAN'S ABSENCE.
WE GOT OUR CLOCKS CLEANED BY A TIN MAN?
THAT... IS GONNA HAUNT ME.
WHERE HAVE YOU BEEN, DJINN?
I ATTEMPTED TO DISCOVER THE SOURCE OF THE ALARM SO WE MIGHT CONTINUE OUR WORK UNDETECTED.
YOU DISAPPEARED BEFORE THAT.
I BELIEVE YOU ARE MISTAKEN.
DID ROUNDHOUSE GE THE JOB DONE?
Uh, DOES MY MOM FENG SHUI THE HOUSE TWICE A MONTH?
I GUESS YOU GUYS WOULDN'T KNOW THAT. BUT, SHE DOES.
AND WE GOT FULL REMOTE ACCESS INTO THE ***BAT-COMPUTER.***

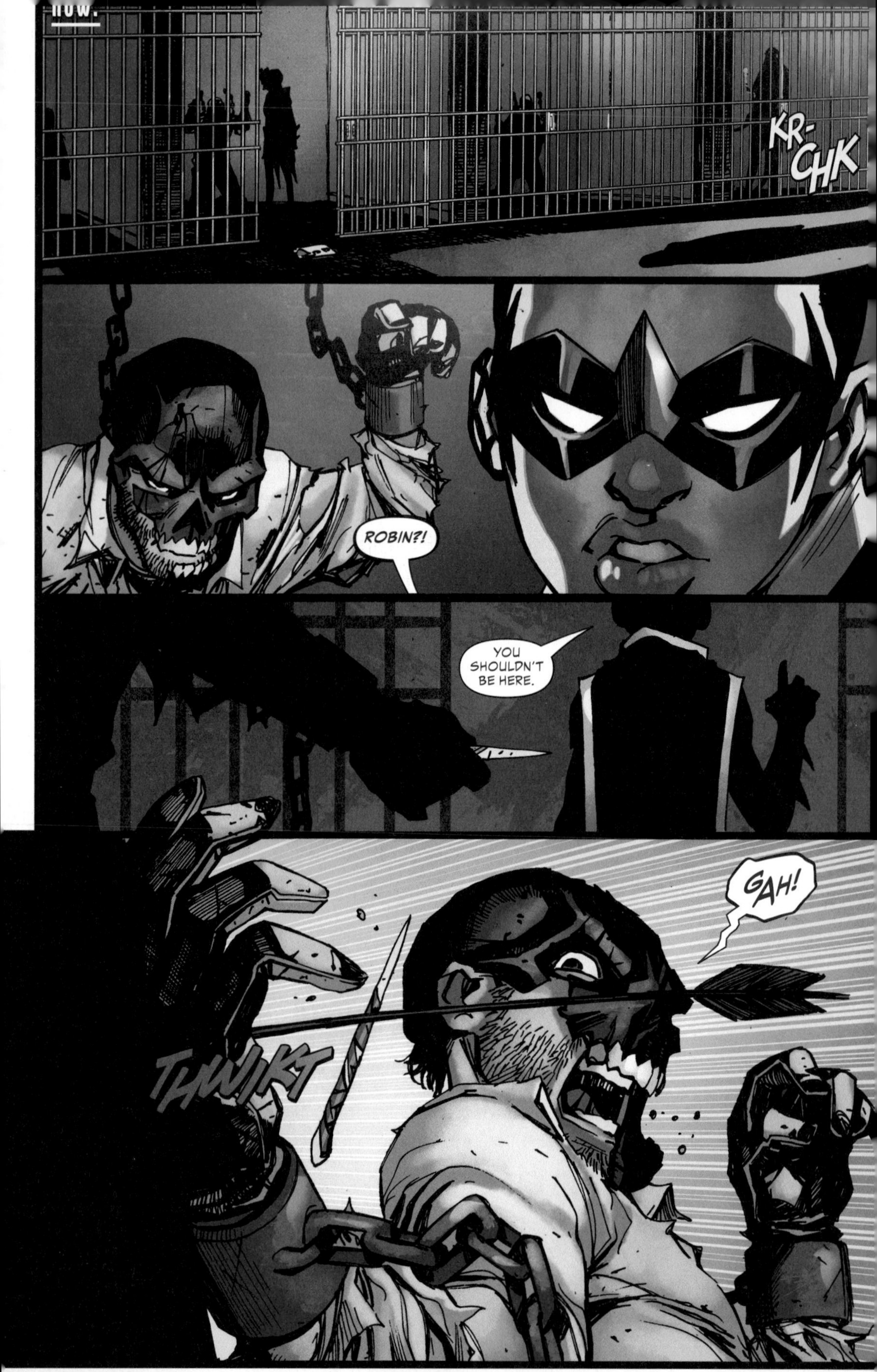
NOW.
KR-CHK
ROBIN?!
YOU SHOULDN'T BE HERE.
GAH!
THWIKT

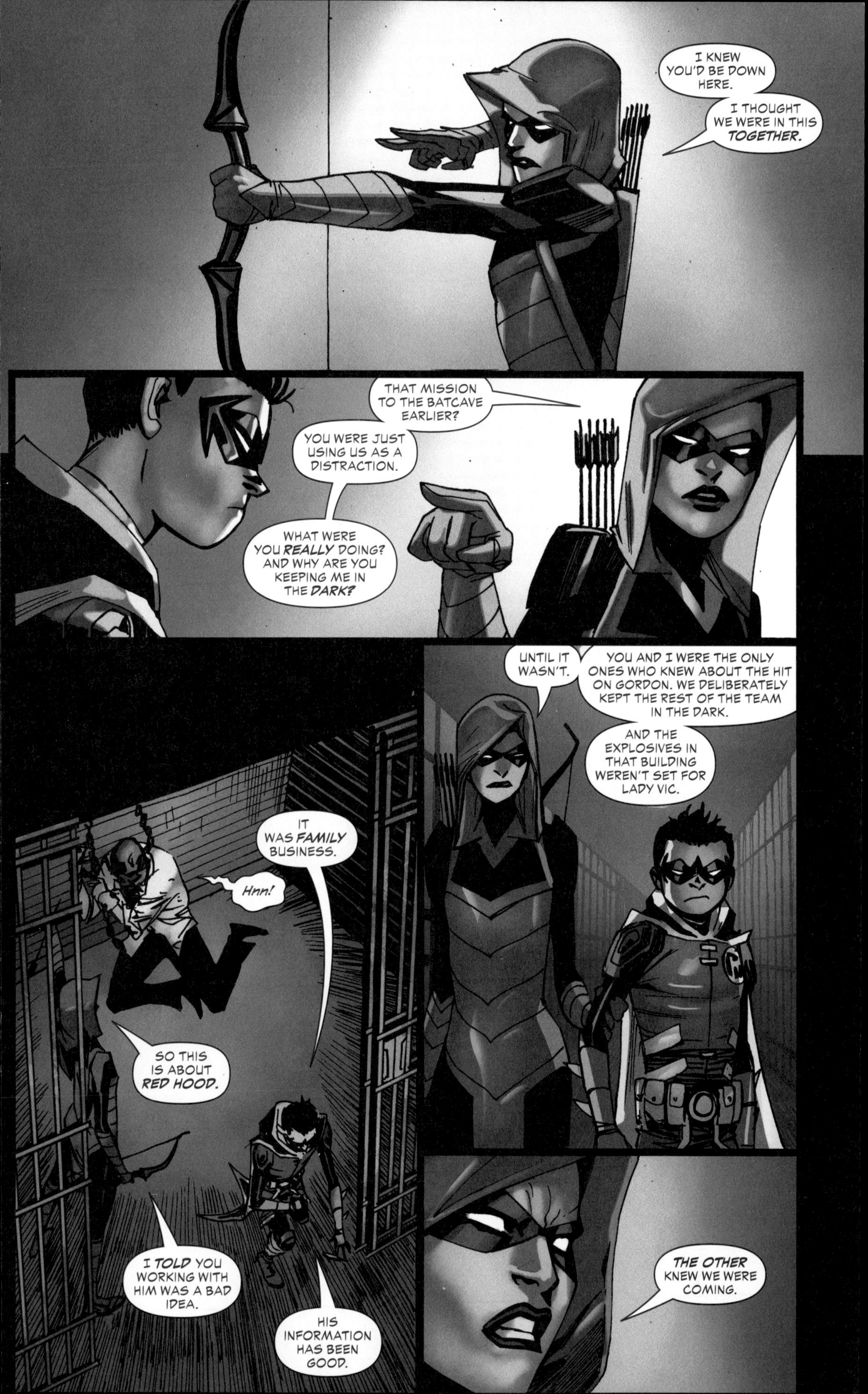
I KNEW YOU'D BE DOWN HERE.
I THOUGHT WE WERE IN THIS *TOGETHER.*
THAT MISSION TO THE BATCAVE EARLIER?
YOU WERE JUST USING US AS A DISTRACTION.
WHAT WERE YOU *REALLY* DOING? AND WHY ARE YOU KEEPING ME IN THE *DARK?*
YOU AND I WERE THE ONLY ONES WHO KNEW ABOUT THE HIT ON GORDON. WE DELIBERATELY KEPT THE REST OF THE TEAM IN THE DARK.
UNTIL IT WASN'T.
AND THE EXPLOSIVES IN THAT BUILDING WEREN'T SET FOR LADY VIC.
IT WAS *FAMILY* BUSINESS.
Hnn!
SO THIS IS ABOUT *RED HOOD.*
I *TOLD* YOU WORKING WITH HIM WAS A BAD IDEA.
HIS INFORMATION HAS BEEN GOOD.
THE OTHER KNEW WE WERE COMING.

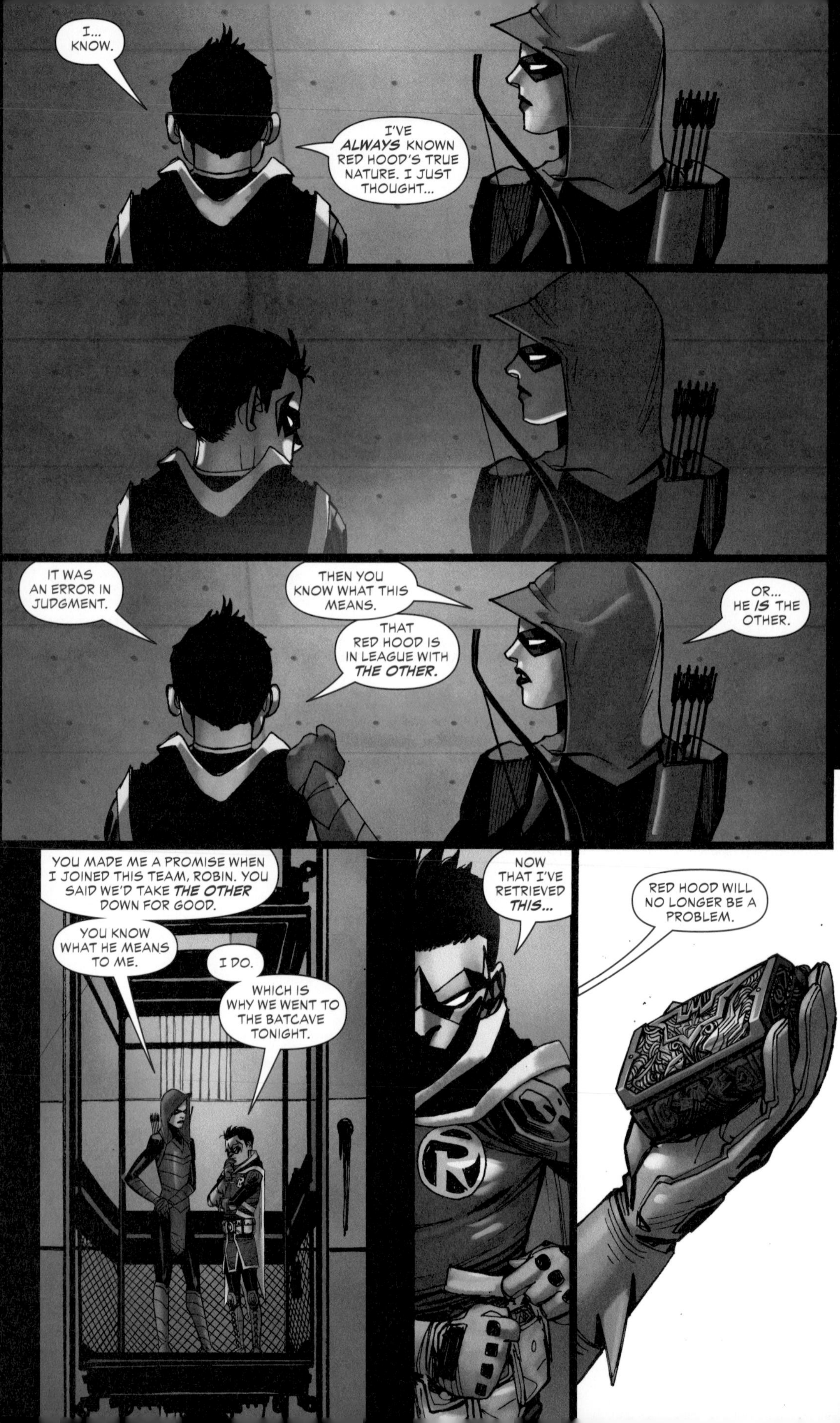
I... KNOW.
I'VE *ALWAYS* KNOWN RED HOOD'S TRUE NATURE. I JUST THOUGHT...
IT WAS AN ERROR IN JUDGMENT.
THEN YOU KNOW WHAT THIS MEANS.
THAT RED HOOD IS IN LEAGUE WITH *THE OTHER.*
OR... HE *IS* THE OTHER.
YOU MADE ME A PROMISE WHEN I JOINED THIS TEAM, ROBIN. YOU SAID WE'D TAKE *THE OTHER* DOWN FOR GOOD.
YOU KNOW WHAT HE MEANS TO ME.
I DO.
WHICH IS WHY WE WENT TO THE BATCAVE TONIGHT.
NOW THAT I'VE RETRIEVED *THIS...*
RED HOOD WILL NO LONGER BE A PROBLEM.

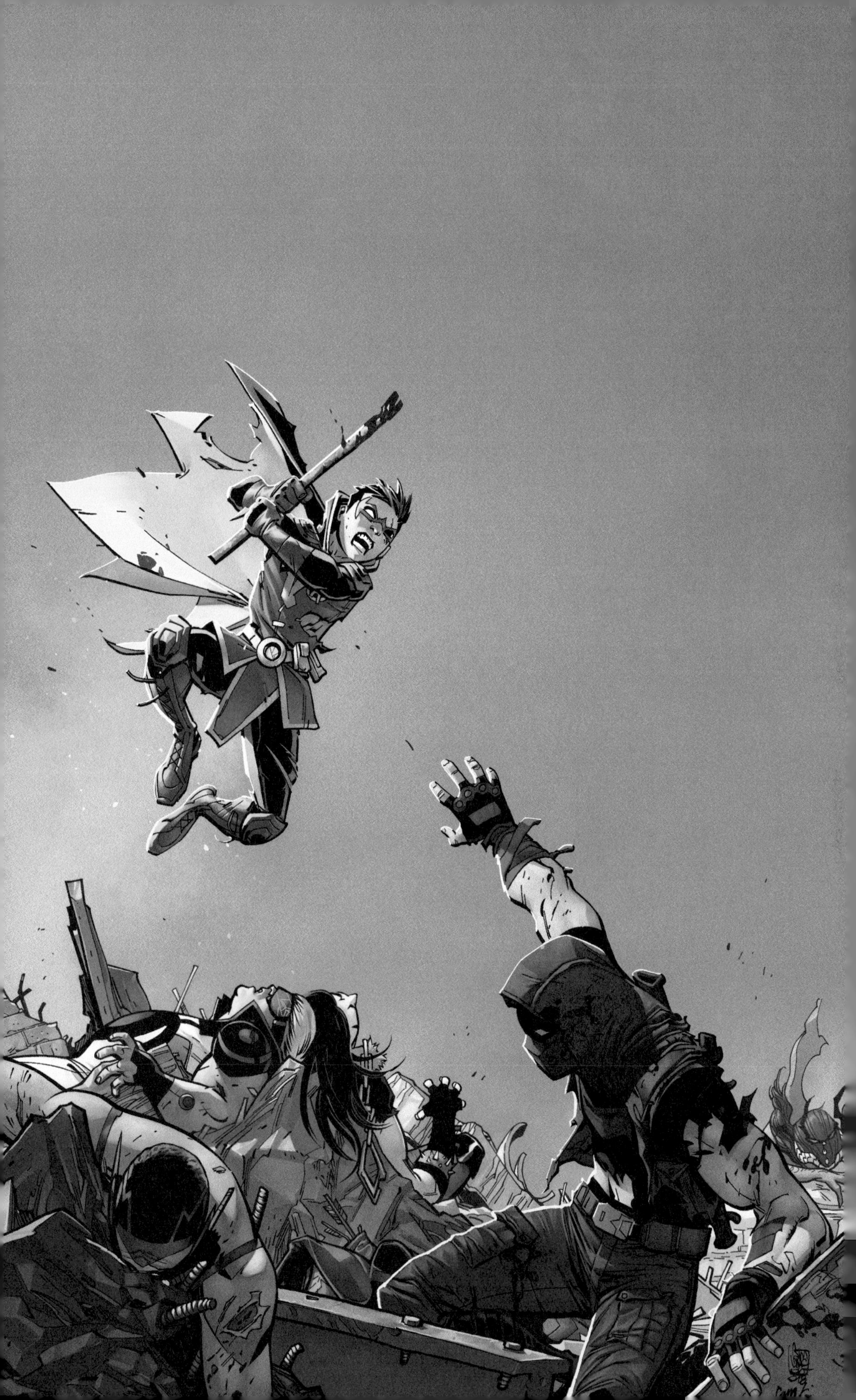

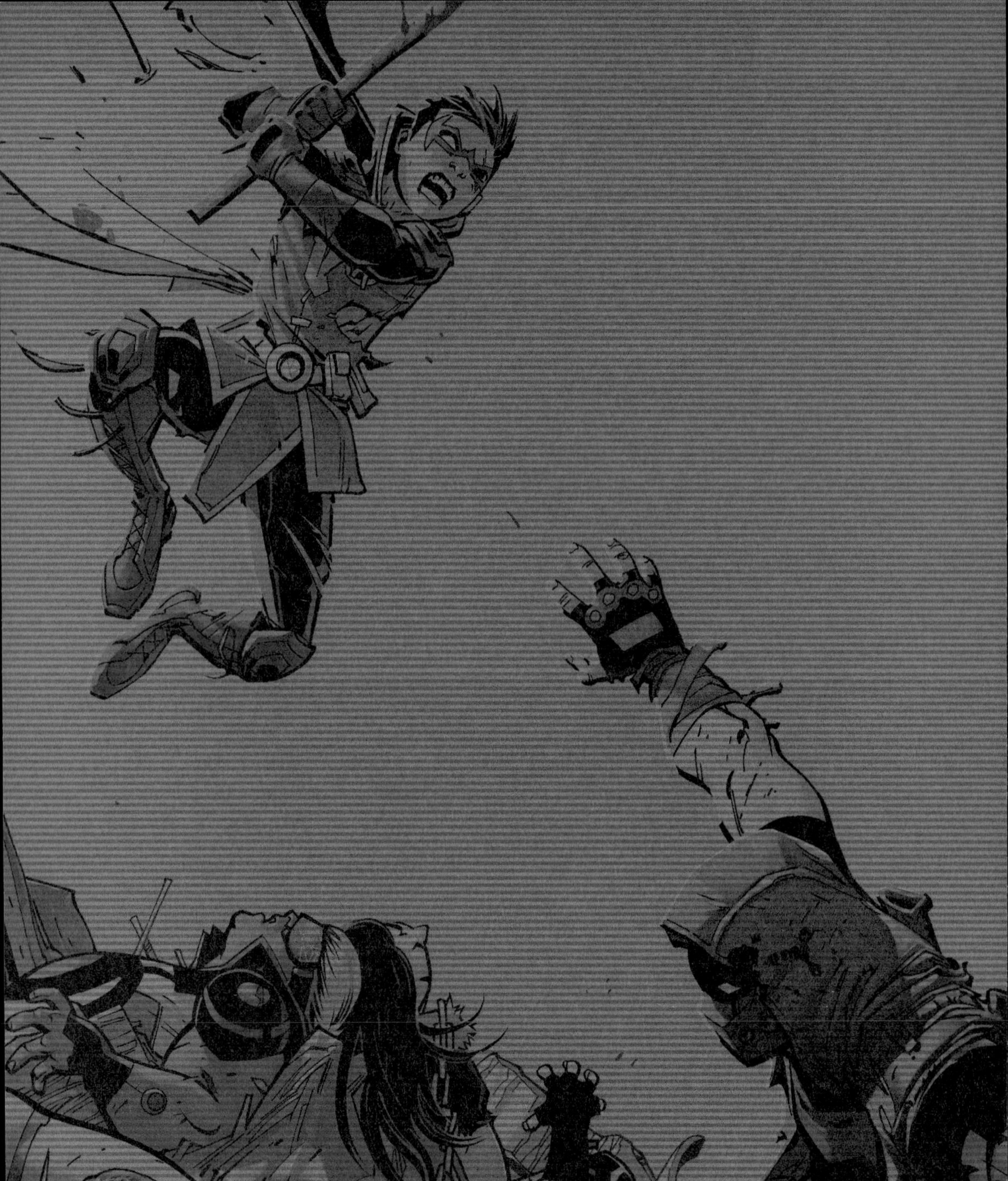

TEEN TITANS
ANNUAL #1

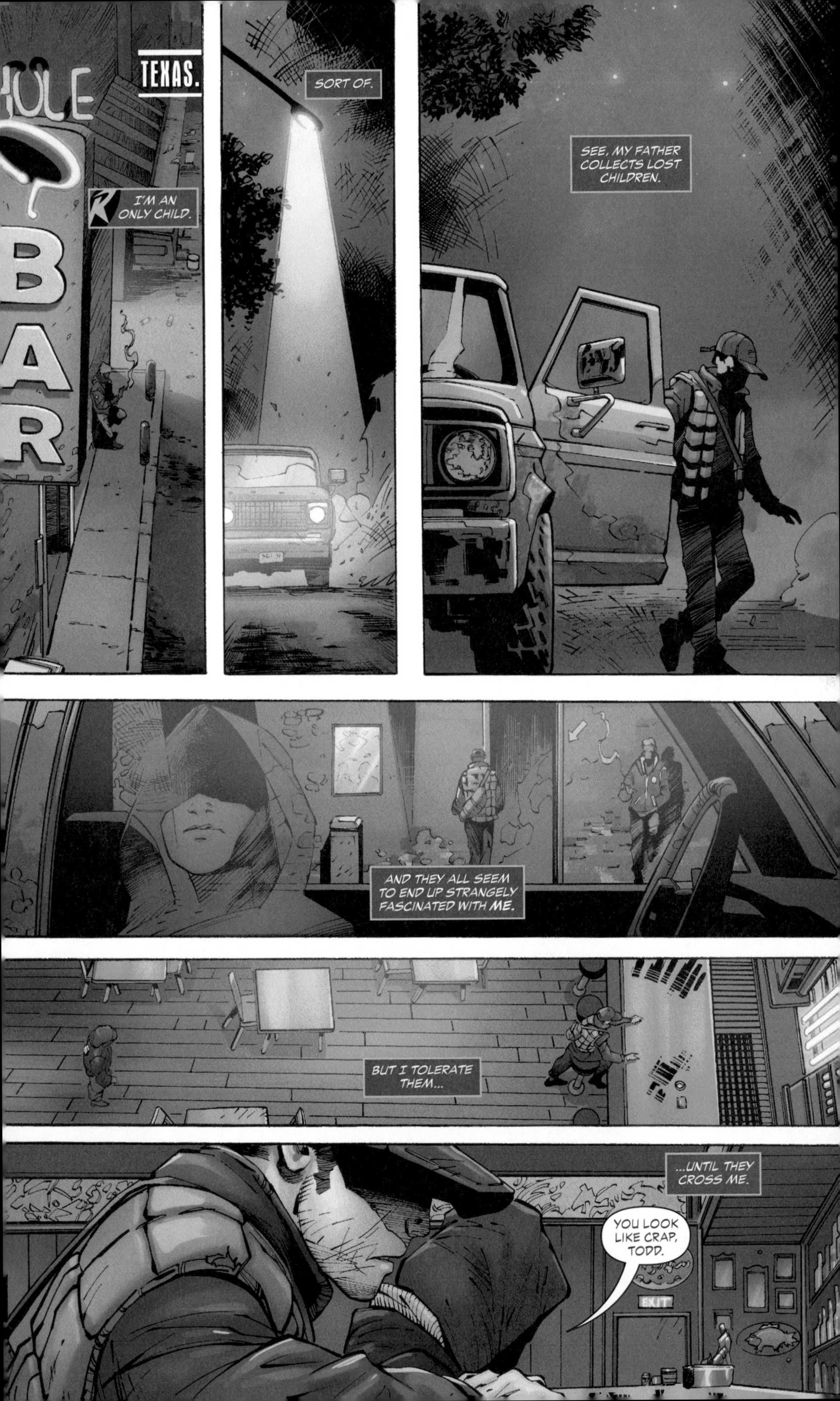

TEXAS.
HOLE
BAR
I'M AN ONLY CHILD.
SORT OF.
SEE, MY FATHER COLLECTS LOST CHILDREN.
AND THEY ALL SEEM TO END UP STRANGELY FASCINATED WITH ME.
BUT I TOLERATE THEM...
...UNTIL THEY CROSS ME.
YOU LOOK LIKE CRAP, TODD.
EXIT

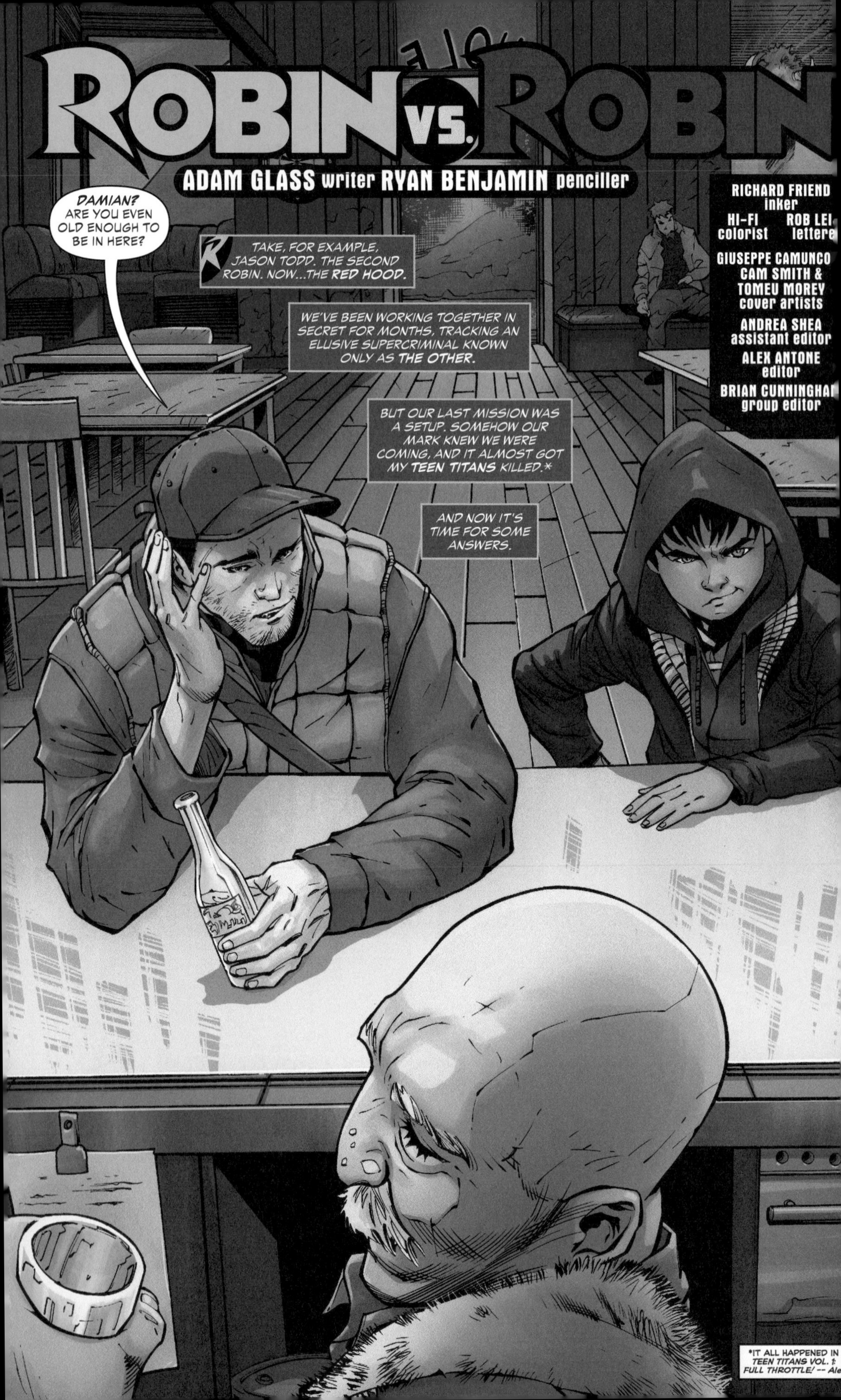
ROBIN VS. ROBIN
ADAM GLASS writer RYAN BENJAMIN penciller
RICHARD FRIEND inker
HI-FI colorist
ROB LEI lettere
GIUSEPPE CAMUNCO CAM SMITH & TOMEU MOREY cover artists
ANDREA SHEA assistant editor
ALEX ANTONE editor
BRIAN CUNNINGHAI group editor
DAMIAN? ARE YOU EVEN OLD ENOUGH TO BE IN HERE?
TAKE, FOR EXAMPLE, JASON TODD. THE SECOND ROBIN. NOW...THE RED HOOD.
WE'VE BEEN WORKING TOGETHER IN SECRET FOR MONTHS, TRACKING AN ELUSIVE SUPERCRIMINAL KNOWN ONLY AS THE OTHER.
BUT OUR LAST MISSION WAS A SETUP. SOMEHOW OUR MARK KNEW WE WERE COMING, AND IT ALMOST GOT MY TEEN TITANS KILLED.*
AND NOW IT'S TIME FOR SOME ANSWERS.
*IT ALL HAPPENED IN TEEN TITANS VOL. 1: FULL THROTTLE! -- Ale

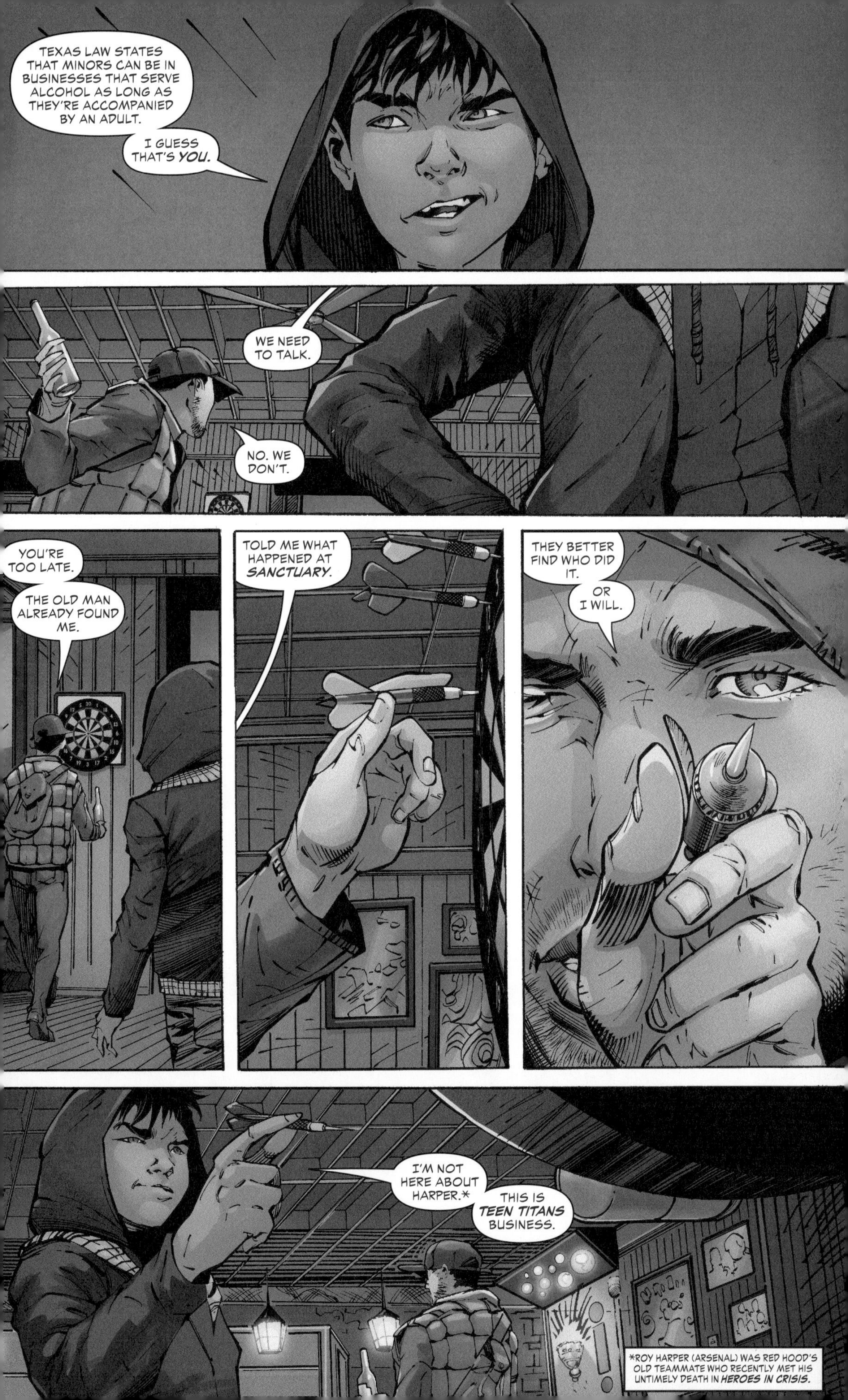
TEXAS LAW STATES THAT MINORS CAN BE IN BUSINESSES THAT SERVE ALCOHOL AS LONG AS THEY'RE ACCOMPANIED BY AN ADULT.
I GUESS THAT'S YOU.
WE NEED TO TALK.
NO. WE DON'T.
YOU'RE TOO LATE.
THE OLD MAN ALREADY FOUND ME.
TOLD ME WHAT HAPPENED AT SANCTUARY.
THEY BETTER FIND WHO DID IT.
OR I WILL.
I'M NOT HERE ABOUT HARPER.*
THIS IS TEEN TITANS BUSINESS.
*ROY HARPER (ARSENAL) WAS RED HOOD'S OLD TEAMMATE WHO RECENTLY MET HIS UNTIMELY DEATH IN HEROES IN CRISIS.

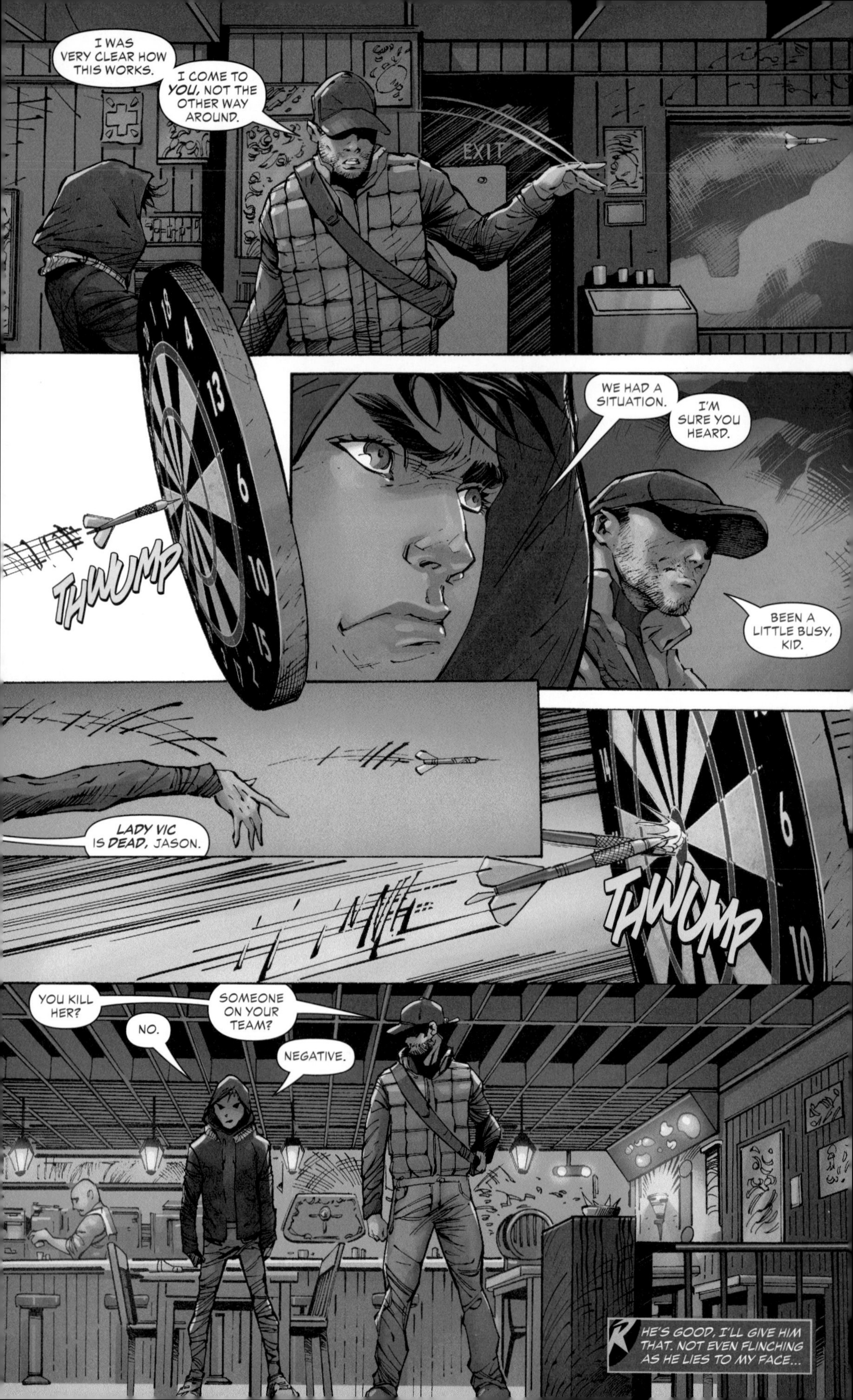
I WAS VERY CLEAR HOW THIS WORKS.
I COME TO YOU, NOT THE OTHER WAY AROUND.
EXIT
WE HAD A SITUATION.
I'M SURE YOU HEARD.
THWUMP
BEEN A LITTLE BUSY, KID.
LADY VIC IS DEAD, JASON.
THWUMP
YOU KILL HER?
NO.
SOMEONE ON YOUR TEAM?
NEGATIVE.
HE'S GOOD, I'LL GIVE HIM THAT. NOT EVEN FLINCHING AS HE LIES TO MY FACE...

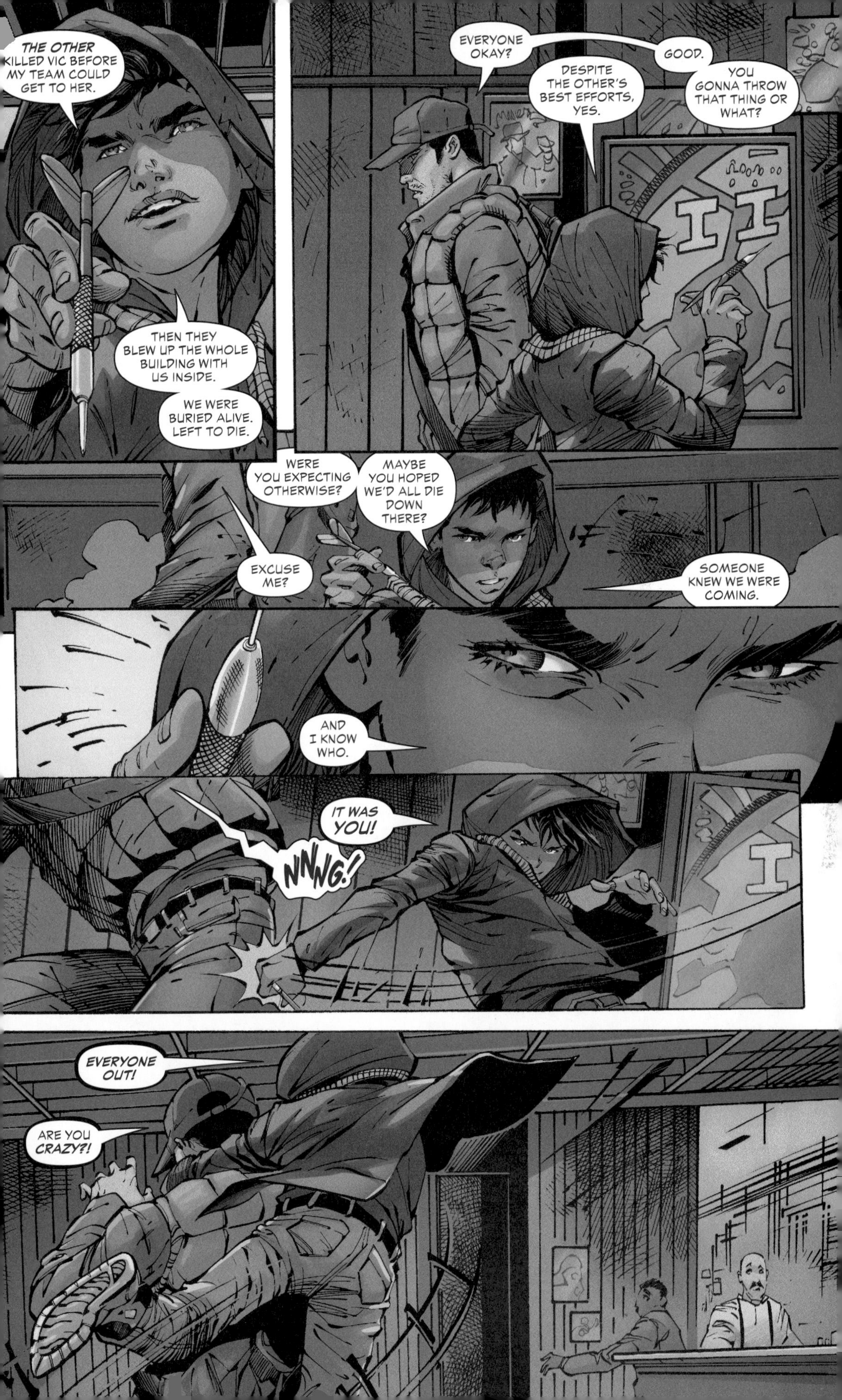
THE OTHER KILLED VIC BEFORE MY TEAM COULD GET TO HER.
THEN THEY BLEW UP THE WHOLE BUILDING WITH US INSIDE.
WE WERE BURIED ALIVE. LEFT TO DIE.
EVERYONE OKAY?
DESPITE THE OTHER'S BEST EFFORTS, YES.
GOOD.
YOU GONNA THROW THAT THING OR WHAT?
WERE YOU EXPECTING OTHERWISE?
MAYBE YOU HOPED WE'D ALL DIE DOWN THERE?
EXCUSE ME?
SOMEONE KNEW WE WERE COMING.
AND I KNOW WHO.
IT WAS YOU!
NNNG!
EVERYONE OUT!
ARE YOU CRAZY?!

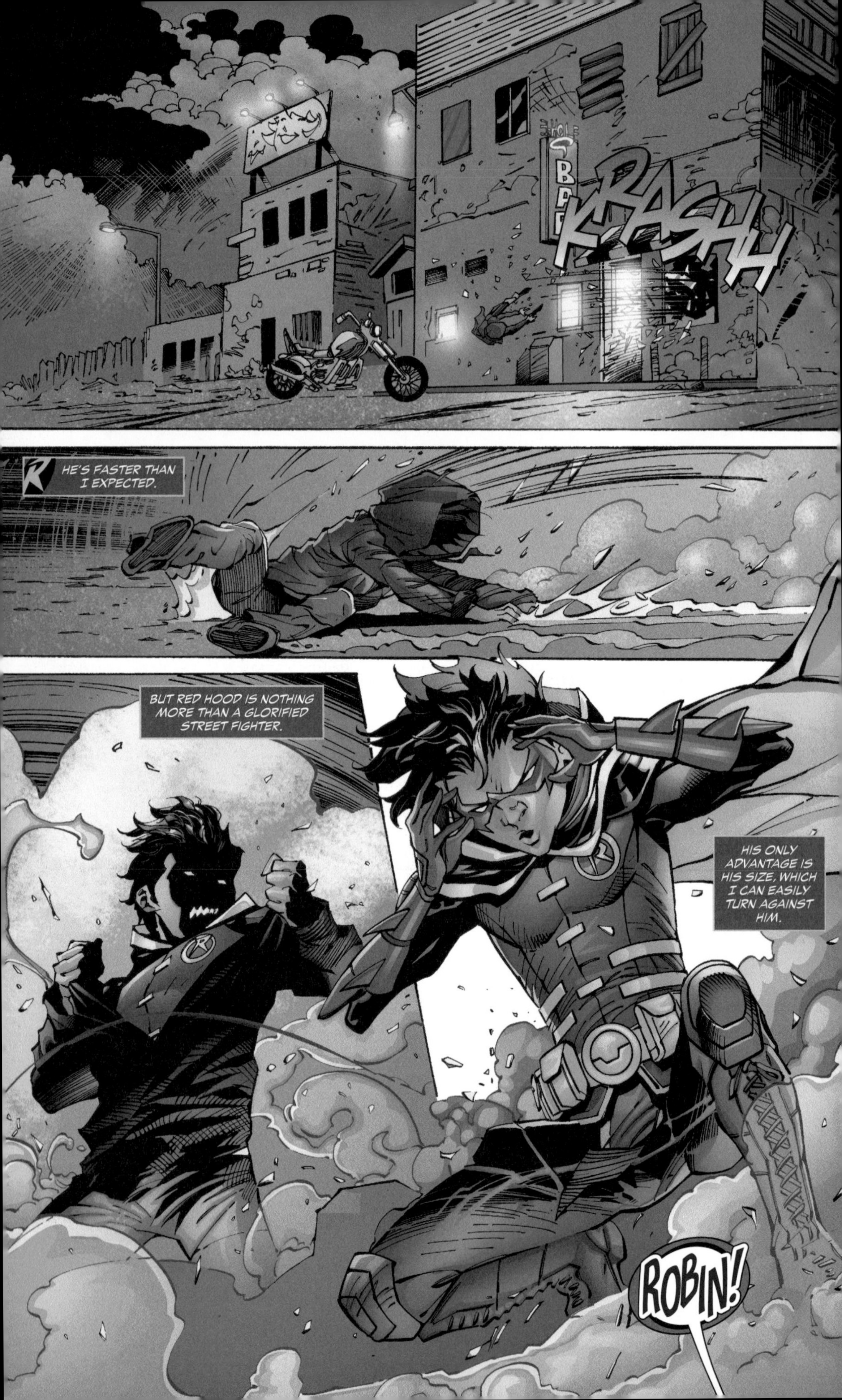
KRASHH
HE'S FASTER THAN I EXPECTED.
BUT RED HOOD IS NOTHING MORE THAN A GLORIFIED STREET FIGHTER.
HIS ONLY ADVANTAGE IS HIS SIZE, WHICH I CAN EASILY TURN AGAINST HIM.
ROBIN!

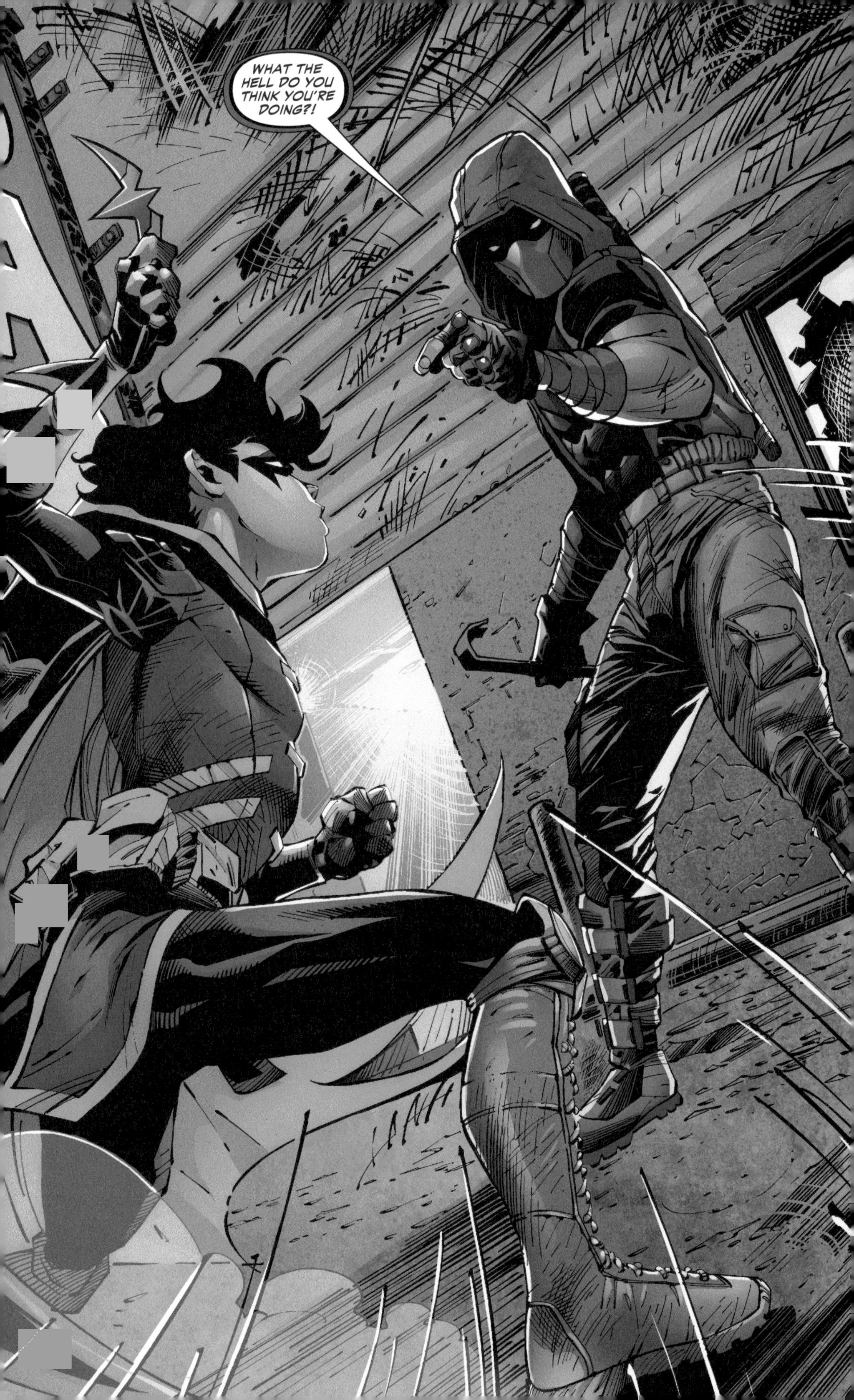
WHAT THE HELL DO YOU THINK YOU'RE DOING?!

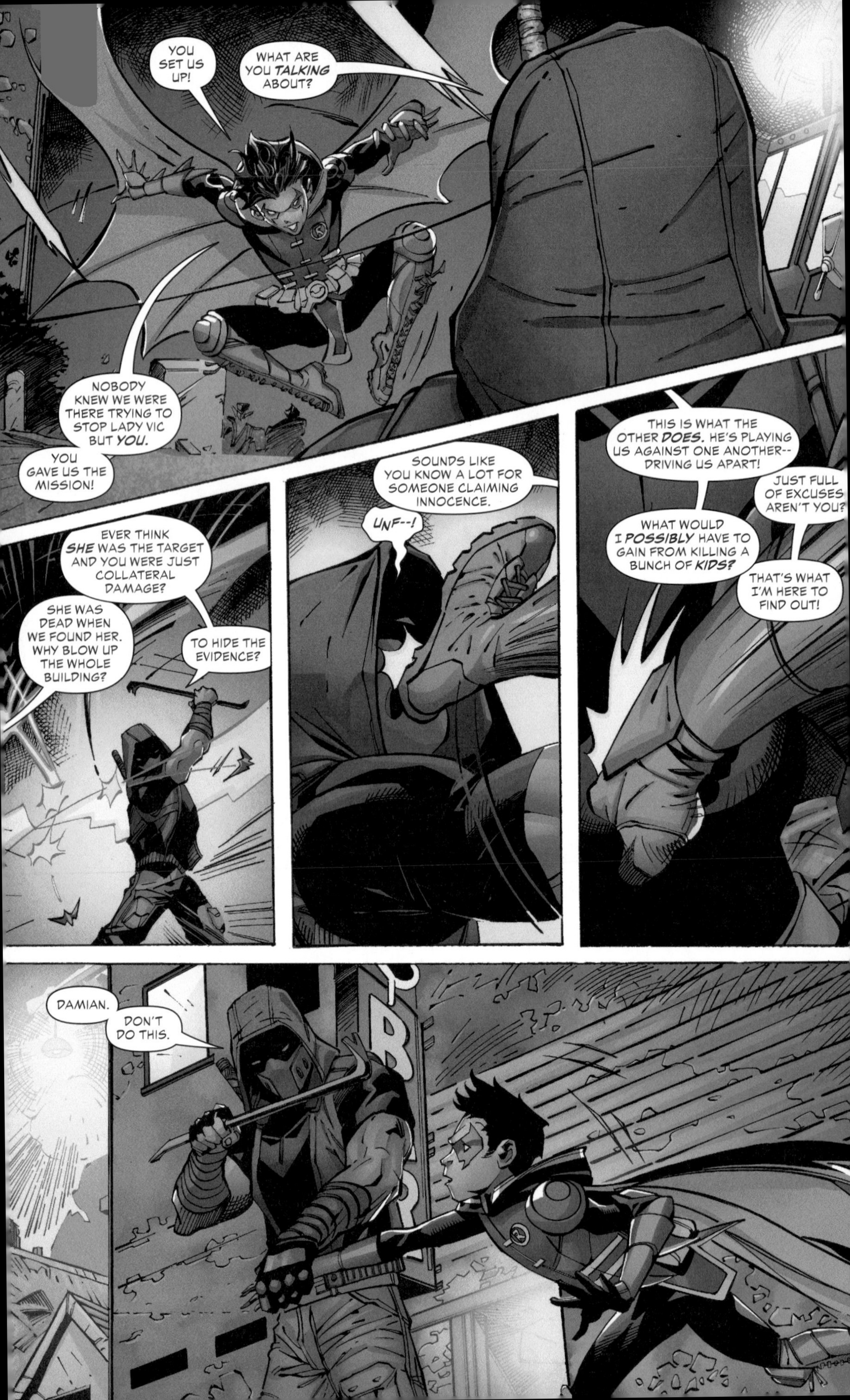

YOU SET US UP!
WHAT ARE YOU *TALKING* ABOUT?
NOBODY KNEW WE WERE THERE TRYING TO STOP LADY VIC BUT *YOU.*
YOU GAVE US THE MISSION!
EVER THINK *SHE* WAS THE TARGET AND YOU WERE JUST COLLATERAL DAMAGE?
SHE WAS DEAD WHEN WE FOUND HER. WHY BLOW UP THE WHOLE BUILDING?
TO HIDE THE EVIDENCE?
SOUNDS LIKE YOU KNOW A LOT FOR SOMEONE CLAIMING INNOCENCE.
UNF--!
THIS IS WHAT THE OTHER *DOES.* HE'S PLAYING US AGAINST ONE ANOTHER-- DRIVING US APART!
JUST FULL OF EXCUSES AREN'T YOU?
WHAT WOULD I *POSSIBLY* HAVE TO GAIN FROM KILLING A BUNCH OF *KIDS?*
THAT'S WHAT I'M HERE TO FIND OUT!
DAMIAN.
DON'T DO THIS.

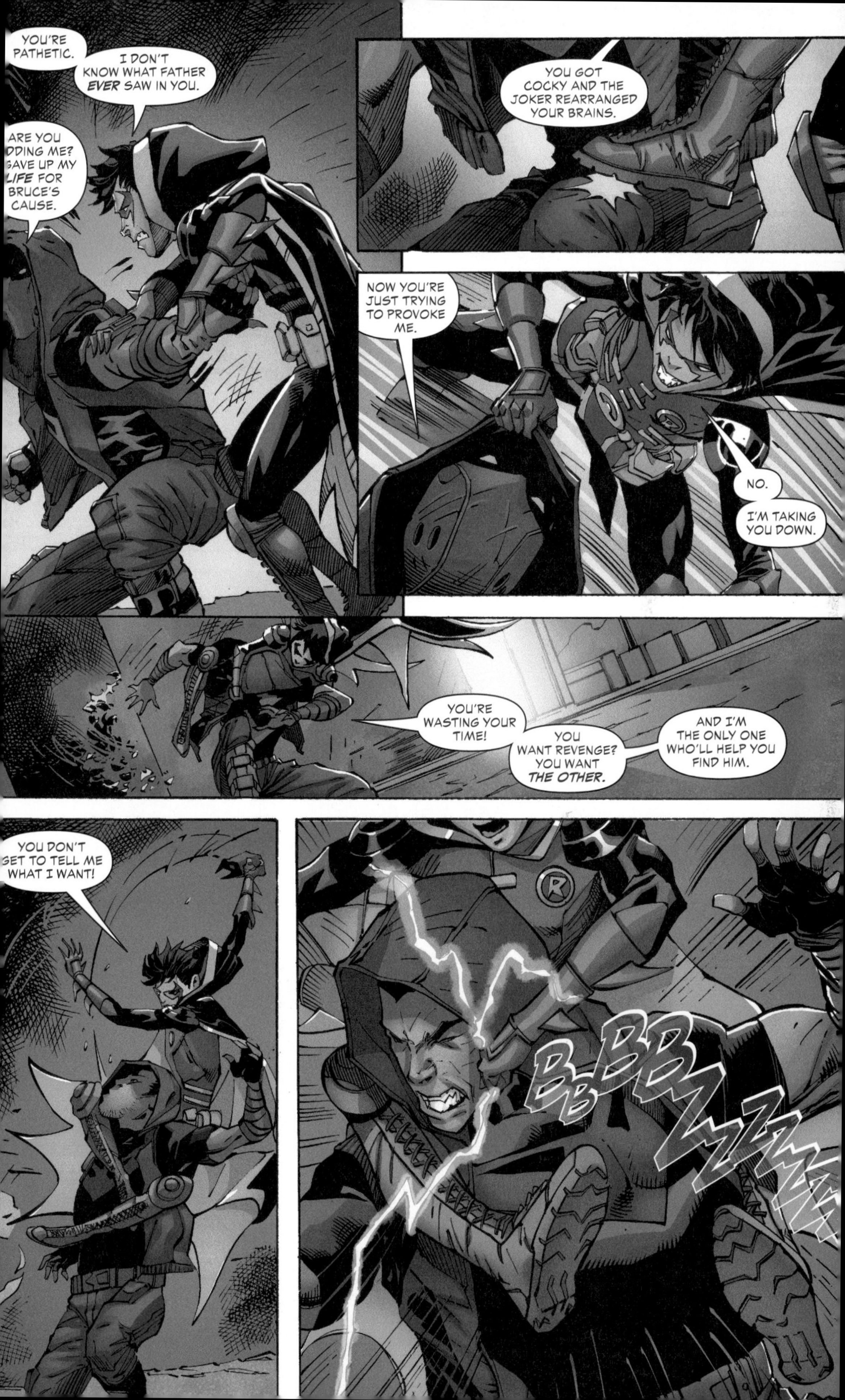
YOU'RE PATHETIC.
I DON'T KNOW WHAT FATHER EVER SAW IN YOU.
ARE YOU ...DDING ME? ...GAVE UP MY LIFE FOR BRUCE'S CAUSE.
YOU GOT COCKY AND THE JOKER REARRANGED YOUR BRAINS.
NOW YOU'RE JUST TRYING TO PROVOKE ME.
NO.
I'M TAKING YOU DOWN.
YOU'RE WASTING YOUR TIME!
YOU WANT REVENGE? YOU WANT THE OTHER.
AND I'M THE ONLY ONE WHO'LL HELP YOU FIND HIM.
YOU DON'T GET TO TELL ME WHAT I WANT!
BBBBZZZZZ

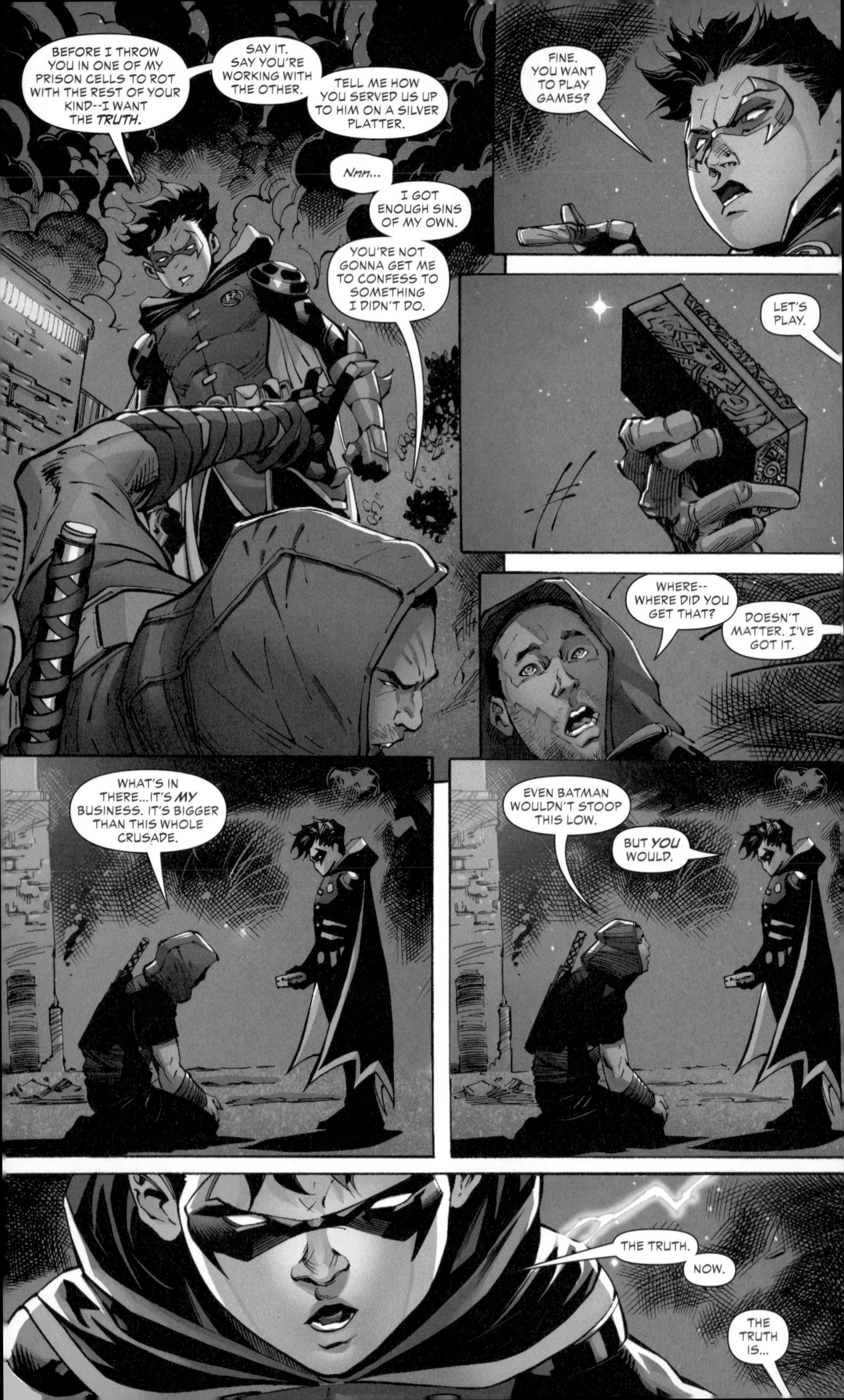
BEFORE I THROW YOU IN ONE OF MY PRISON CELLS TO ROT WITH THE REST OF YOUR KIND--I WANT THE *TRUTH.*
SAY IT. SAY YOU'RE WORKING WITH THE OTHER.
TELL ME HOW YOU SERVED US UP TO HIM ON A SILVER PLATTER.
Nnn...
I GOT ENOUGH SINS OF MY OWN.
YOU'RE NOT GONNA GET ME TO CONFESS TO SOMETHING I DIDN'T DO.
FINE. YOU WANT TO PLAY GAMES?
LET'S PLAY.
WHERE-- WHERE DID YOU GET THAT?
DOESN'T MATTER. I'VE GOT IT.
WHAT'S IN THERE...IT'S *MY* BUSINESS. IT'S BIGGER THAN THIS WHOLE CRUSADE.
EVEN BATMAN WOULDN'T STOOP THIS LOW.
BUT *YOU* WOULD.
THE TRUTH.
NOW.
THE TRUTH IS...

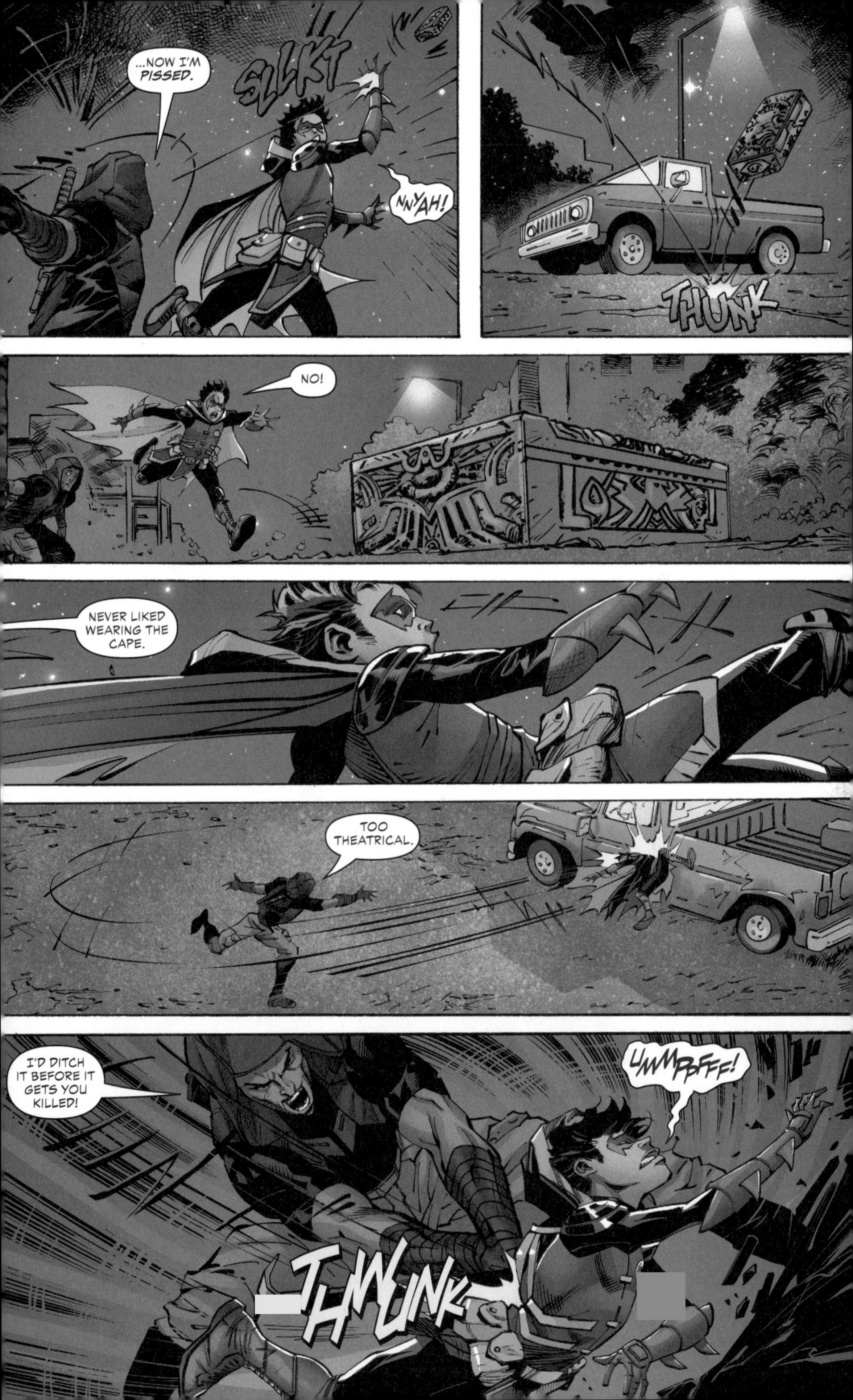
...NOW I'M PISSED.
SLLKT
NNYAH!
THUNK
NO!
NEVER LIKED WEARING THE CAPE.
TOO THEATRICAL.
I'D DITCH IT BEFORE IT GETS YOU KILLED!
UMMPFFF!
THWUNK

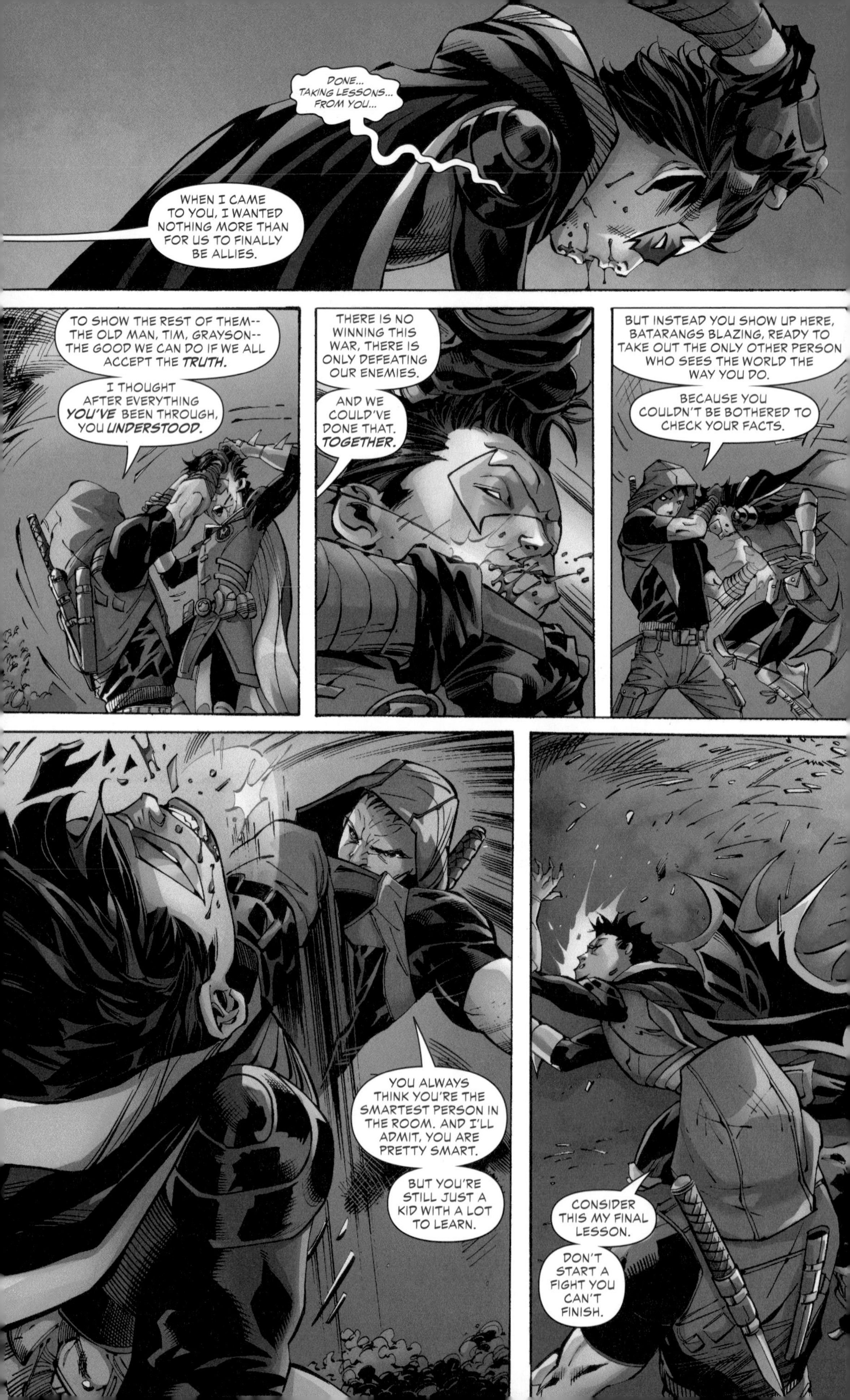
DONE... TAKING LESSONS... FROM YOU...
WHEN I CAME TO YOU, I WANTED NOTHING MORE THAN FOR US TO FINALLY BE ALLIES.
TO SHOW THE REST OF THEM-- THE OLD MAN, TIM, GRAYSON-- THE GOOD WE CAN DO IF WE ALL ACCEPT THE *TRUTH.*
I THOUGHT AFTER EVERYTHING *YOU'VE* BEEN THROUGH, YOU *UNDERSTOOD.*
THERE IS NO WINNING THIS WAR, THERE IS ONLY DEFEATING OUR ENEMIES.
AND WE COULD'VE DONE THAT. *TOGETHER.*
BUT INSTEAD YOU SHOW UP HERE, BATARANGS BLAZING, READY TO TAKE OUT THE ONLY OTHER PERSON WHO SEES THE WORLD THE WAY YOU DO.
BECAUSE YOU COULDN'T BE BOTHERED TO CHECK YOUR FACTS.
YOU ALWAYS THINK YOU'RE THE SMARTEST PERSON IN THE ROOM. AND I'LL ADMIT, YOU ARE PRETTY SMART.
BUT YOU'RE STILL JUST A KID WITH A LOT TO LEARN.
CONSIDER THIS MY FINAL LESSON.
DON'T START A FIGHT YOU CAN'T FINISH.

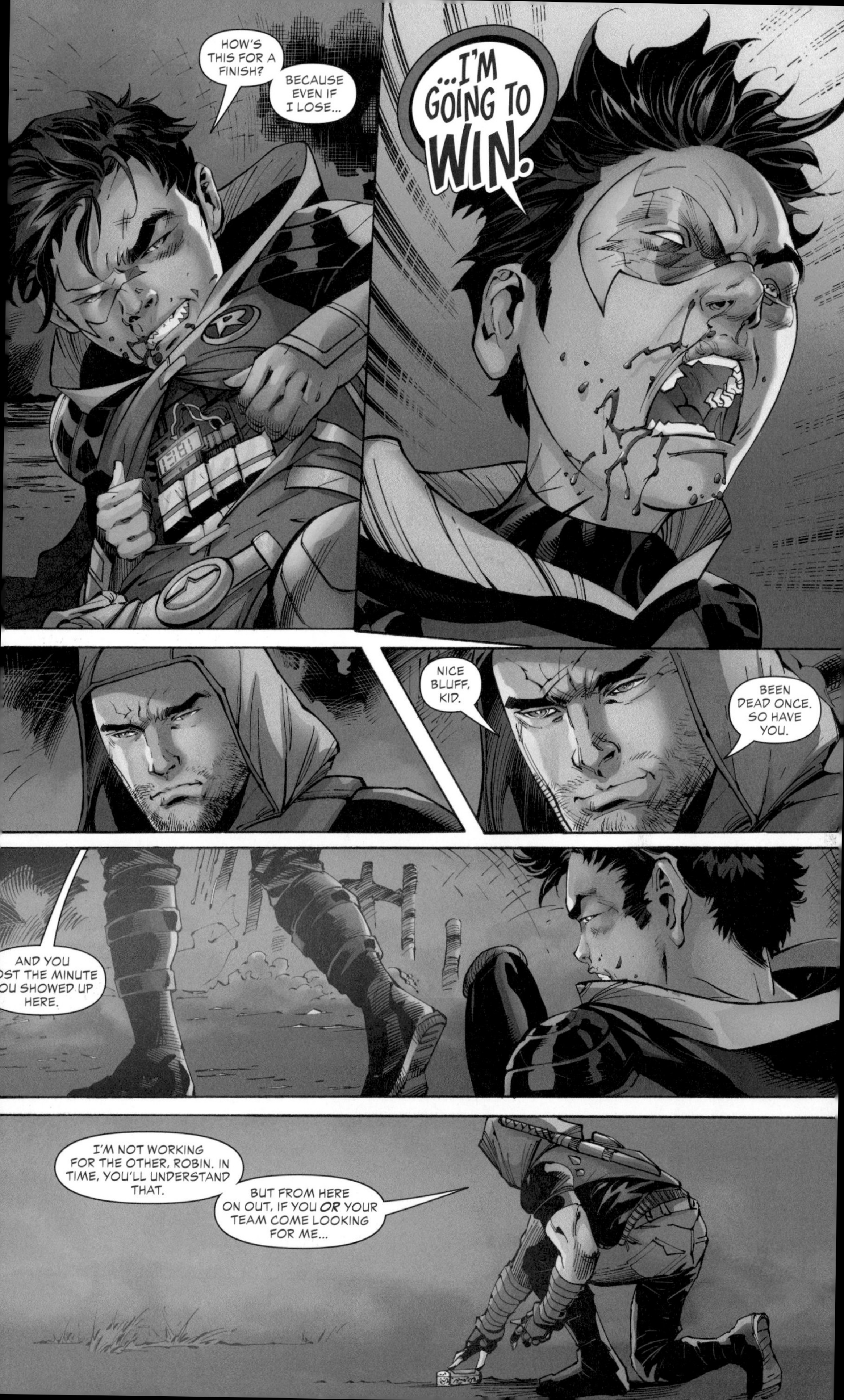
HOW'S THIS FOR A FINISH?
BECAUSE EVEN IF I LOSE...
...I'M GOING TO WIN.
NICE BLUFF, KID.
BEEN DEAD ONCE. SO HAVE YOU.
AND YOU OST THE MINUTE OU SHOWED UP HERE.
I'M NOT WORKING FOR THE OTHER, ROBIN. IN TIME, YOU'LL UNDERSTAND THAT.
BUT FROM HERE ON OUT, IF YOU OR YOUR TEAM COME LOOKING FOR ME...

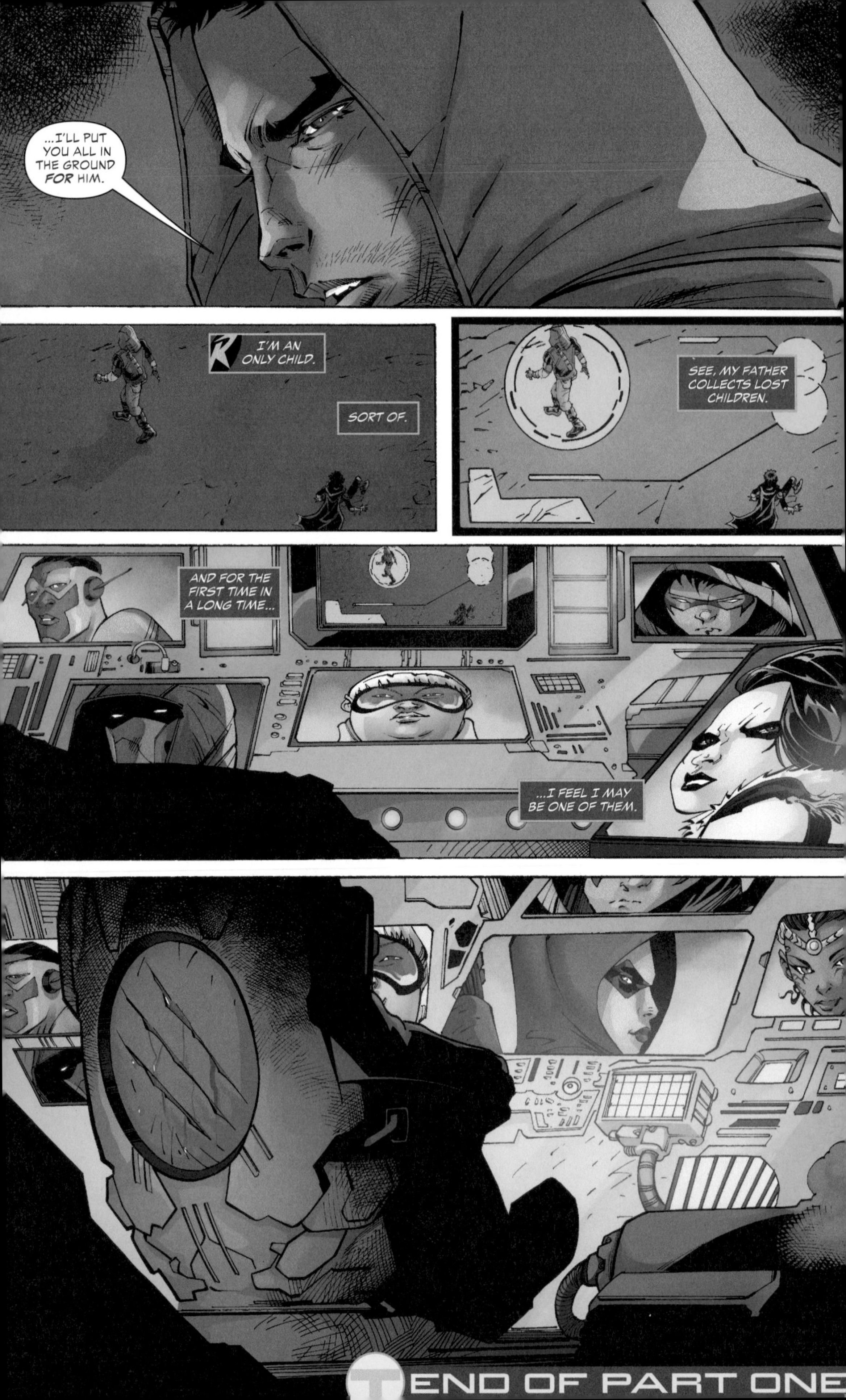
...I'LL PUT YOU ALL IN THE GROUND FOR HIM.
I'M AN ONLY CHILD.
SORT OF.
SEE, MY FATHER COLLECTS LOST CHILDREN.
AND FOR THE FIRST TIME IN A LONG TIME...
...I FEEL I MAY BE ONE OF THEM.
END OF PART ONE

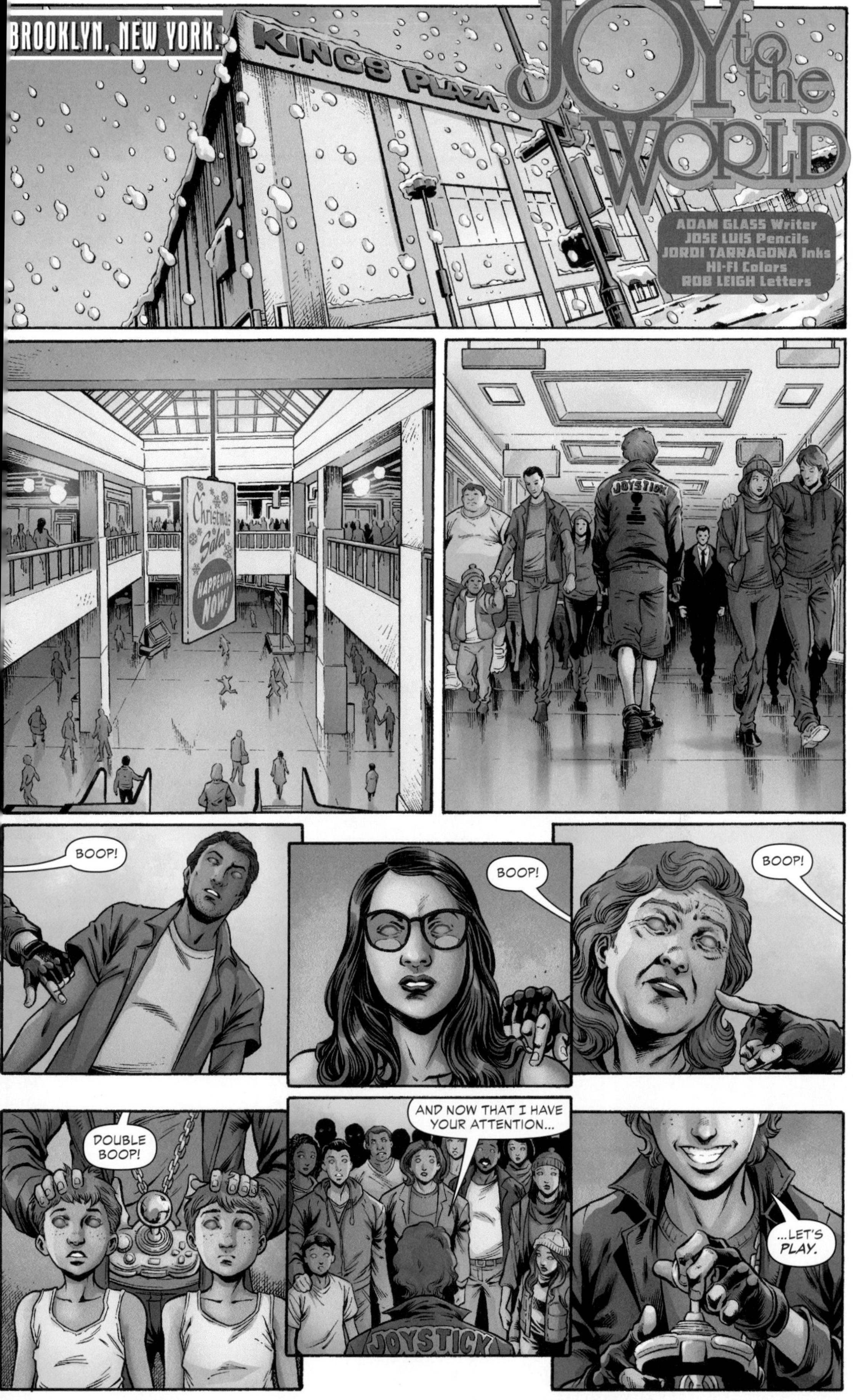
BROOKLYN, NEW YORK.
KINGS PLAZA
JOY to the WORLD
ADAM GLASS Writer
JOSE LUIS Pencils
JORDI TARRAGONA Inks
HI-FI Colors
ROB LEIGH Letters
Christmas Sales HAPPENING NOW!
JOYSTICK
BOOP!
BOOP!
BOOP!
DOUBLE BOOP!
AND NOW THAT I HAVE YOUR ATTENTION...
...LET'S PLAY.
JOYSTICK

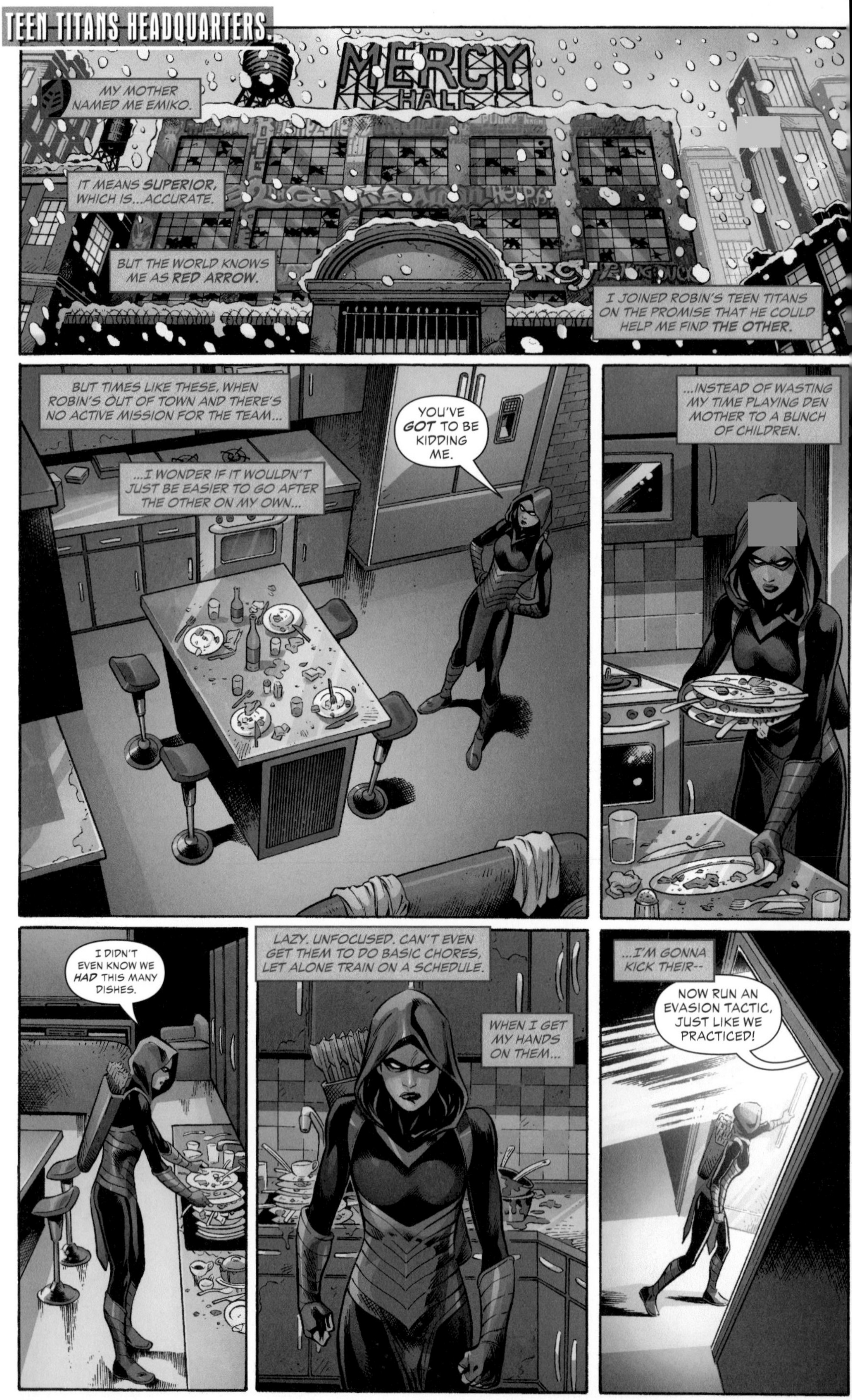
TEEN TITANS HEADQUARTERS.
MERCY HALL
MY MOTHER NAMED ME EMIKO.
IT MEANS SUPERIOR, WHICH IS...ACCURATE.
BUT THE WORLD KNOWS ME AS RED ARROW.
I JOINED ROBIN'S TEEN TITANS ON THE PROMISE THAT HE COULD HELP ME FIND THE OTHER.
BUT TIMES LIKE THESE, WHEN ROBIN'S OUT OF TOWN AND THERE'S NO ACTIVE MISSION FOR THE TEAM...
...I WONDER IF IT WOULDN'T JUST BE EASIER TO GO AFTER THE OTHER ON MY OWN...
YOU'VE GOT TO BE KIDDING ME.
...INSTEAD OF WASTING MY TIME PLAYING DEN MOTHER TO A BUNCH OF CHILDREN.
I DIDN'T EVEN KNOW WE HAD THIS MANY DISHES.
LAZY. UNFOCUSED. CAN'T EVEN GET THEM TO DO BASIC CHORES, LET ALONE TRAIN ON A SCHEDULE.
WHEN I GET MY HANDS ON THEM...
...I'M GONNA KICK THEIR--
NOW RUN AN EVASION TACTIC, JUST LIKE WE PRACTICED!

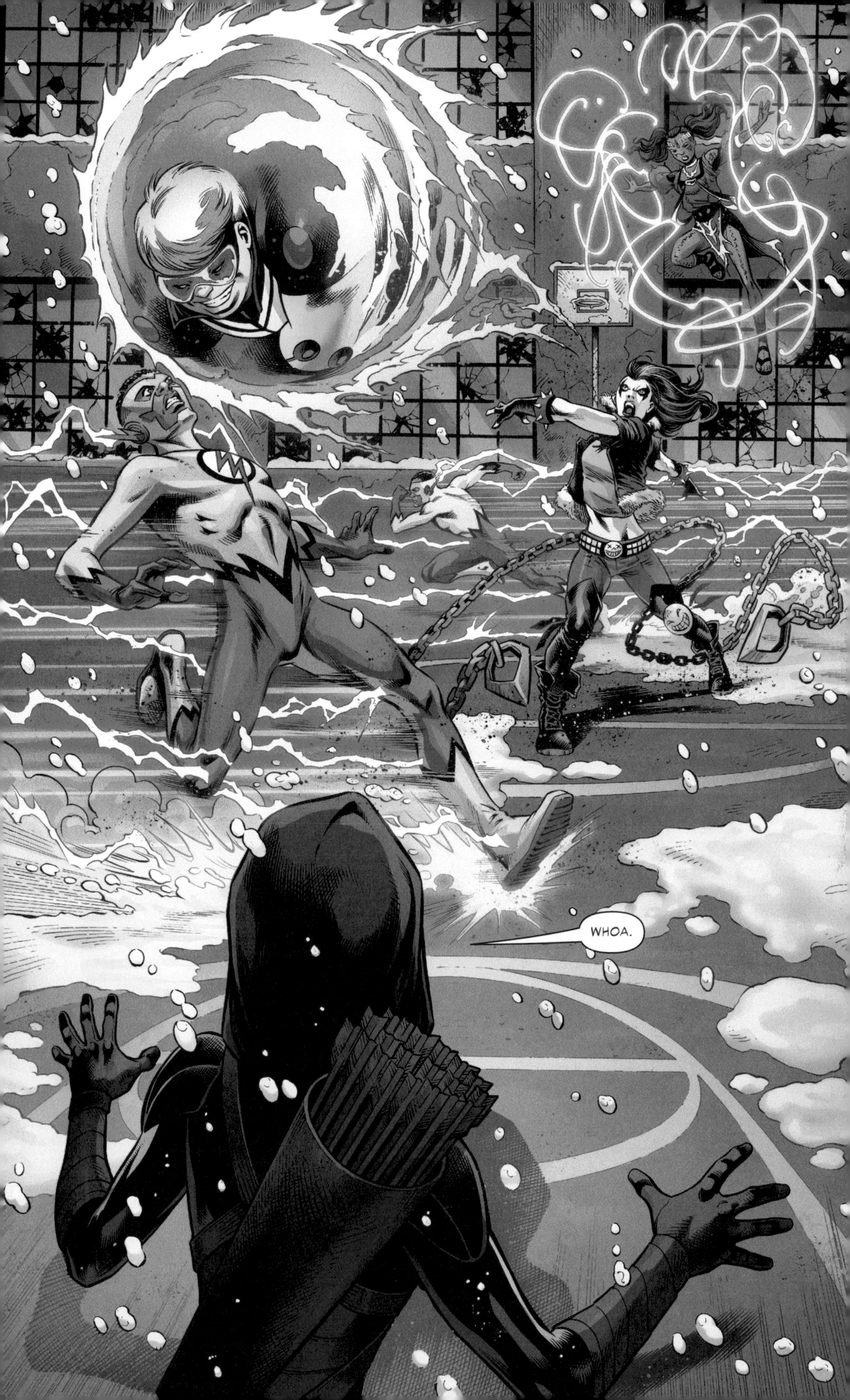
WHOA.

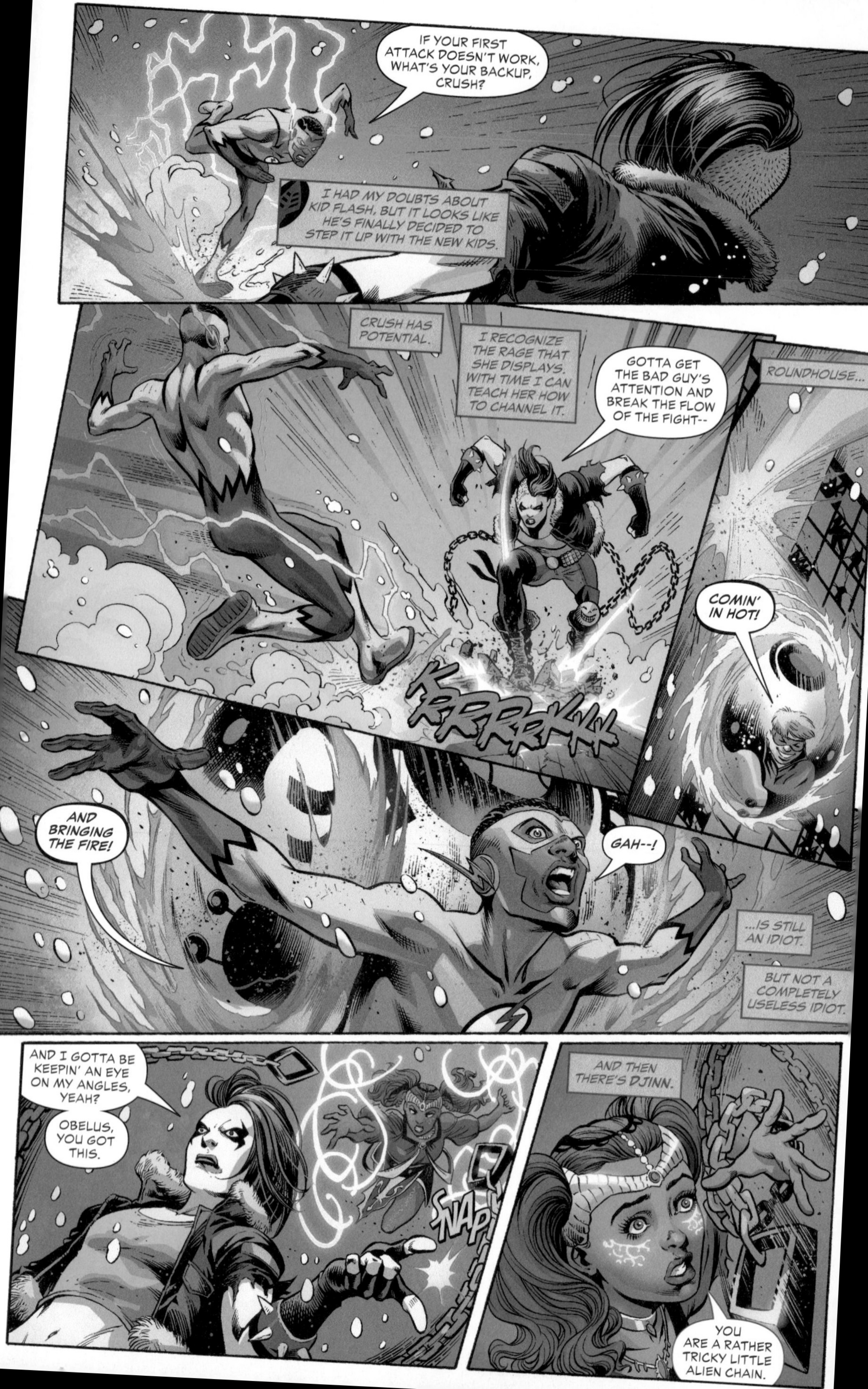
IF YOUR FIRST ATTACK DOESN'T WORK, WHAT'S YOUR BACKUP, CRUSH?
I HAD MY DOUBTS ABOUT KID FLASH. BUT IT LOOKS LIKE HE'S FINALLY DECIDED TO STEP IT UP WITH THE NEW KIDS.
CRUSH HAS POTENTIAL.
I RECOGNIZE THE RAGE THAT SHE DISPLAYS. WITH TIME I CAN TEACH HER HOW TO CHANNEL IT.
GOTTA GET THE BAD GUY'S ATTENTION AND BREAK THE FLOW OF THE FIGHT--
KRRRRKKK
ROUNDHOUSE...
COMIN' IN HOT!
AND BRINGING THE FIRE!
GAH--!
...IS STILL AN IDIOT.
BUT NOT A COMPLETELY USELESS IDIOT.
AND I GOTTA BE KEEPIN' AN EYE ON MY ANGLES, YEAH?
OBELUS, YOU GOT THIS.
SNAP
AND THEN THERE'S DJINN.
YOU ARE A RATHER TRICKY LITTLE ALIEN CHAIN.

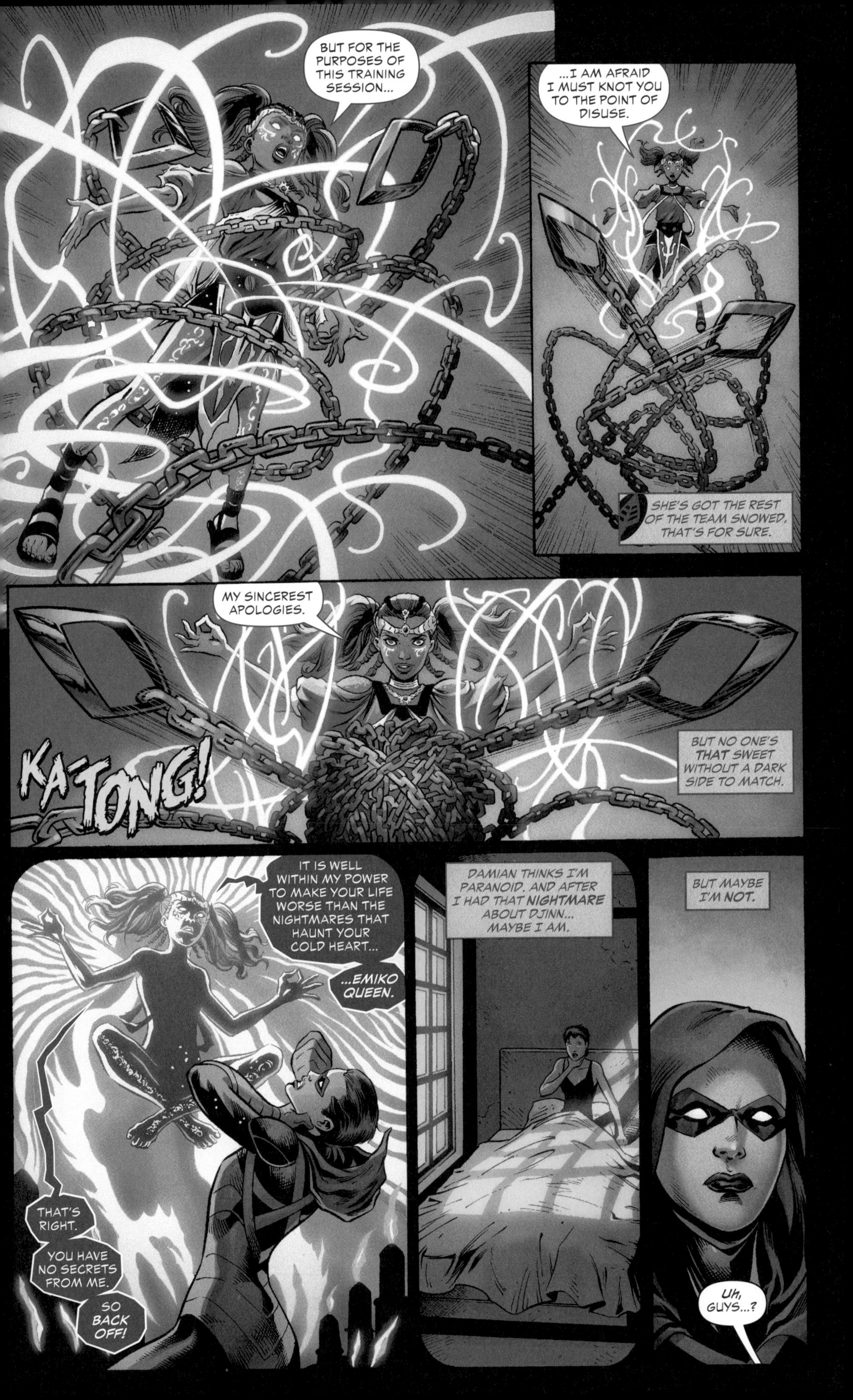
BUT FOR THE PURPOSES OF THIS TRAINING SESSION...
...I AM AFRAID I MUST KNOT YOU TO THE POINT OF DISUSE.
SHE'S GOT THE REST OF THE TEAM SNOWED, THAT'S FOR SURE.
MY SINCEREST APOLOGIES.
KA-TONG!
BUT NO ONE'S THAT SWEET WITHOUT A DARK SIDE TO MATCH.
IT IS WELL WITHIN MY POWER TO MAKE YOUR LIFE WORSE THAN THE NIGHTMARES THAT HAUNT YOUR COLD HEART...
...EMIKO QUEEN.
THAT'S RIGHT.
YOU HAVE NO SECRETS FROM ME.
SO BACK OFF!
DAMIAN THINKS I'M PARANOID. AND AFTER I HAD THAT NIGHTMARE ABOUT DJINN... MAYBE I AM.
BUT MAYBE I'M NOT.
Uh, GUYS...?

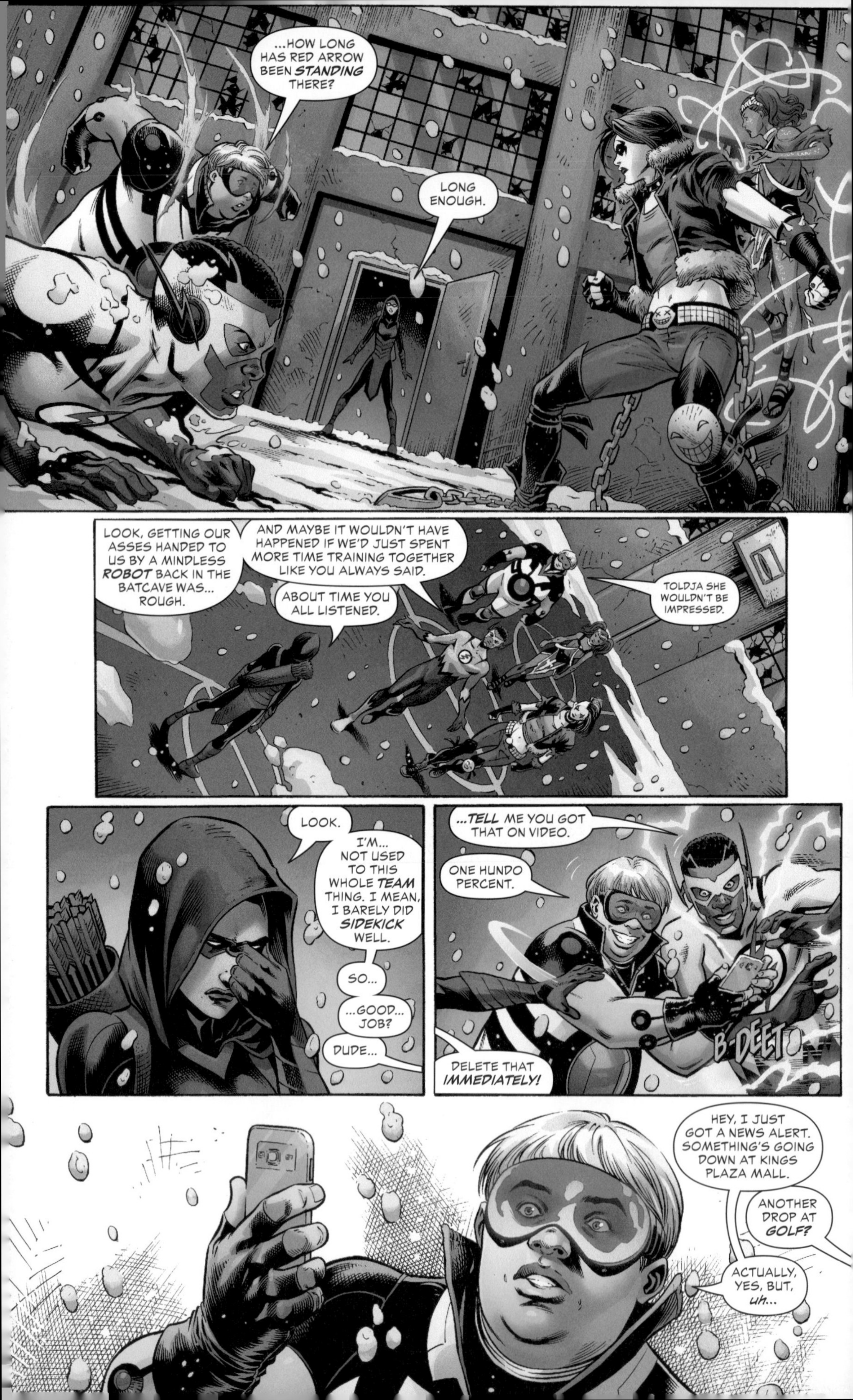
...HOW LONG HAS RED ARROW BEEN STANDING THERE?
LONG ENOUGH.
LOOK, GETTING OUR ASSES HANDED TO US BY A MINDLESS ROBOT BACK IN THE BATCAVE WAS... ROUGH.
AND MAYBE IT WOULDN'T HAVE HAPPENED IF WE'D JUST SPENT MORE TIME TRAINING TOGETHER LIKE YOU ALWAYS SAID.
ABOUT TIME YOU ALL LISTENED.
TOLDJA SHE WOULDN'T BE IMPRESSED.
LOOK.
I'M... NOT USED TO THIS WHOLE TEAM THING. I MEAN, I BARELY DID SIDEKICK WELL.
SO...
...GOOD... JOB?
DUDE...
...TELL ME YOU GOT THAT ON VIDEO.
ONE HUNDO PERCENT.
B-DEET
DELETE THAT IMMEDIATELY!
HEY, I JUST GOT A NEWS ALERT. SOMETHING'S GOING DOWN AT KINGS PLAZA MALL.
ANOTHER DROP AT GOLF?
ACTUALLY, YES, BUT, uh...

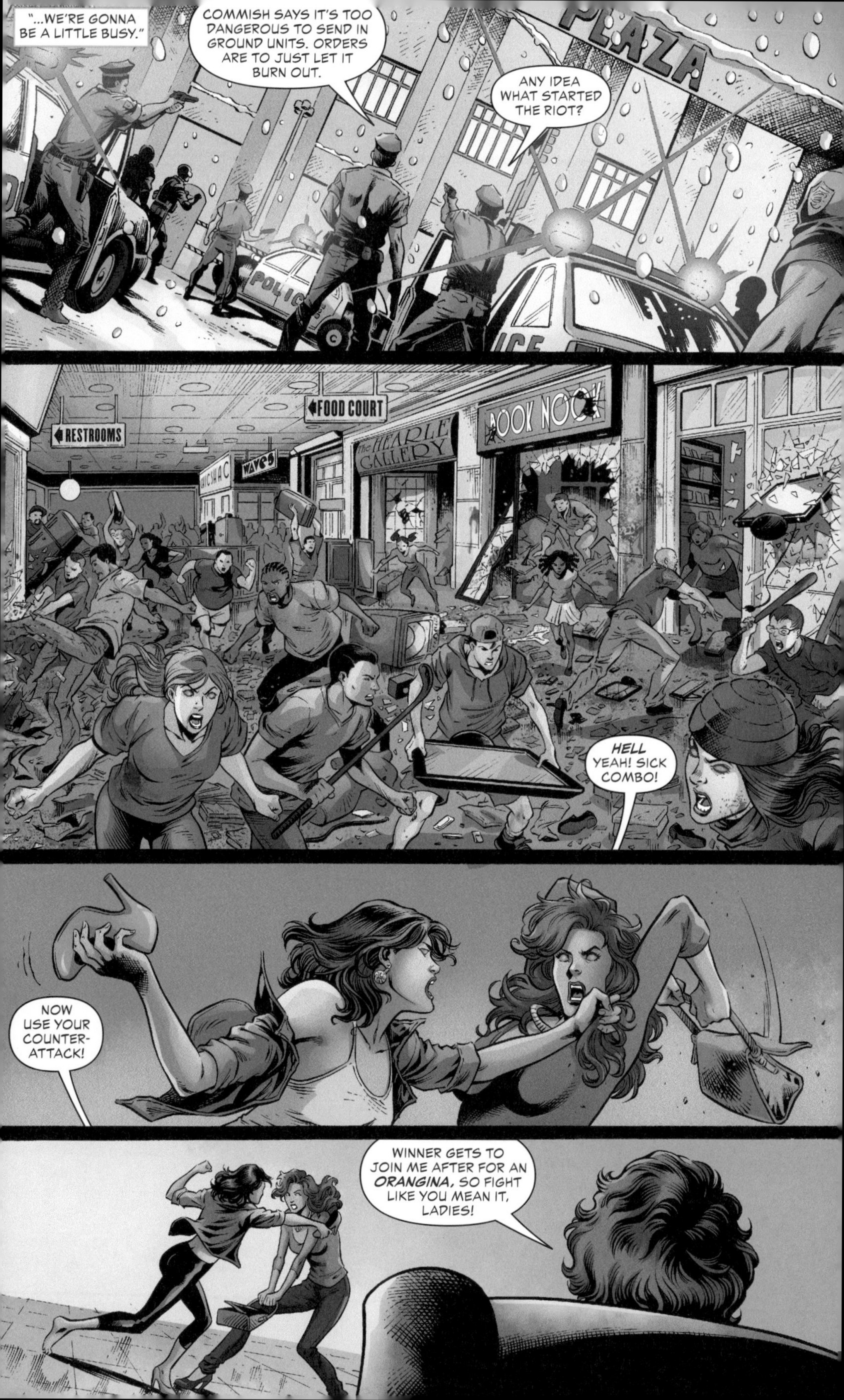
"...WE'RE GONNA BE A LITTLE BUSY."
COMMISH SAYS IT'S TOO DANGEROUS TO SEND IN GROUND UNITS. ORDERS ARE TO JUST LET IT BURN OUT.
ANY IDEA WHAT STARTED THE RIOT?
PLAZA
POLICE
RESTROOMS
FOOD COURT
BOOK NOOK
The HEARLE GALLERY
WAVES
HELL YEAH! SICK COMBO!
NOW USE YOUR COUNTER-ATTACK!
WINNER GETS TO JOIN ME AFTER FOR AN ORANGINA, SO FIGHT LIKE YOU MEAN IT, LADIES!

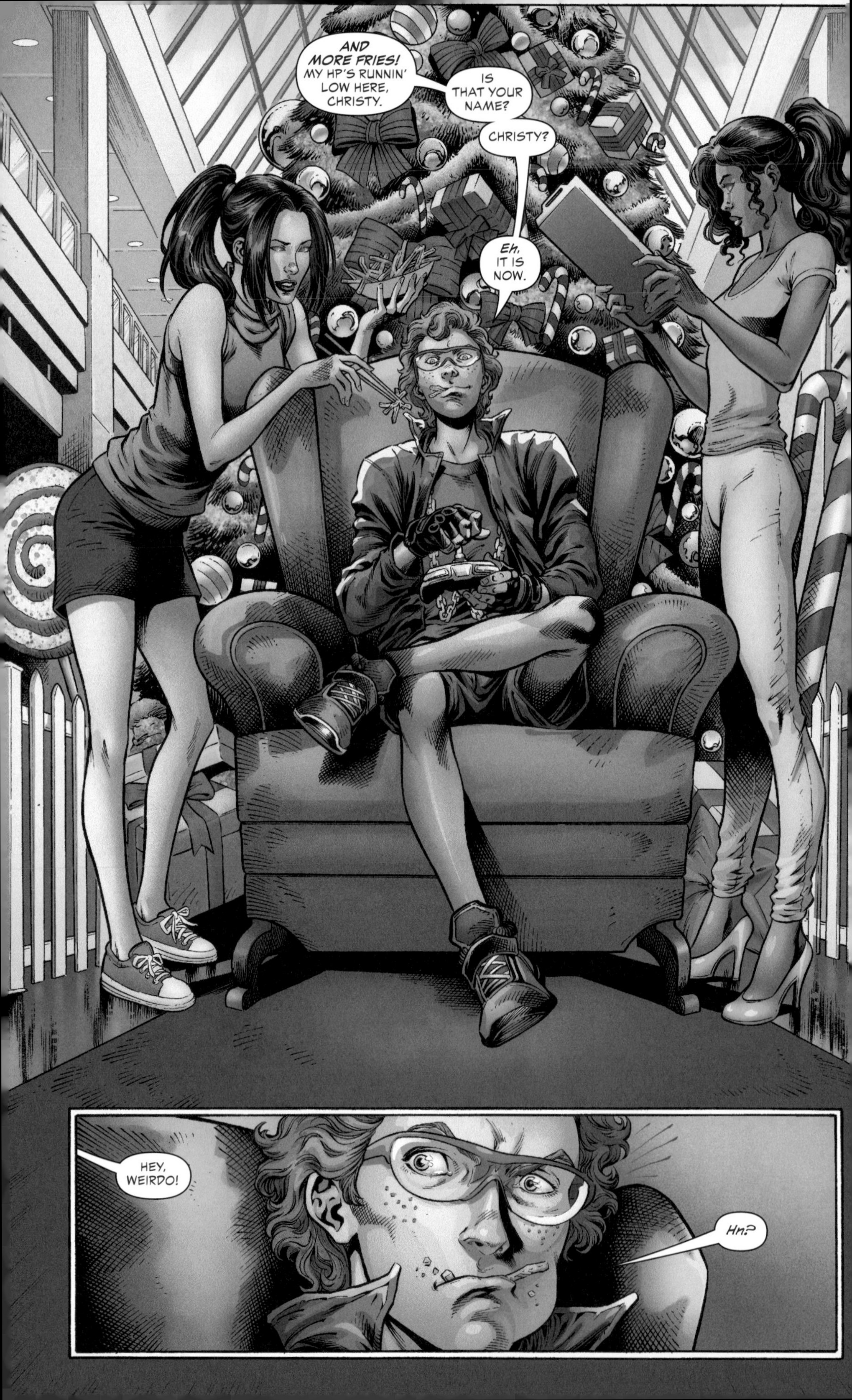
AND MORE FRIES! MY HP'S RUNNIN' LOW HERE, CHRISTY.
IS THAT YOUR NAME?
CHRISTY?
Eh, IT IS NOW.
HEY, WEIRDO!
Hn?

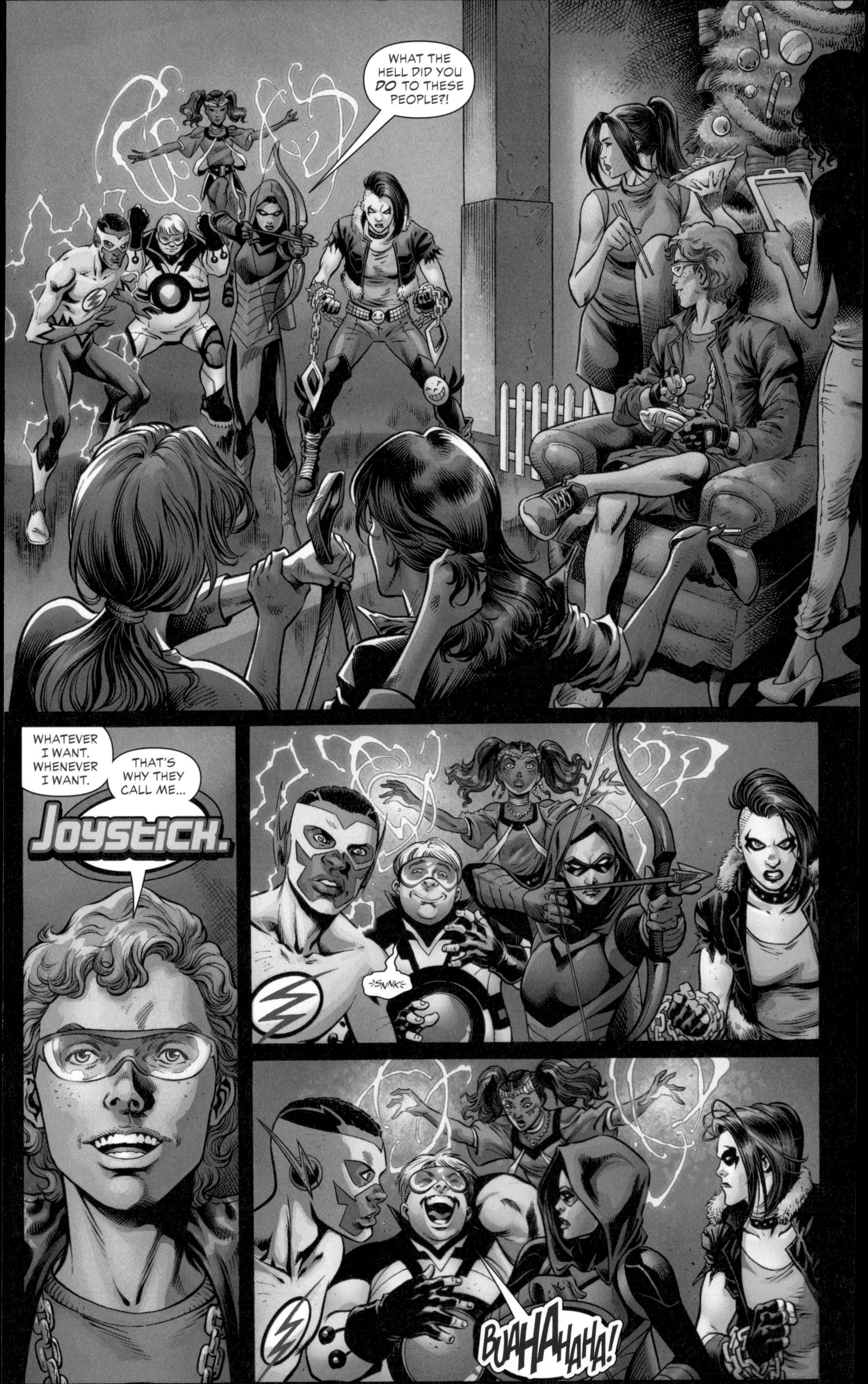
WHAT THE HELL DID YOU DO TO THESE PEOPLE?!
WHATEVER I WANT. WHENEVER I WANT.
THAT'S WHY THEY CALL ME...
Joystick.
SNNK
BUAHAHAHA!

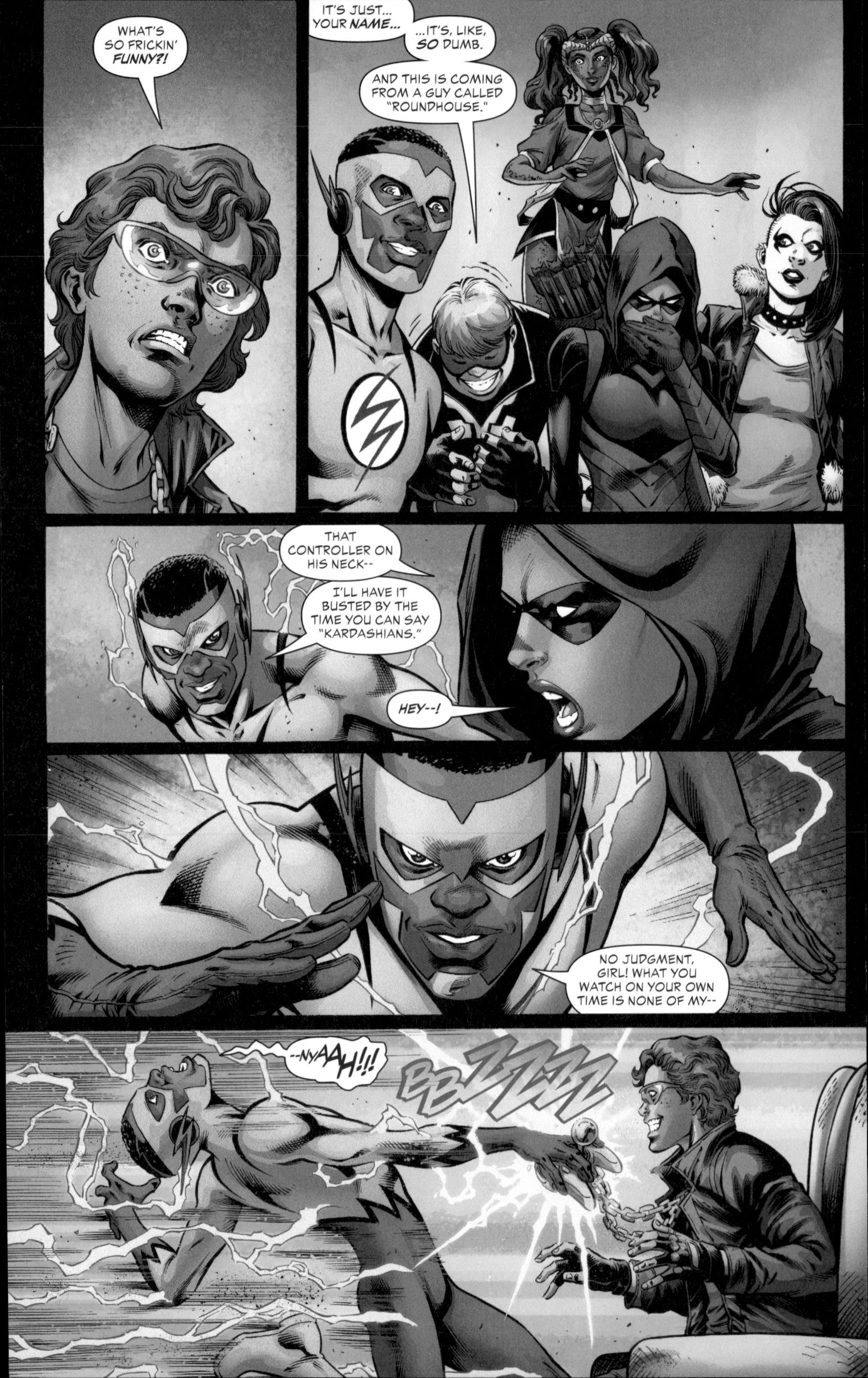

WHAT'S SO FRICKIN' FUNNY?!
IT'S JUST... YOUR NAME...
...IT'S, LIKE, SO DUMB.
AND THIS IS COMING FROM A GUY CALLED "ROUNDHOUSE."
THAT CONTROLLER ON HIS NECK--
I'LL HAVE IT BUSTED BY THE TIME YOU CAN SAY "KARDASHIANS."
HEY--!
NO JUDGMENT, GIRL! WHAT YOU WATCH ON YOUR OWN TIME IS NONE OF MY--
--NYAAH!!!
BBZZZZT

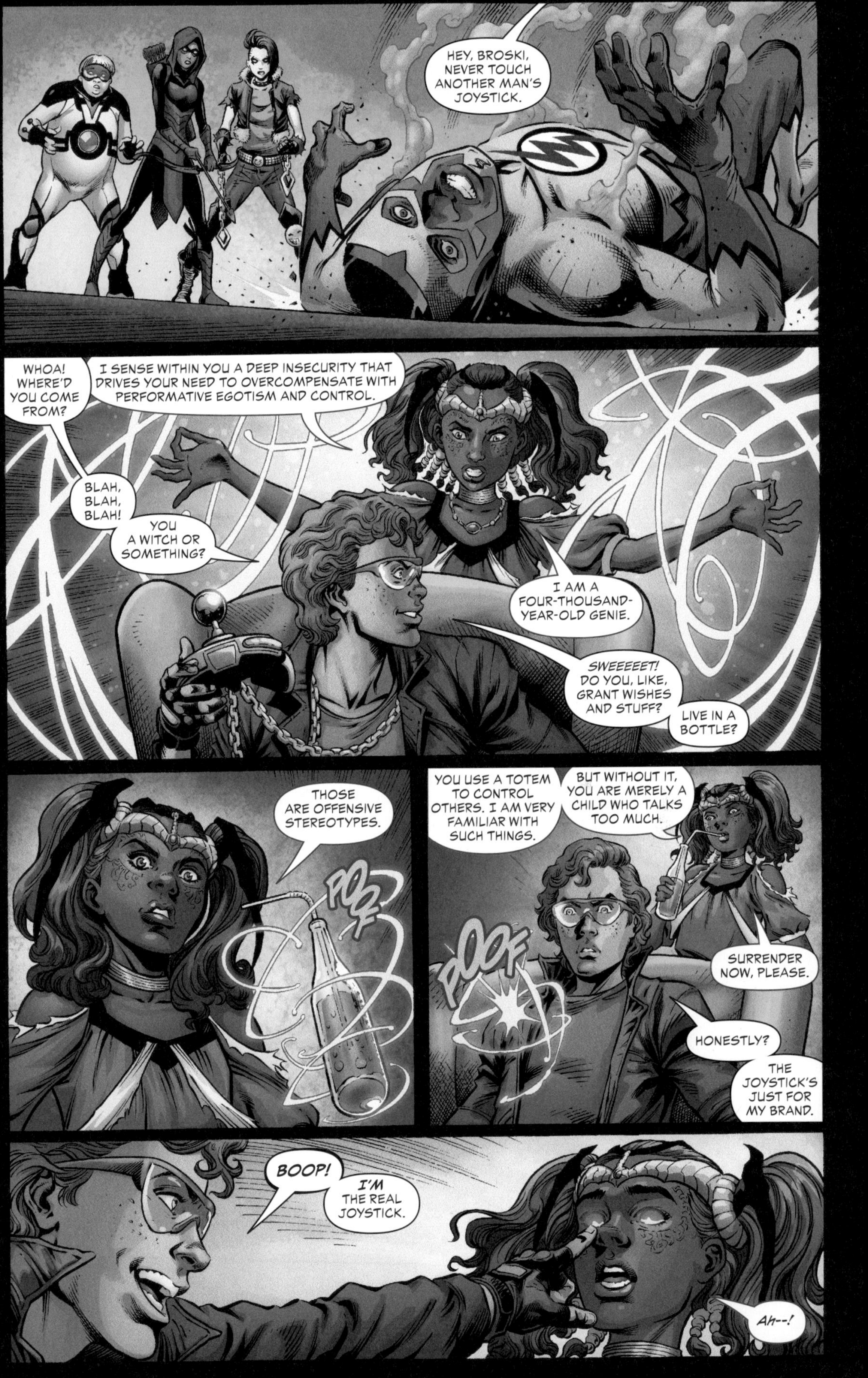
HEY, BROSKI, NEVER TOUCH ANOTHER MAN'S JOYSTICK.
WHOA! WHERE'D YOU COME FROM?
I SENSE WITHIN YOU A DEEP INSECURITY THAT DRIVES YOUR NEED TO OVERCOMPENSATE WITH PERFORMATIVE EGOTISM AND CONTROL.
BLAH, BLAH, BLAH!
YOU A WITCH OR SOMETHING?
I AM A FOUR-THOUSAND-YEAR-OLD GENIE.
SWEEEEET! DO YOU, LIKE, GRANT WISHES AND STUFF?
LIVE IN A BOTTLE?
THOSE ARE OFFENSIVE STEREOTYPES.
POOF
YOU USE A TOTEM TO CONTROL OTHERS. I AM VERY FAMILIAR WITH SUCH THINGS.
BUT WITHOUT IT, YOU ARE MERELY A CHILD WHO TALKS TOO MUCH.
POOF
SURRENDER NOW, PLEASE.
HONESTLY?
THE JOYSTICK'S JUST FOR MY BRAND.
BOOP!
I'M THE REAL JOYSTICK.
Ah--!

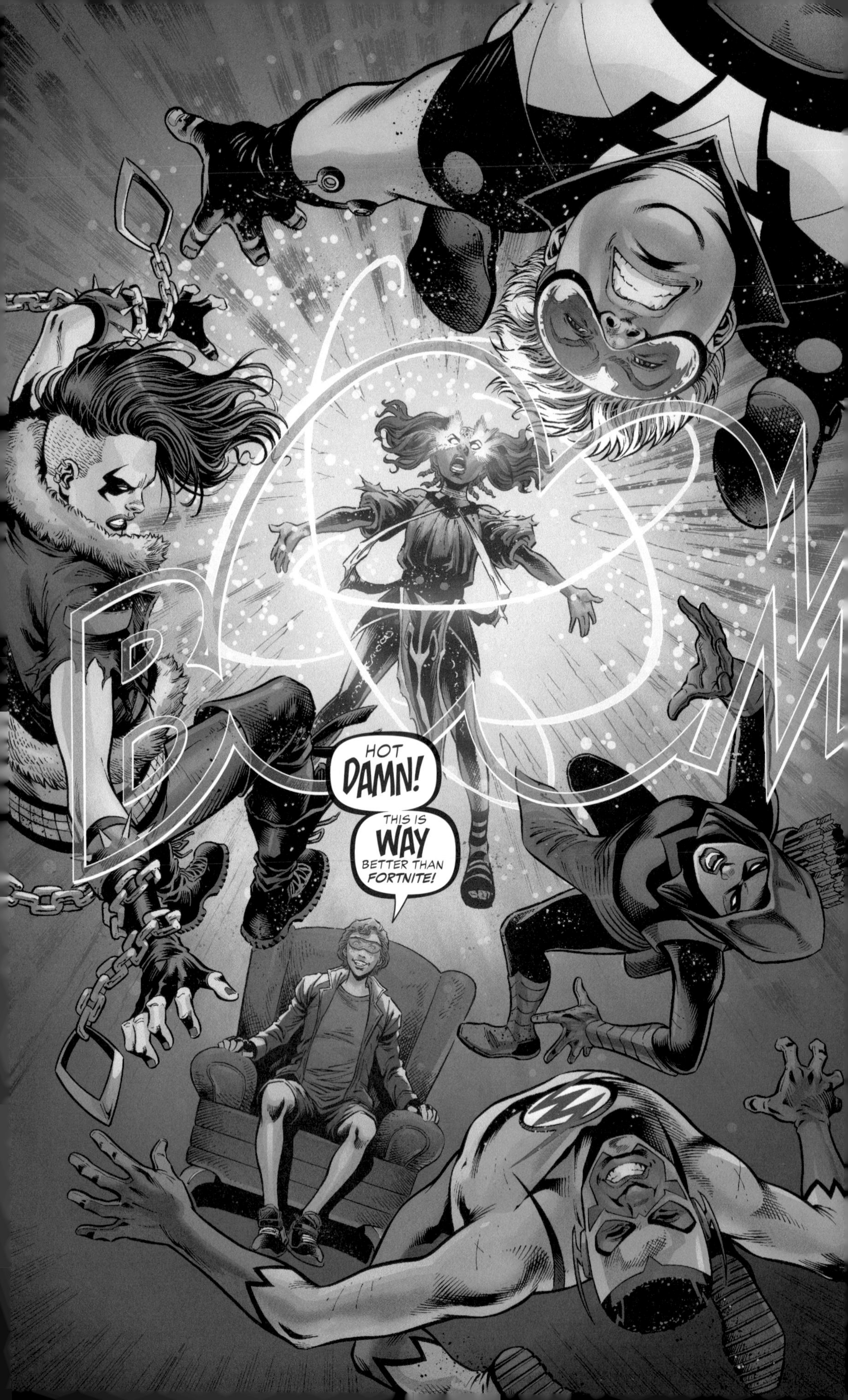
BOOM
HOT DAMN!
THIS IS WAY BETTER THAN FORTNITE!

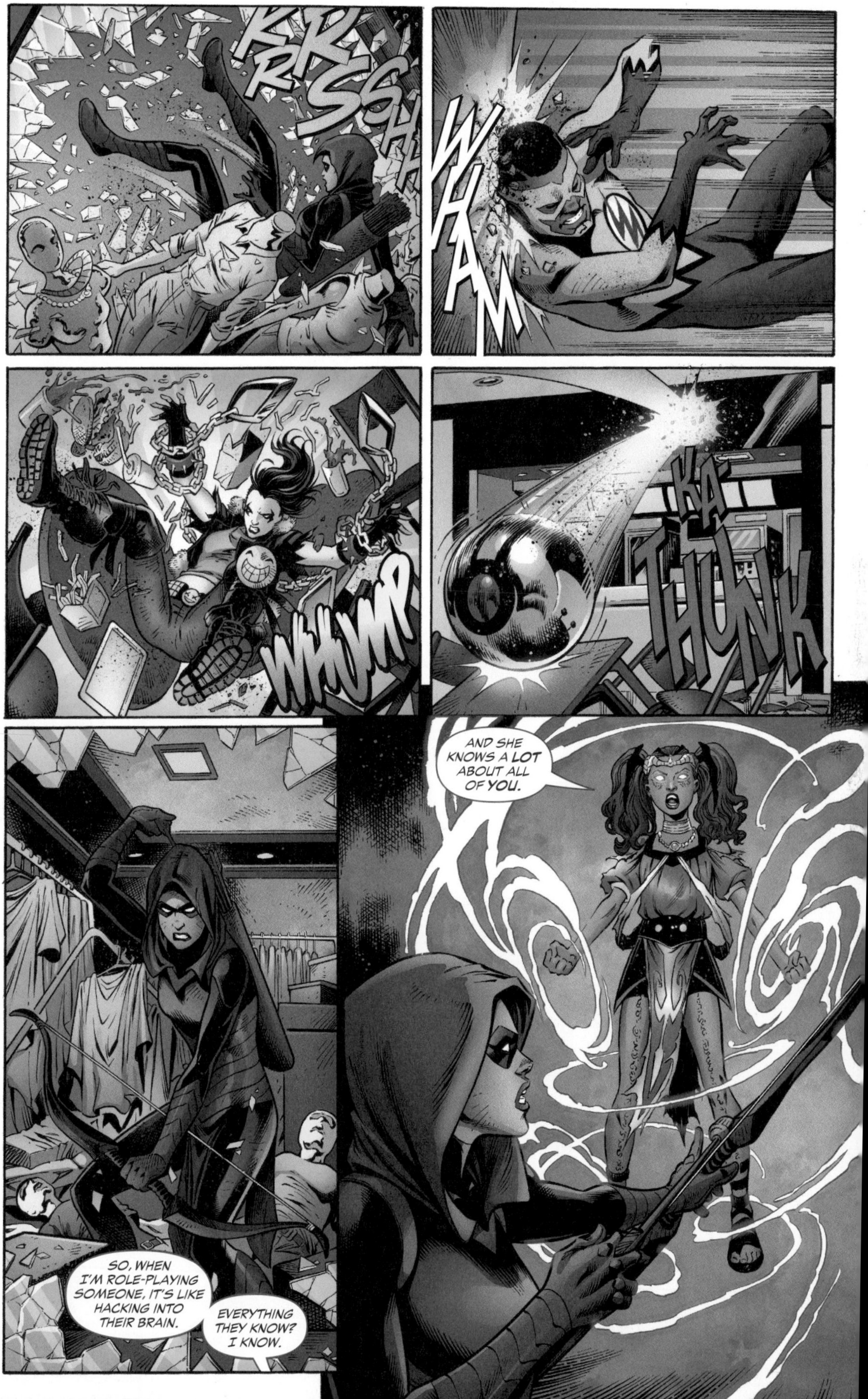
KRRKSSH
WHAM
WHUMP
KA-THUNK
SO, WHEN I'M ROLE-PLAYING SOMEONE, IT'S LIKE HACKING INTO THEIR BRAIN.
EVERYTHING THEY KNOW? I KNOW.
AND SHE KNOWS A LOT ABOUT ALL OF YOU.

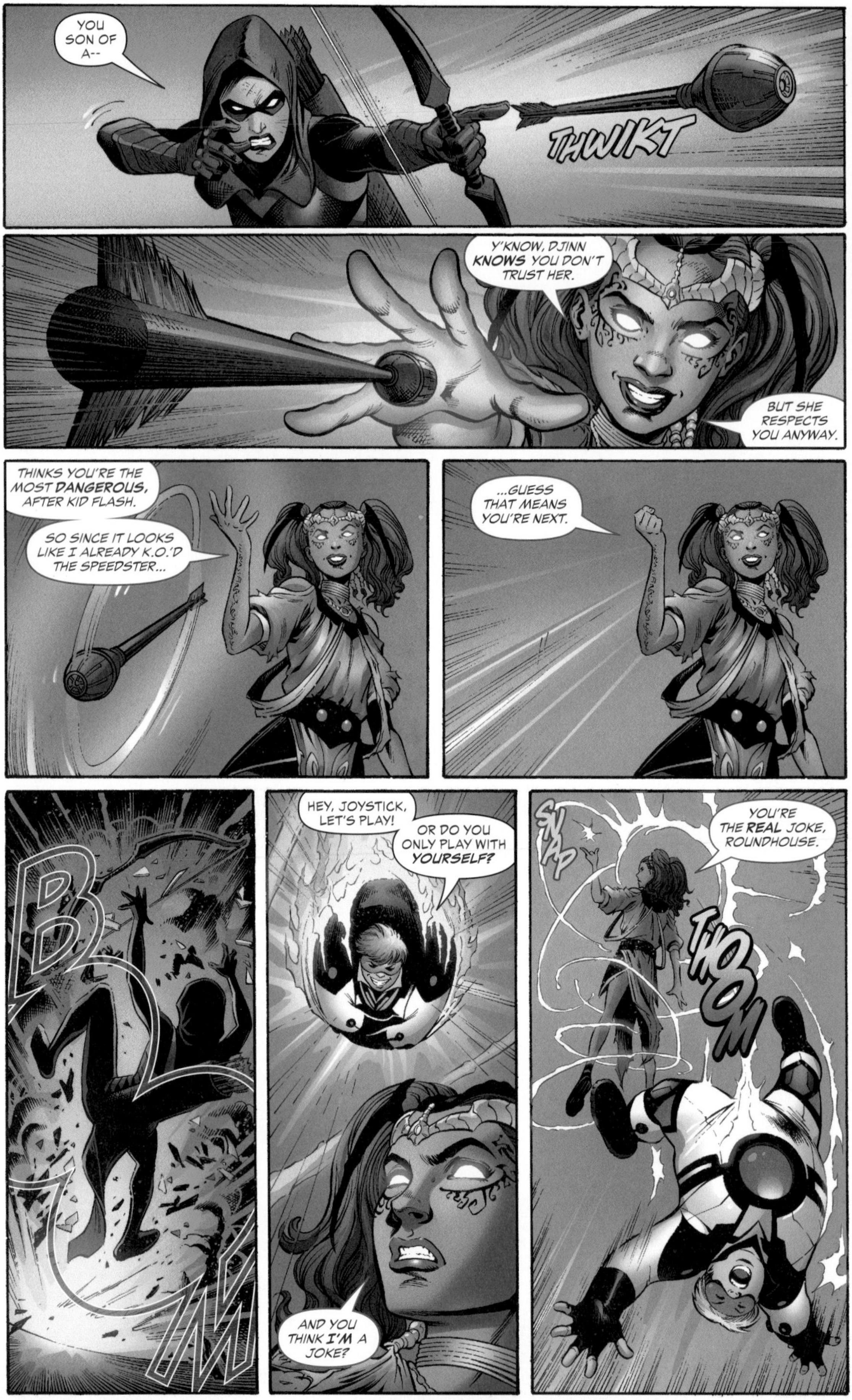
YOU SON OF A--
THWIKT
Y'KNOW, DJINN KNOWS YOU DON'T TRUST HER.
BUT SHE RESPECTS YOU ANYWAY.
THINKS YOU'RE THE MOST DANGEROUS, AFTER KID FLASH.
SO SINCE IT LOOKS LIKE I ALREADY K.O.'D THE SPEEDSTER...
...GUESS THAT MEANS YOU'RE NEXT.
BLAM
HEY, JOYSTICK, LET'S PLAY!
OR DO YOU ONLY PLAY WITH YOURSELF?
AND YOU THINK I'M A JOKE?
SNAP
YOU'RE THE REAL JOKE, ROUNDHOUSE.
THOOM

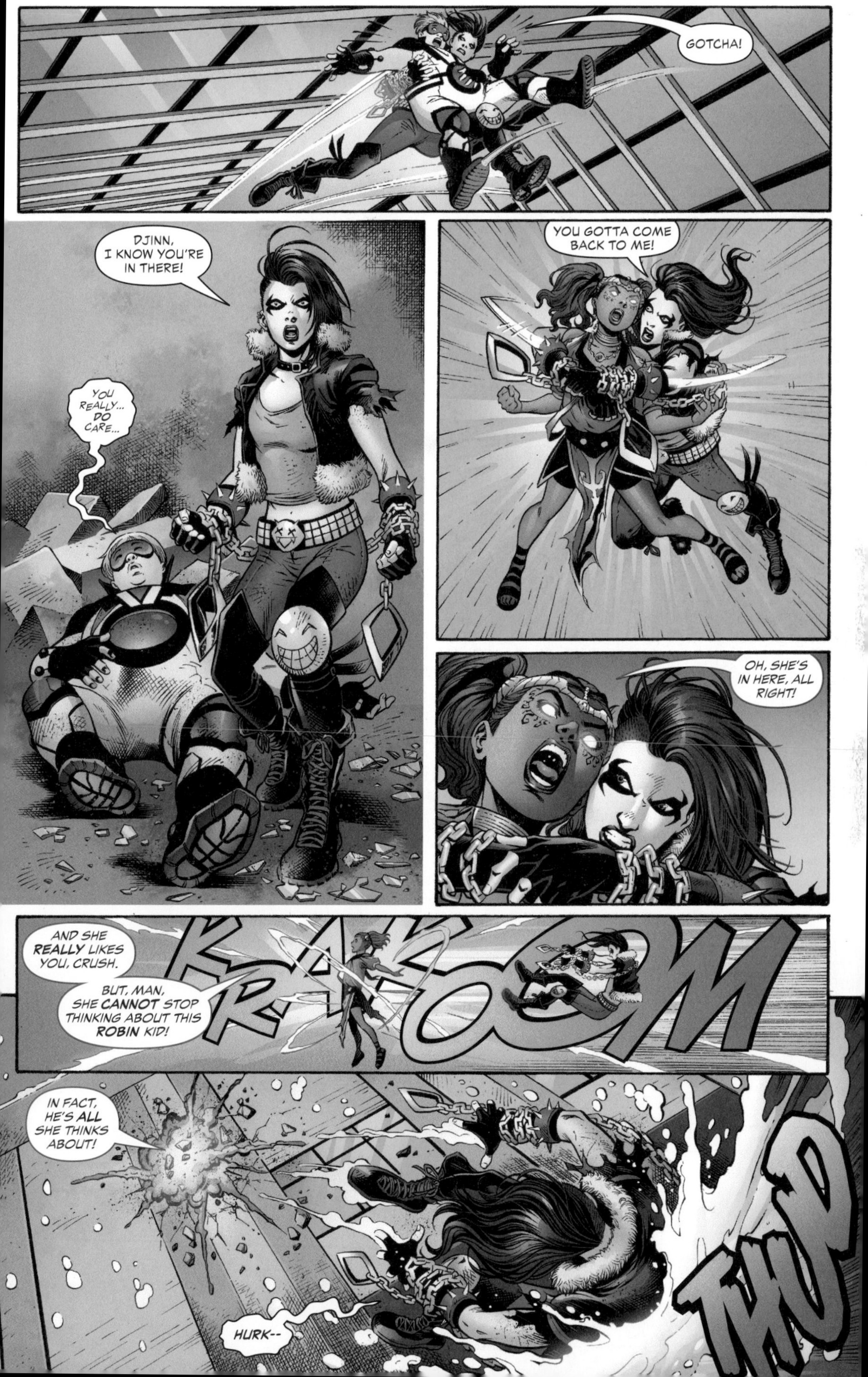
GOTCHA!
DJINN, I KNOW YOU'RE IN THERE!
YOU REALLY... DO CARE...
YOU GOTTA COME BACK TO ME!
OH, SHE'S IN HERE, ALL RIGHT!
AND SHE REALLY LIKES YOU, CRUSH.
BUT, MAN, SHE CANNOT STOP THINKING ABOUT THIS ROBIN KID!
KRAKOOM
IN FACT, HE'S ALL SHE THINKS ABOUT!
HURK--
THUD

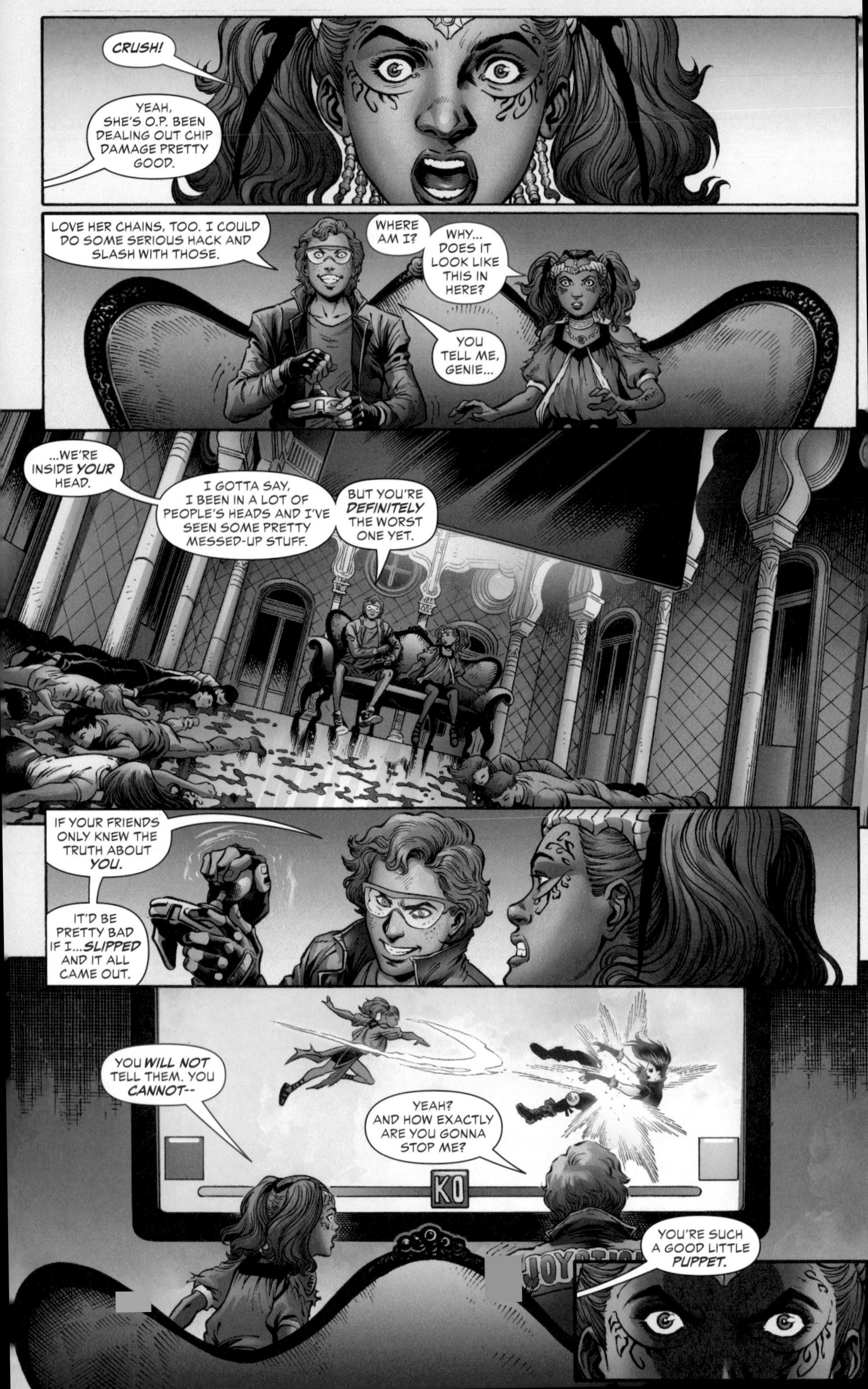
CRUSH!
YEAH, SHE'S O.P. BEEN DEALING OUT CHIP DAMAGE PRETTY GOOD.
LOVE HER CHAINS, TOO. I COULD DO SOME SERIOUS HACK AND SLASH WITH THOSE.
WHERE AM I?
WHY... DOES IT LOOK LIKE THIS IN HERE?
YOU TELL ME, GENIE...
...WE'RE INSIDE YOUR HEAD.
I GOTTA SAY, I BEEN IN A LOT OF PEOPLE'S HEADS AND I'VE SEEN SOME PRETTY MESSED-UP STUFF.
BUT YOU'RE DEFINITELY THE WORST ONE YET.
IF YOUR FRIENDS ONLY KNEW THE TRUTH ABOUT YOU.
IT'D BE PRETTY BAD IF I...SLIPPED AND IT ALL CAME OUT.
YOU WILL NOT TELL THEM. YOU CANNOT--
YEAH? AND HOW EXACTLY ARE YOU GONNA STOP ME?
KO
YOU'RE SUCH A GOOD LITTLE PUPPET.

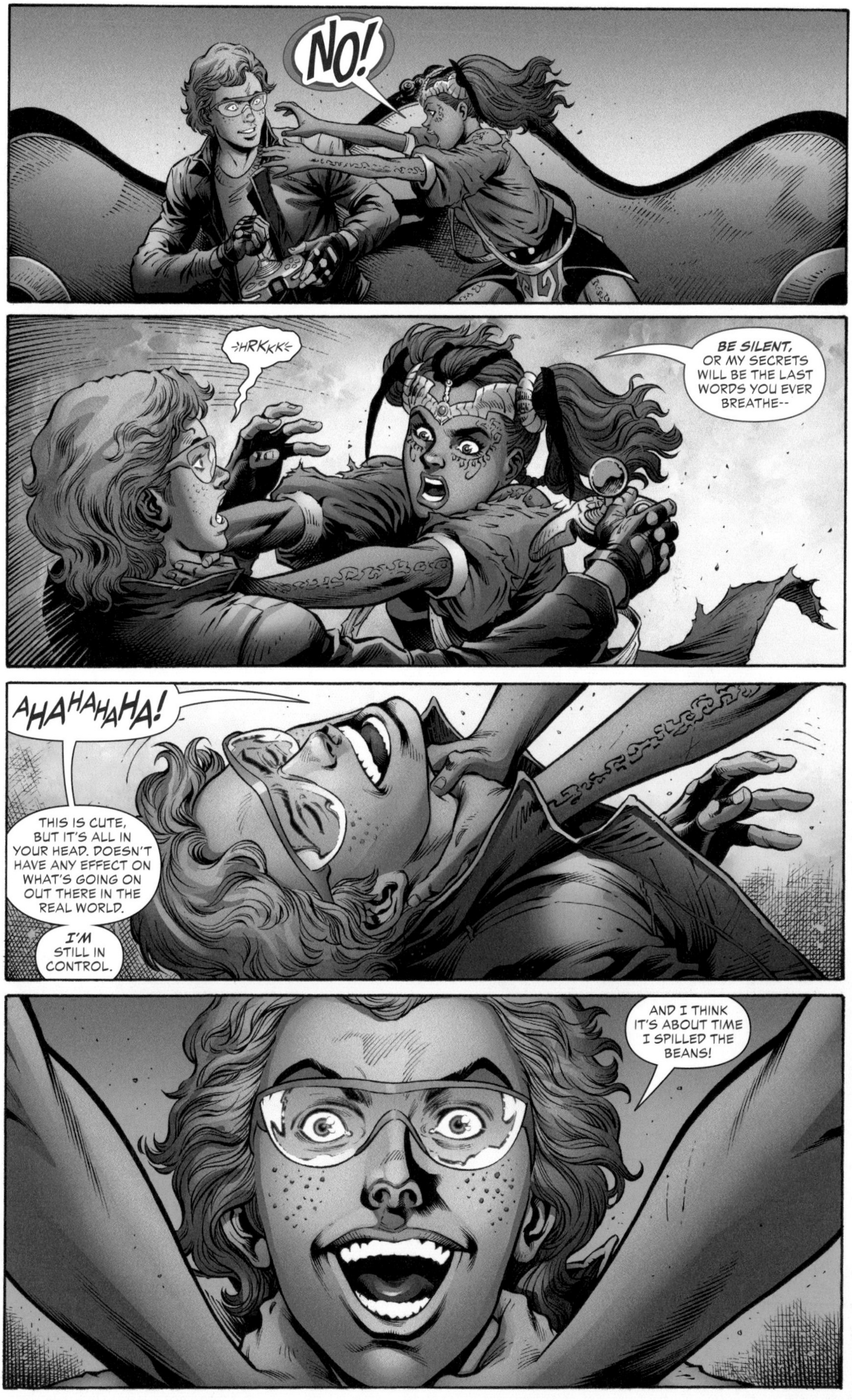
NO!
-HRKKK-
BE SILENT, OR MY SECRETS WILL BE THE LAST WORDS YOU EVER BREATHE--
AHAHAHAHA!
THIS IS CUTE, BUT IT'S ALL IN YOUR HEAD. DOESN'T HAVE ANY EFFECT ON WHAT'S GOING ON OUT THERE IN THE REAL WORLD.
I'M STILL IN CONTROL.
AND I THINK IT'S ABOUT TIME I SPILLED THE BEANS!

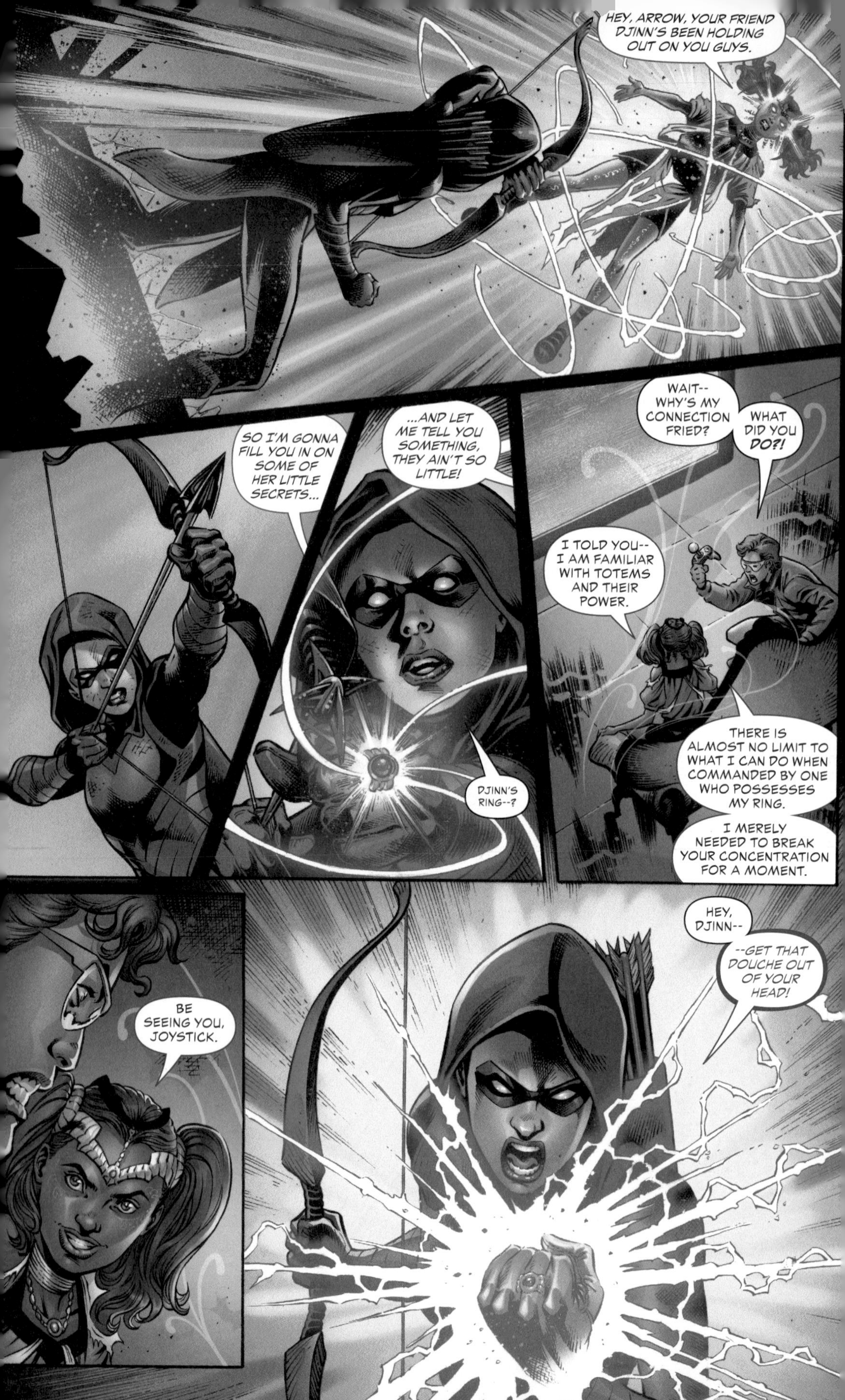
HEY, ARROW, YOUR FRIEND DJINN'S BEEN HOLDING OUT ON YOU GUYS.
SO I'M GONNA FILL YOU IN ON SOME OF HER LITTLE SECRETS...
...AND LET ME TELL YOU SOMETHING, THEY AIN'T SO LITTLE!
DJINN'S RING--?
WAIT-- WHY'S MY CONNECTION FRIED?
WHAT DID YOU DO?!
I TOLD YOU-- I AM FAMILIAR WITH TOTEMS AND THEIR POWER.
THERE IS ALMOST NO LIMIT TO WHAT I CAN DO WHEN COMMANDED BY ONE WHO POSSESSES MY RING.
I MERELY NEEDED TO BREAK YOUR CONCENTRATION FOR A MOMENT.
BE SEEING YOU, JOYSTICK.
HEY, DJINN--
--GET THAT DOUCHE OUT OF YOUR HEAD!

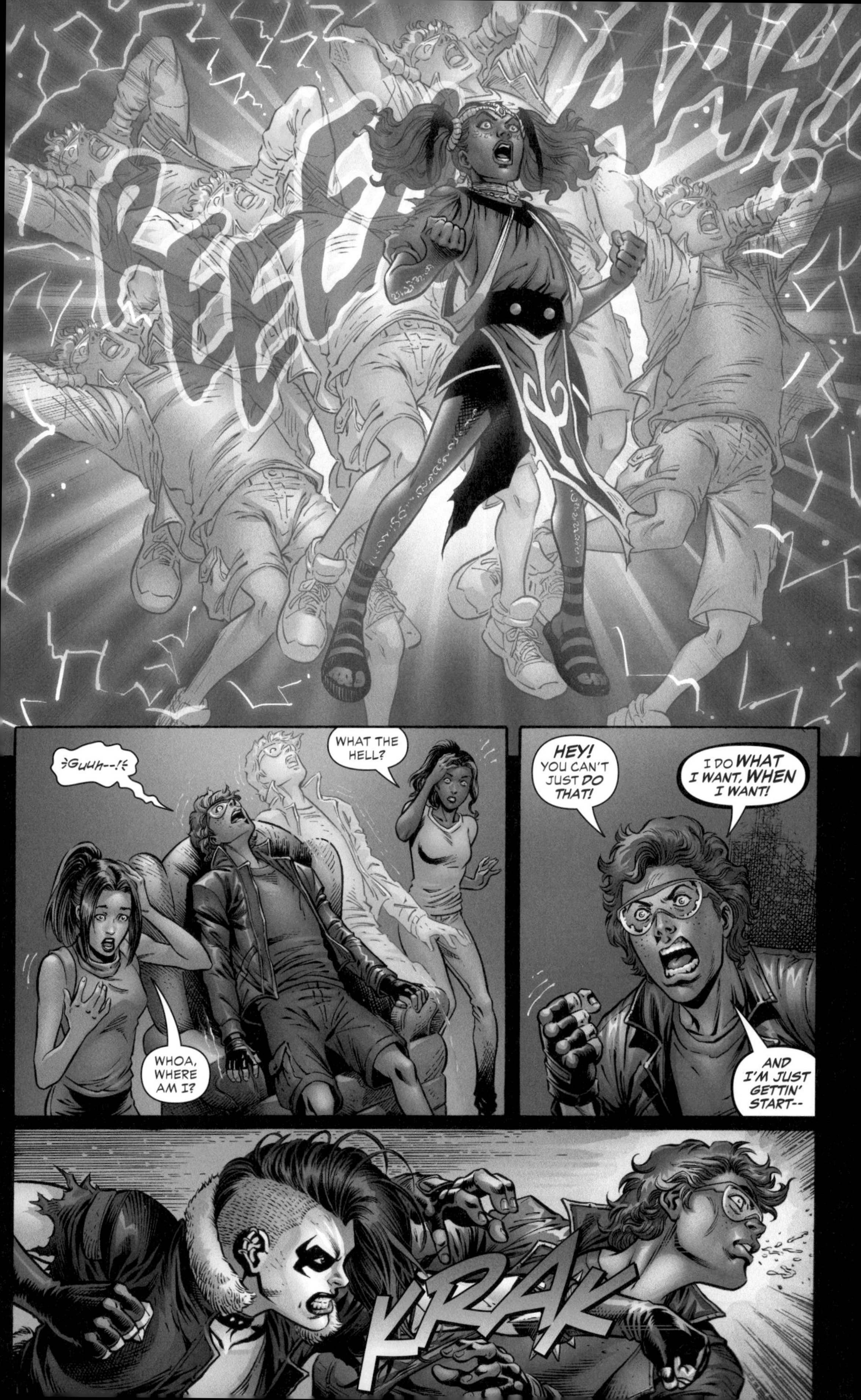

Guuh--!
WHAT THE HELL?
WHOA, WHERE AM I?
HEY! YOU CAN'T JUST DO THAT!
I DO WHAT I WANT, WHEN I WANT!
AND I'M JUST GETTIN' START--
KRAK

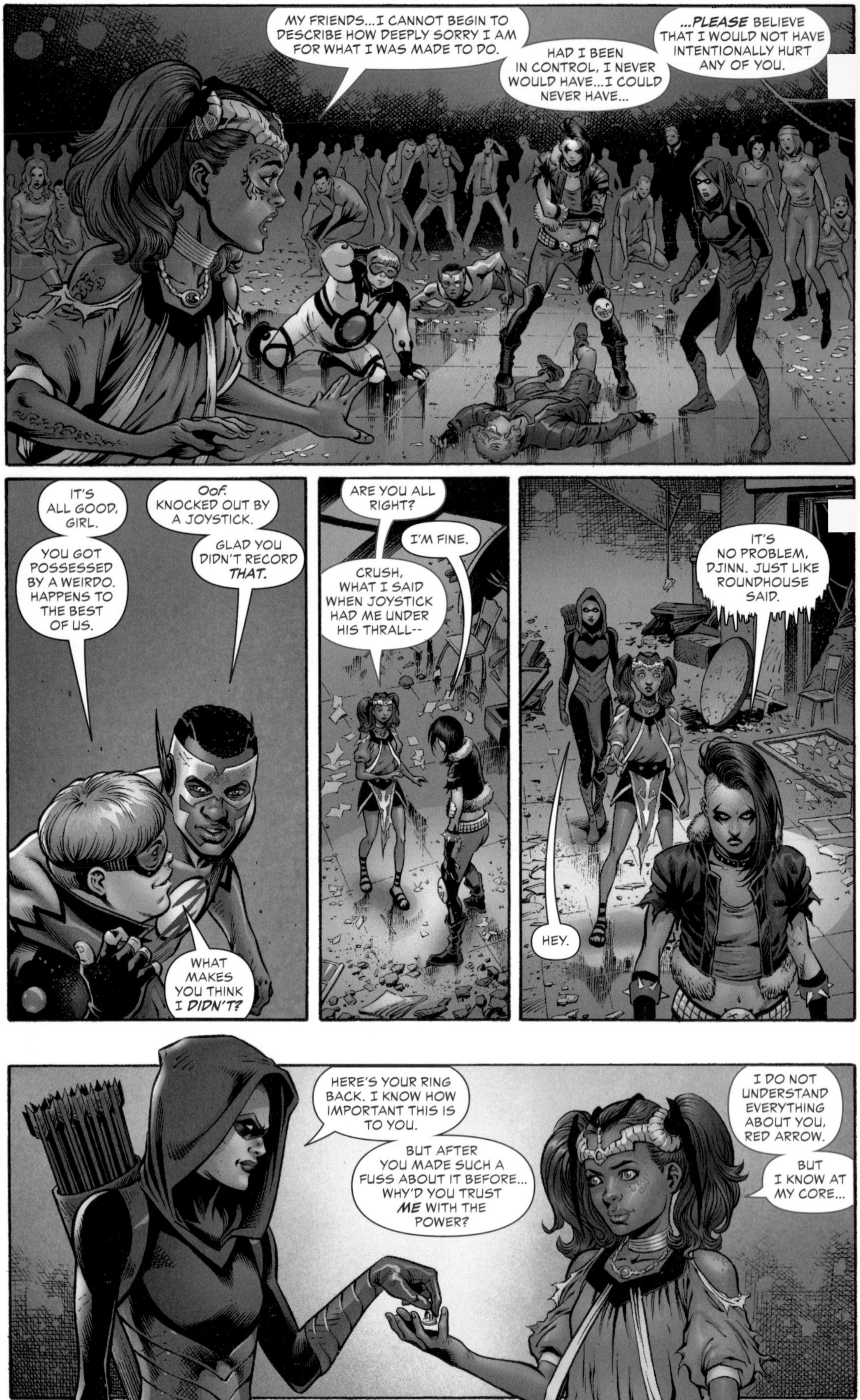
MY FRIENDS...I CANNOT BEGIN TO DESCRIBE HOW DEEPLY SORRY I AM FOR WHAT I WAS MADE TO DO.
HAD I BEEN IN CONTROL, I NEVER WOULD HAVE...I COULD NEVER HAVE...
...*PLEASE* BELIEVE THAT I WOULD NOT HAVE INTENTIONALLY HURT ANY OF YOU.
IT'S ALL GOOD, GIRL.
YOU GOT POSSESSED BY A WEIRDO. HAPPENS TO THE BEST OF US.
Oof. KNOCKED OUT BY A JOYSTICK.
GLAD YOU DIDN'T RECORD *THAT.*
WHAT MAKES YOU THINK I *DIDN'T?*
ARE YOU ALL RIGHT?
I'M FINE.
CRUSH, WHAT I SAID WHEN JOYSTICK HAD ME UNDER HIS THRALL--
IT'S NO PROBLEM, DJINN. JUST LIKE ROUNDHOUSE SAID.
HEY.
HERE'S YOUR RING BACK. I KNOW HOW IMPORTANT THIS IS TO YOU.
BUT AFTER YOU MADE SUCH A FUSS ABOUT IT BEFORE... WHY'D YOU TRUST *ME* WITH THE POWER?
I DO NOT UNDERSTAND EVERYTHING ABOUT YOU, RED ARROW.
BUT I KNOW AT MY CORE...

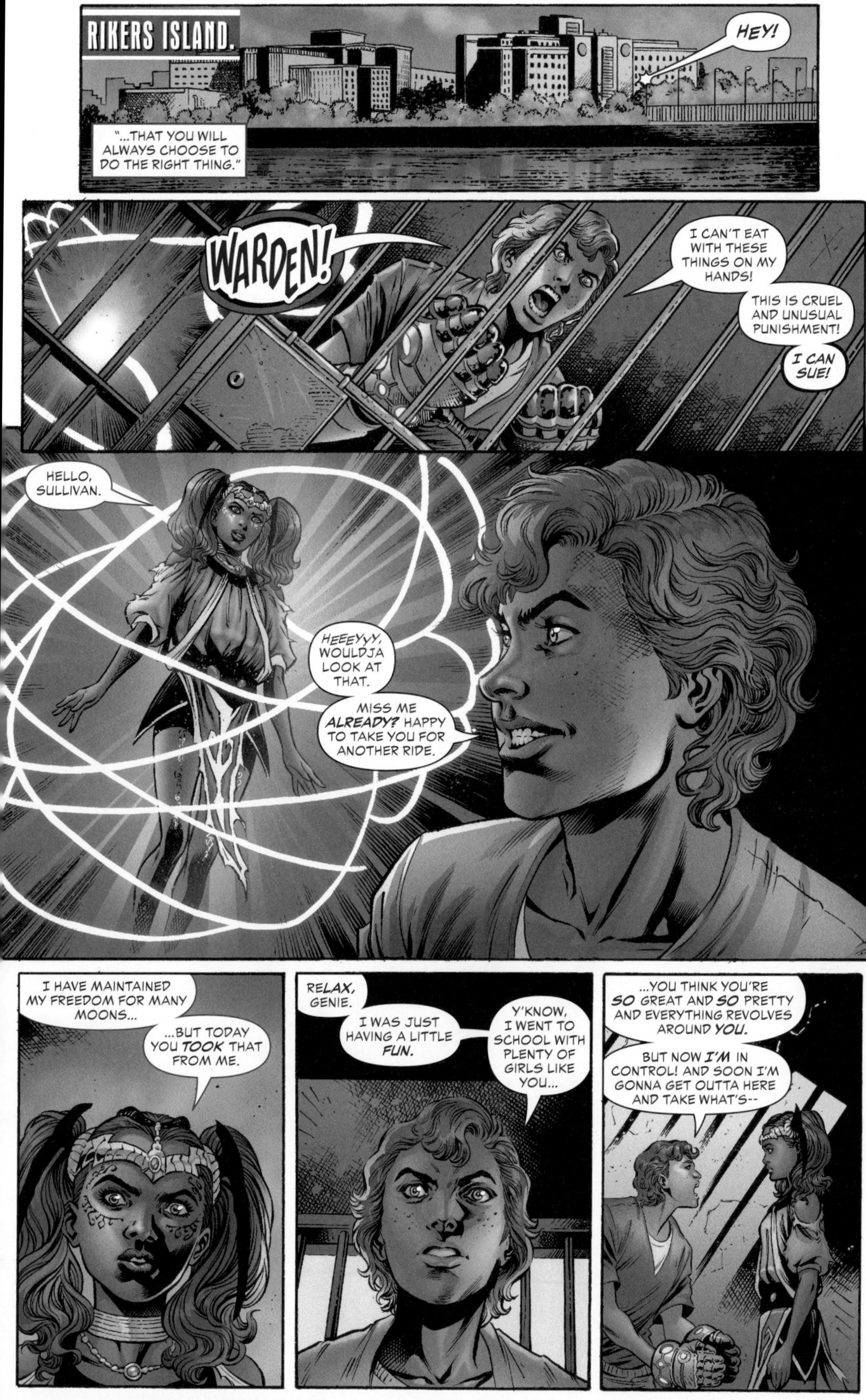
RIKERS ISLAND.
"...THAT YOU WILL ALWAYS CHOOSE TO DO THE RIGHT THING."
HEY!
WARDEN!
I CAN'T EAT WITH THESE THINGS ON MY HANDS!
THIS IS CRUEL AND UNUSUAL PUNISHMENT!
I CAN SUE!
HELLO, SULLIVAN.
HEEEYYY, WOULDJA LOOK AT THAT.
MISS ME ALREADY? HAPPY TO TAKE YOU FOR ANOTHER RIDE.
I HAVE MAINTAINED MY FREEDOM FOR MANY MOONS...
...BUT TODAY YOU TOOK THAT FROM ME.
RELAX, GENIE.
I WAS JUST HAVING A LITTLE FUN.
Y'KNOW, I WENT TO SCHOOL WITH PLENTY OF GIRLS LIKE YOU...
...YOU THINK YOU'RE SO GREAT AND SO PRETTY AND EVERYTHING REVOLVES AROUND YOU.
BUT NOW I'M IN CONTROL! AND SOON I'M GONNA GET OUTTA HERE AND TAKE WHAT'S--

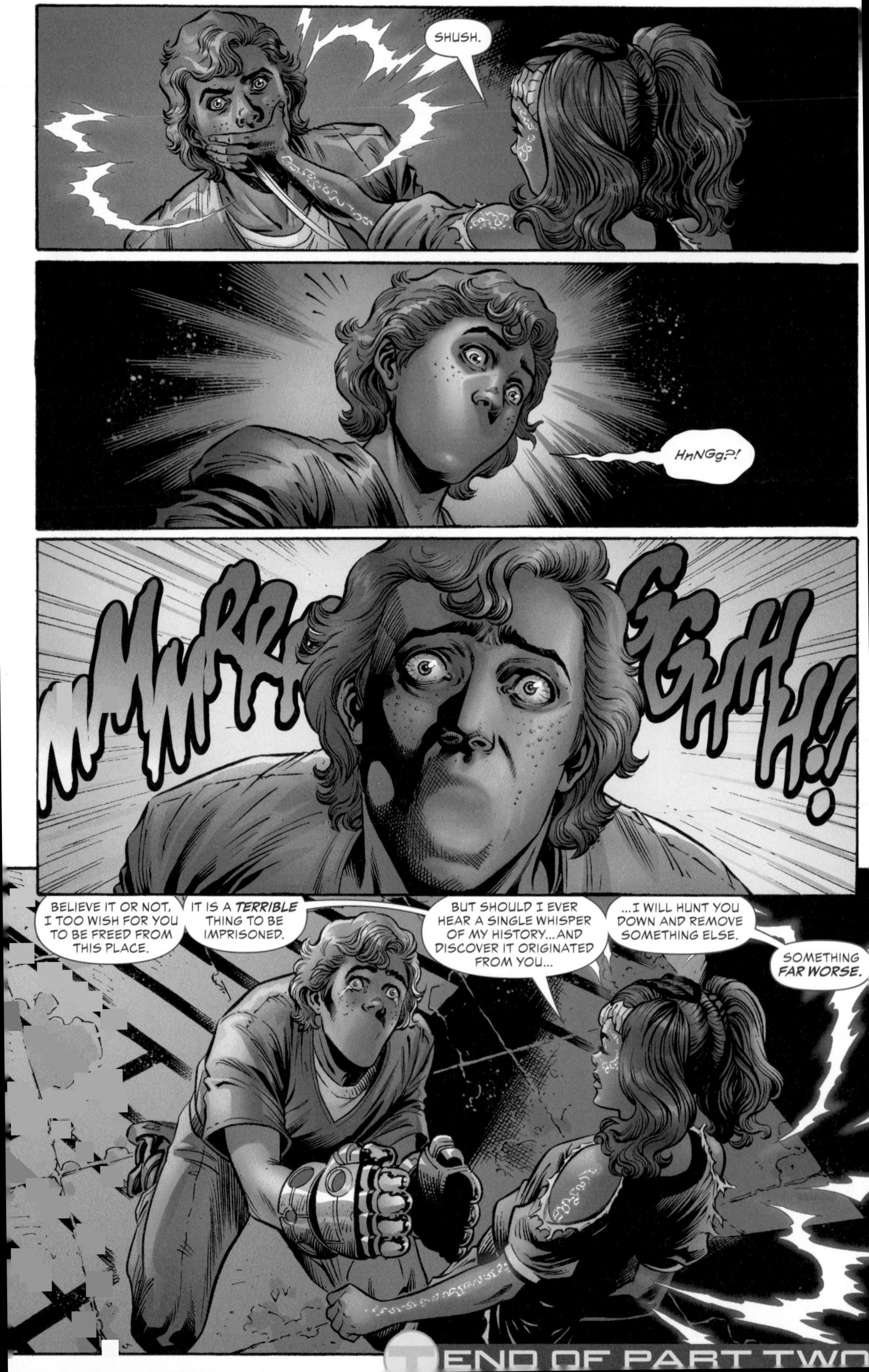
SHUSH.
HnNGg?!
MMMRRAAGGHH!!
BELIEVE IT OR NOT, I TOO WISH FOR YOU TO BE FREED FROM THIS PLACE.
IT IS A *TERRIBLE* THING TO BE IMPRISONED.
BUT SHOULD I EVER HEAR A SINGLE WHISPER OF MY HISTORY...AND DISCOVER IT ORIGINATED FROM YOU...
...I WILL HUNT YOU DOWN AND REMOVE SOMETHING ELSE.
SOMETHING *FAR WORSE.*
END OF PART TWO

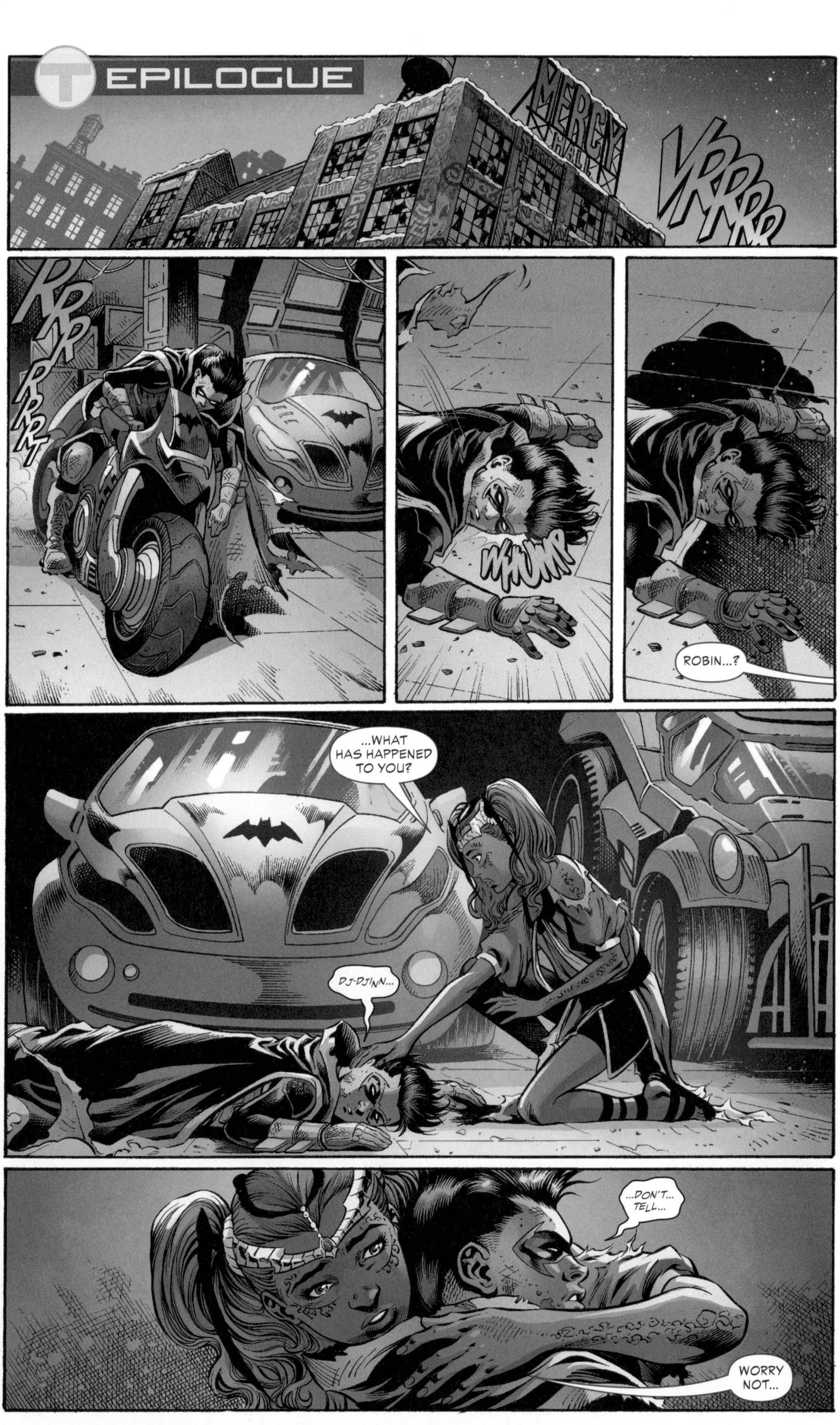
EPILOGUE
MERCY HALL
VRRRRR
RRRRRRRT
WHUMP
ROBIN...?
...WHAT HAS HAPPENED TO YOU?
DJ-DJINN...
...DON'T... TELL...
WORRY NOT...

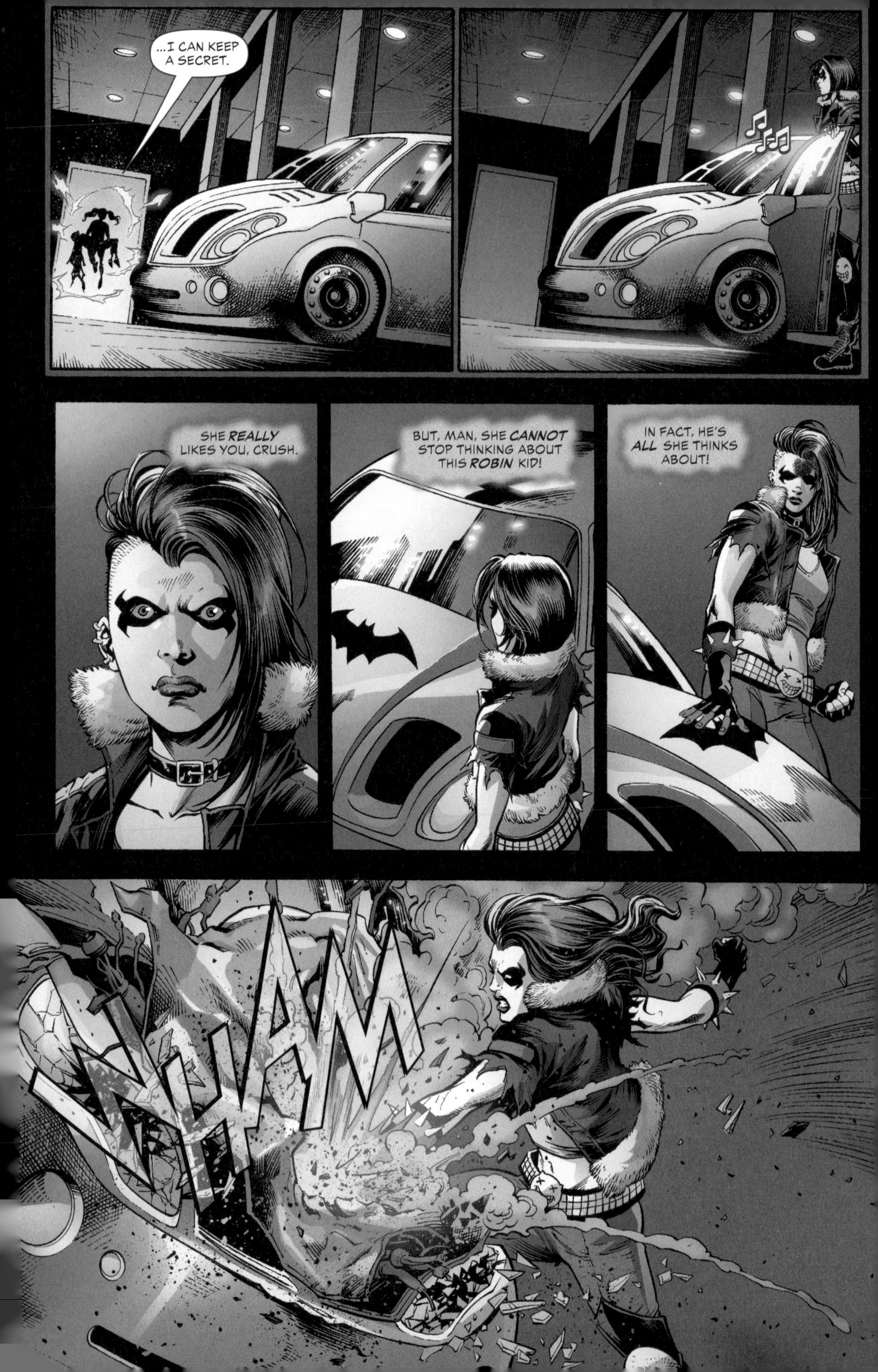
...I CAN KEEP A SECRET.
SHE REALLY LIKES YOU, CRUSH.
BUT, MAN, SHE CANNOT STOP THINKING ABOUT THIS ROBIN KID!
IN FACT, HE'S ALL SHE THINKS ABOUT!
WHAM

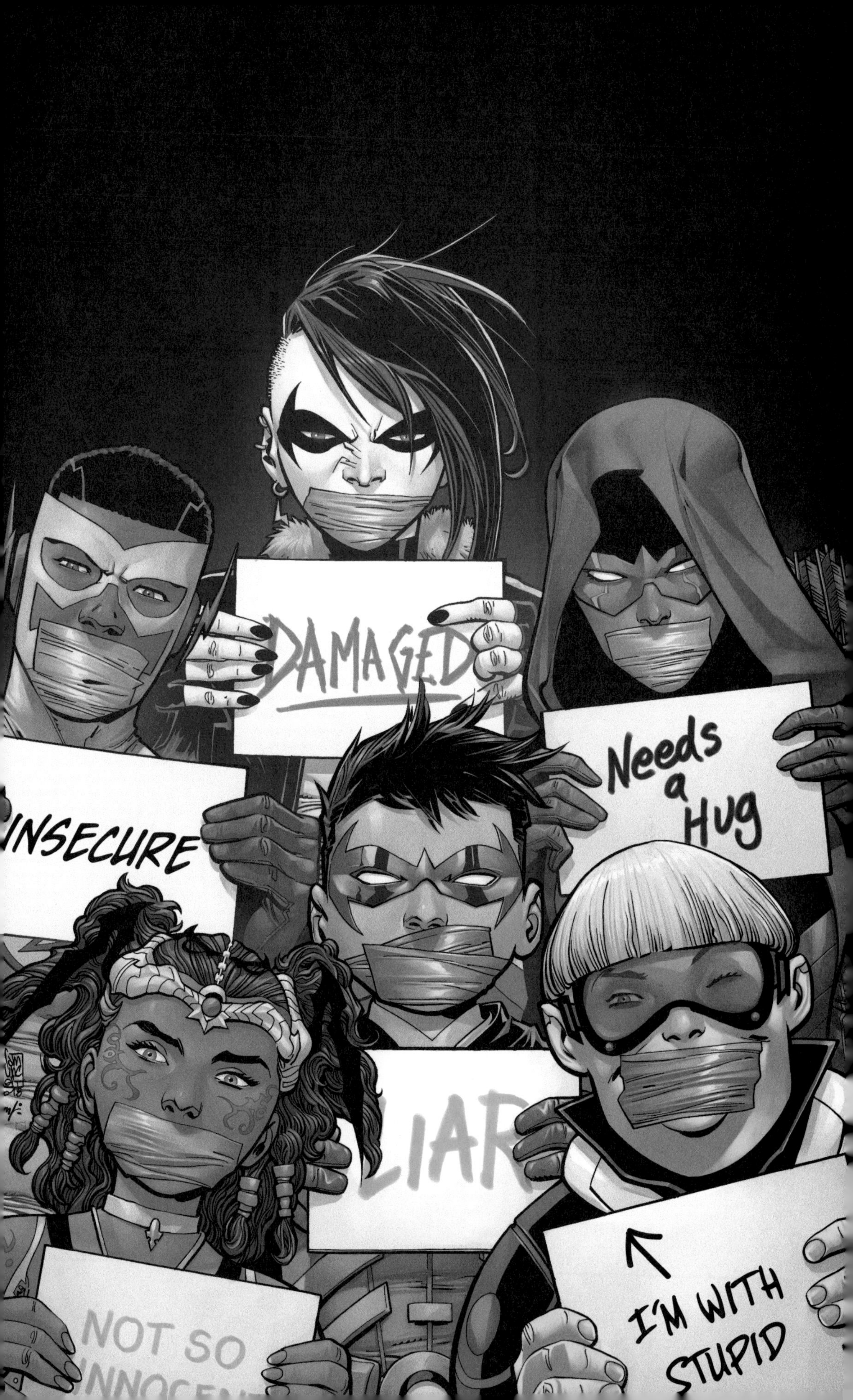
DAMAGED
INSECURE
Needs a Hug
LIAR
NOT SO
I'M WITH STUPID

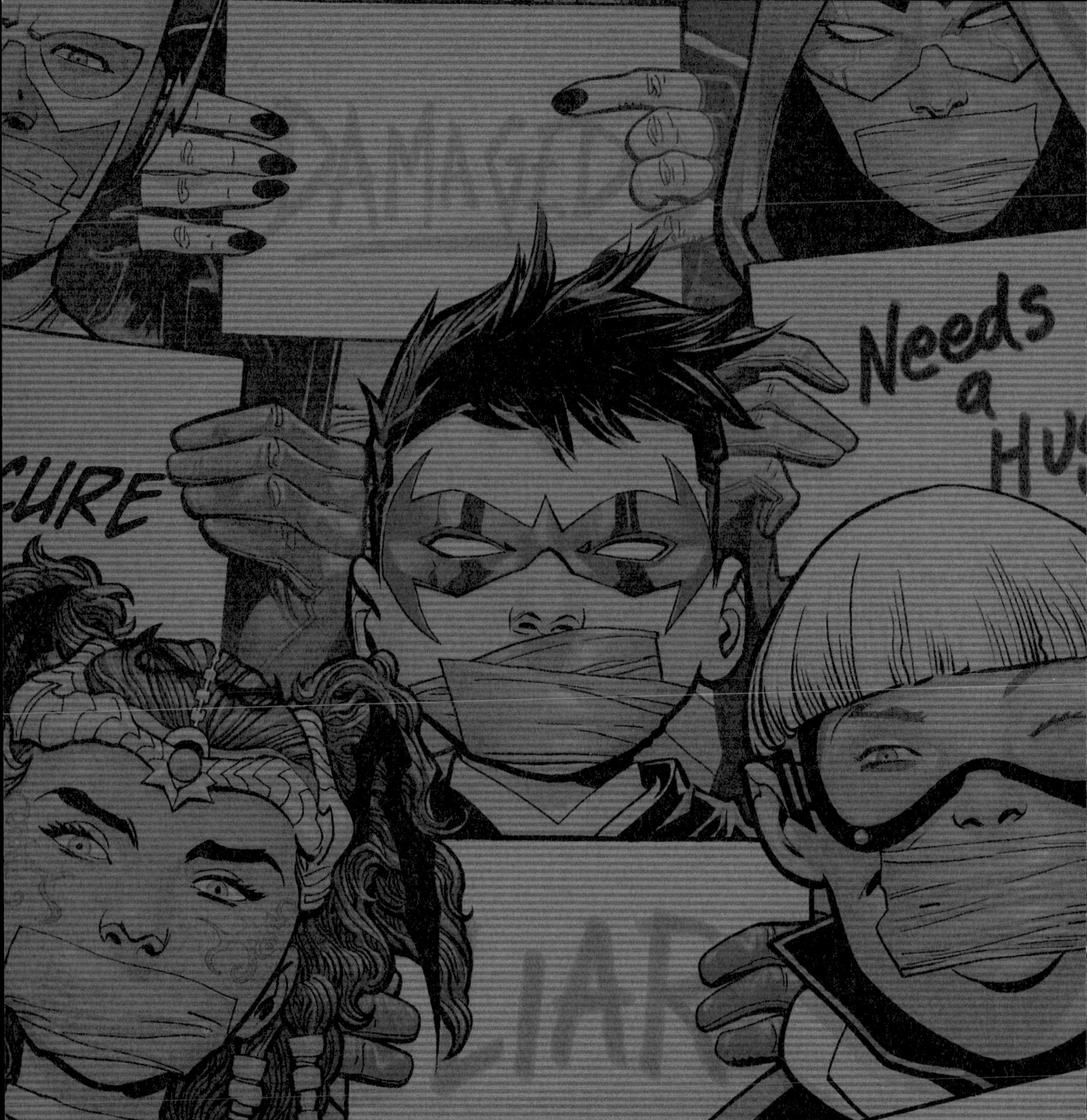
Needs a

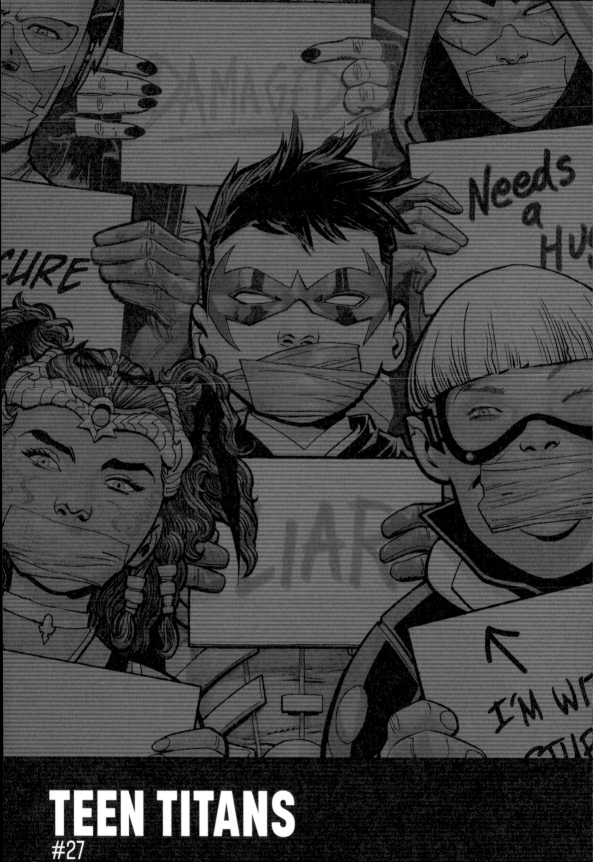

TEEN TITANS
#27

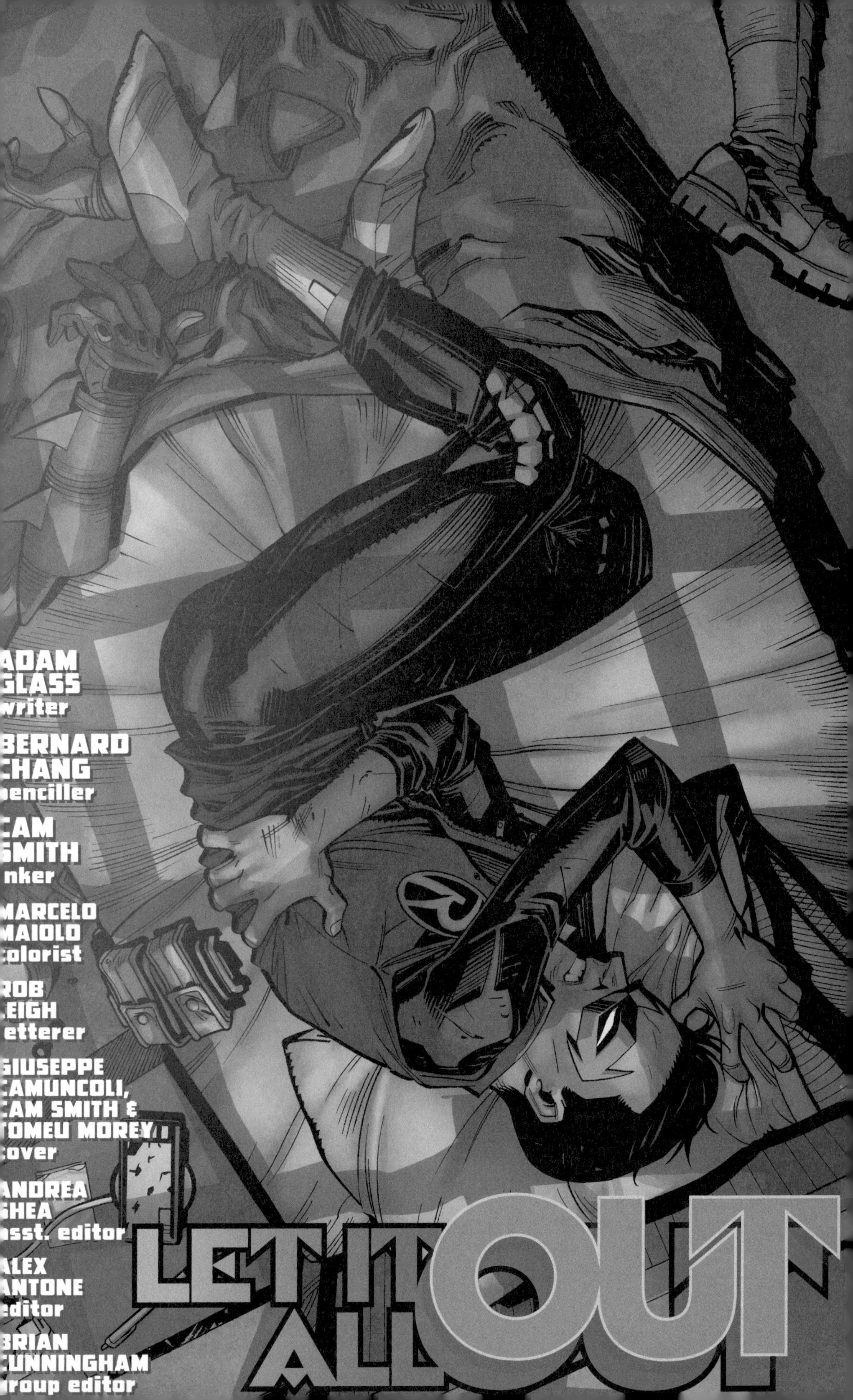

ADAM GLASS writer
BERNARD CHANG penciller
CAM SMITH inker
MARCELO MAIOLO colorist
ROB LEIGH letterer
GIUSEPPE CAMUNCOLI, CAM SMITH & TOMEU MOREY cover
ANDREA SHEA asst. editor
ALEX ANTONE editor
BRIAN CUNNINGHAM group editor
LET IT ALL OUT

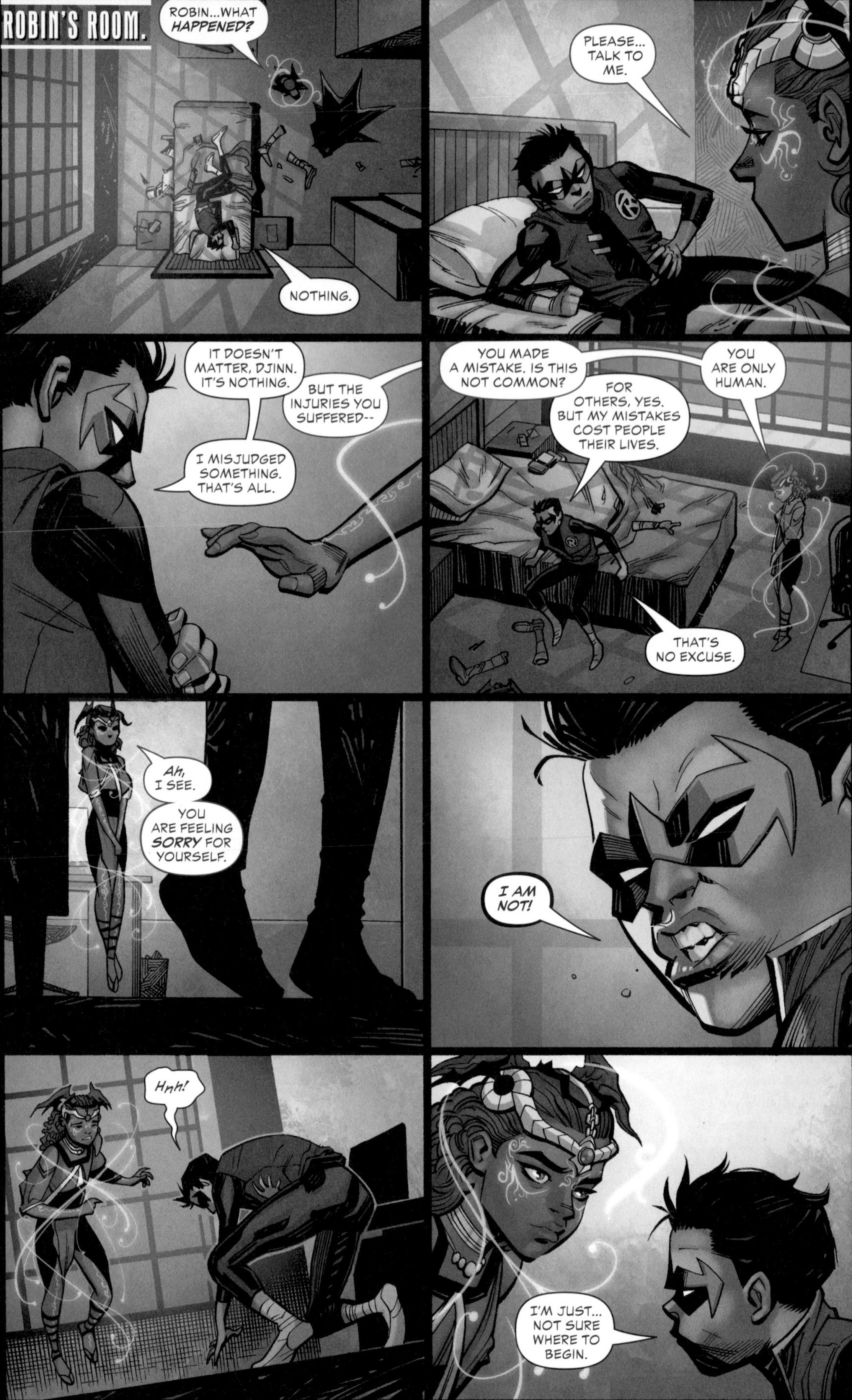
ROBIN'S ROOM.
ROBIN...WHAT *HAPPENED?*
NOTHING.
PLEASE... TALK TO ME.
IT DOESN'T MATTER, DJINN. IT'S NOTHING.
BUT THE INJURIES YOU SUFFERED--
I MISJUDGED SOMETHING. THAT'S ALL.
YOU MADE A MISTAKE. IS THIS NOT COMMON?
YOU ARE ONLY HUMAN.
FOR OTHERS, YES. BUT MY MISTAKES COST PEOPLE THEIR LIVES.
THAT'S NO EXCUSE.
Ah, I SEE.
YOU ARE FEELING ***SORRY*** FOR YOURSELF.
I AM NOT!
Hnh!
I'M JUST... NOT SURE WHERE TO BEGIN.

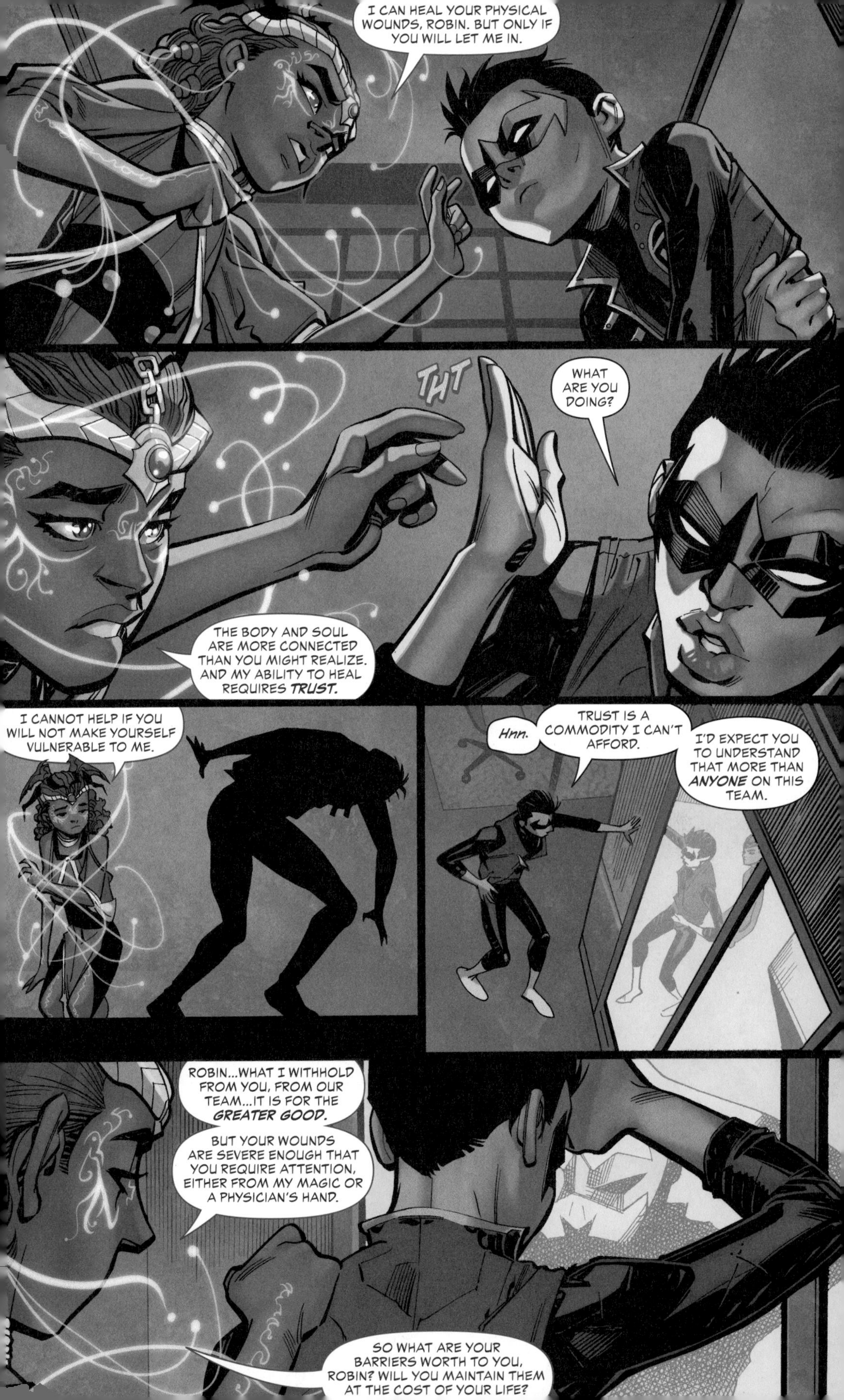
I CAN HEAL YOUR PHYSICAL WOUNDS, ROBIN. BUT ONLY IF YOU WILL LET ME IN.
THT
WHAT ARE YOU DOING?
THE BODY AND SOUL ARE MORE CONNECTED THAN YOU MIGHT REALIZE. AND MY ABILITY TO HEAL REQUIRES *TRUST.*
I CANNOT HELP IF YOU WILL NOT MAKE YOURSELF VULNERABLE TO ME.
Hnn.
TRUST IS A COMMODITY I CAN'T AFFORD.
I'D EXPECT YOU TO UNDERSTAND THAT MORE THAN *ANYONE* ON THIS TEAM.
ROBIN...WHAT I WITHHOLD FROM YOU, FROM OUR TEAM...IT IS FOR THE *GREATER GOOD.*
BUT YOUR WOUNDS ARE SEVERE ENOUGH THAT YOU REQUIRE ATTENTION, EITHER FROM MY MAGIC OR A PHYSICIAN'S HAND.
SO WHAT ARE YOUR BARRIERS WORTH TO YOU, ROBIN? WILL YOU MAINTAIN THEM AT THE COST OF YOUR LIFE?

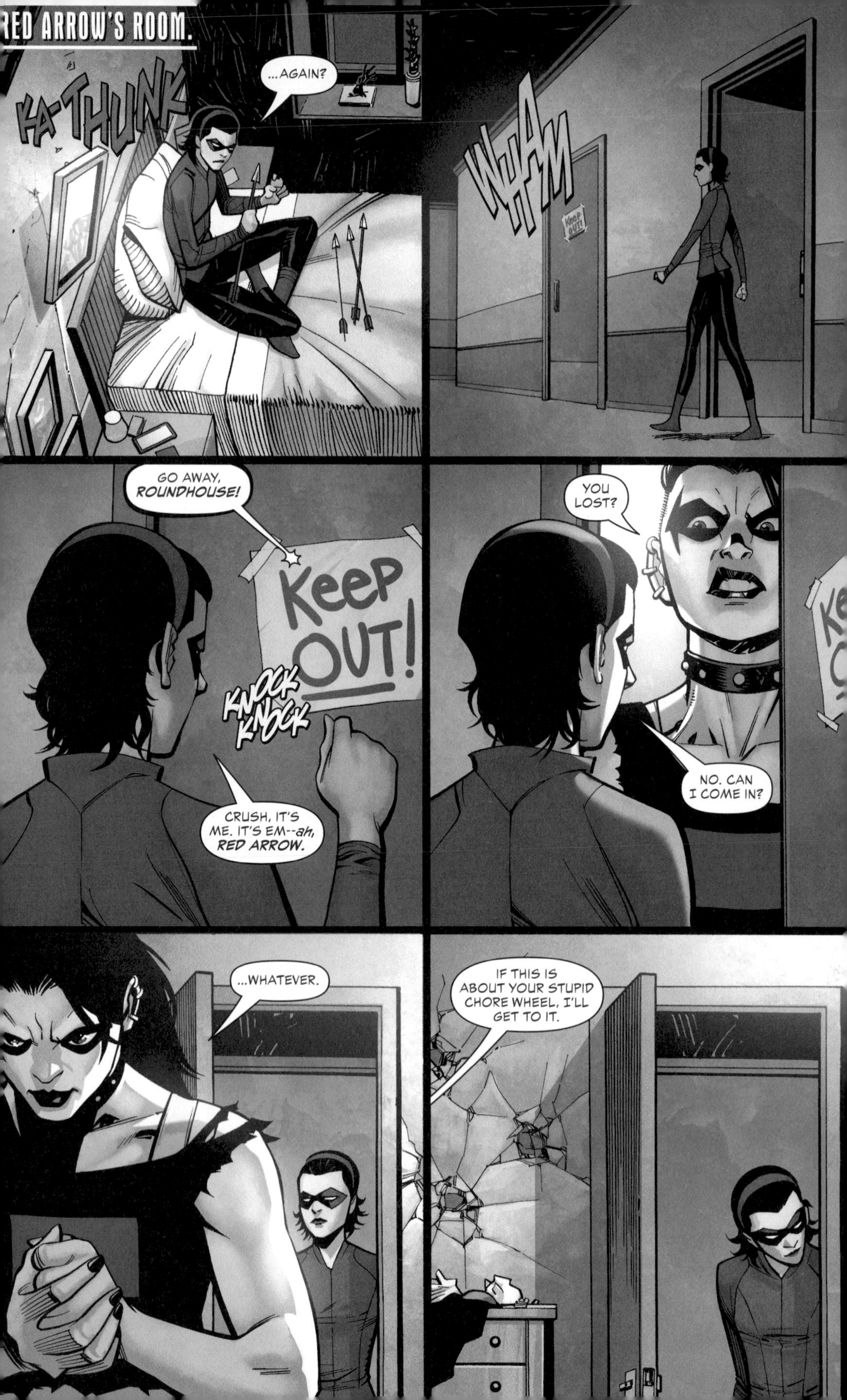

RED ARROW'S ROOM.
KA-THUNK
...AGAIN?
WHAM
KEEP OUT!
GO AWAY, ROUNDHOUSE!
KEEP OUT!
KNOCK KNOCK
CRUSH, IT'S ME. IT'S EM--ah, RED ARROW.
YOU LOST?
NO. CAN I COME IN?
...WHATEVER.
IF THIS IS ABOUT YOUR STUPID CHORE WHEEL, I'LL GET TO IT.

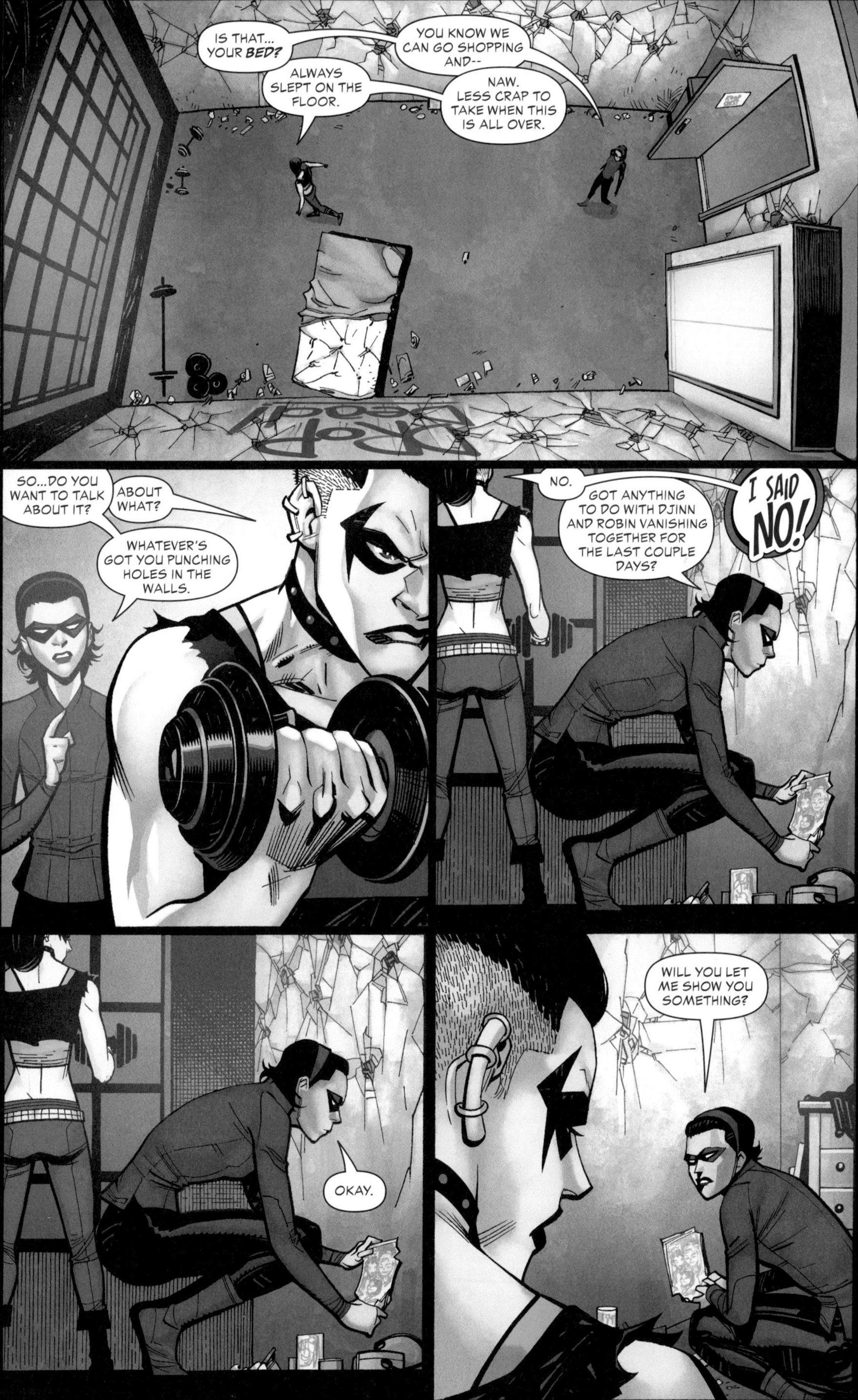
IS THAT... YOUR *BED?*
YOU KNOW WE CAN GO SHOPPING AND--
ALWAYS SLEPT ON THE FLOOR.
NAW. LESS CRAP TO TAKE WHEN THIS IS ALL OVER.
SO...DO YOU WANT TO TALK ABOUT IT?
ABOUT WHAT?
WHATEVER'S GOT YOU PUNCHING HOLES IN THE WALLS.
NO.
GOT ANYTHING TO DO WITH DJINN AND ROBIN VANISHING TOGETHER FOR THE LAST COUPLE DAYS?
I SAID NO!
OKAY.
WILL YOU LET ME SHOW YOU SOMETHING?

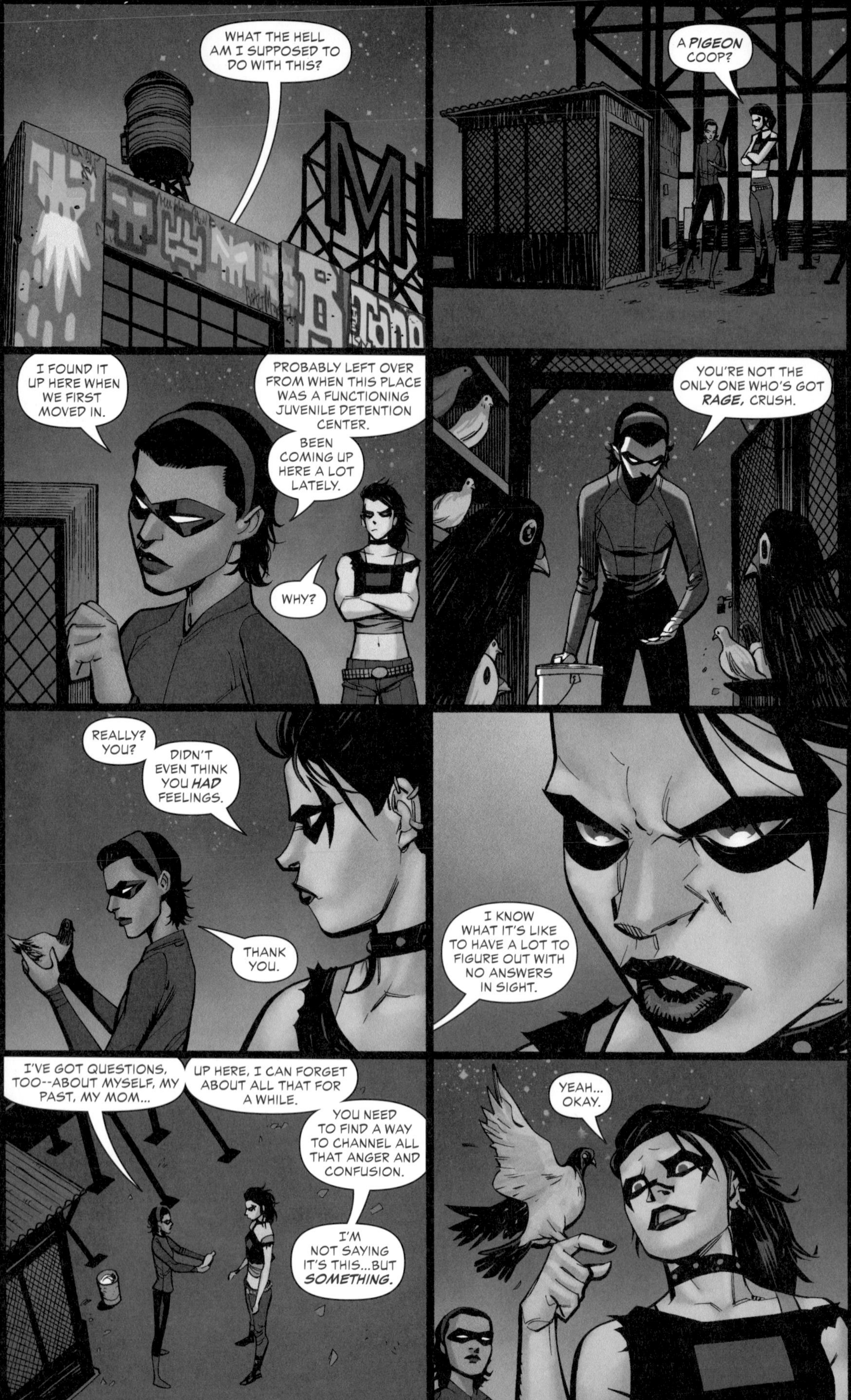
WHAT THE HELL AM I SUPPOSED TO DO WITH THIS?
A PIGEON COOP?
I FOUND IT UP HERE WHEN WE FIRST MOVED IN.
PROBABLY LEFT OVER FROM WHEN THIS PLACE WAS A FUNCTIONING JUVENILE DETENTION CENTER.
BEEN COMING UP HERE A LOT LATELY.
WHY?
YOU'RE NOT THE ONLY ONE WHO'S GOT RAGE, CRUSH.
REALLY? YOU?
DIDN'T EVEN THINK YOU HAD FEELINGS.
THANK YOU.
I KNOW WHAT IT'S LIKE TO HAVE A LOT TO FIGURE OUT WITH NO ANSWERS IN SIGHT.
I'VE GOT QUESTIONS, TOO--ABOUT MYSELF, MY PAST, MY MOM...
UP HERE, I CAN FORGET ABOUT ALL THAT FOR A WHILE.
YOU NEED TO FIND A WAY TO CHANNEL ALL THAT ANGER AND CONFUSION.
I'M NOT SAYING IT'S THIS...BUT SOMETHING.
YEAH... OKAY.

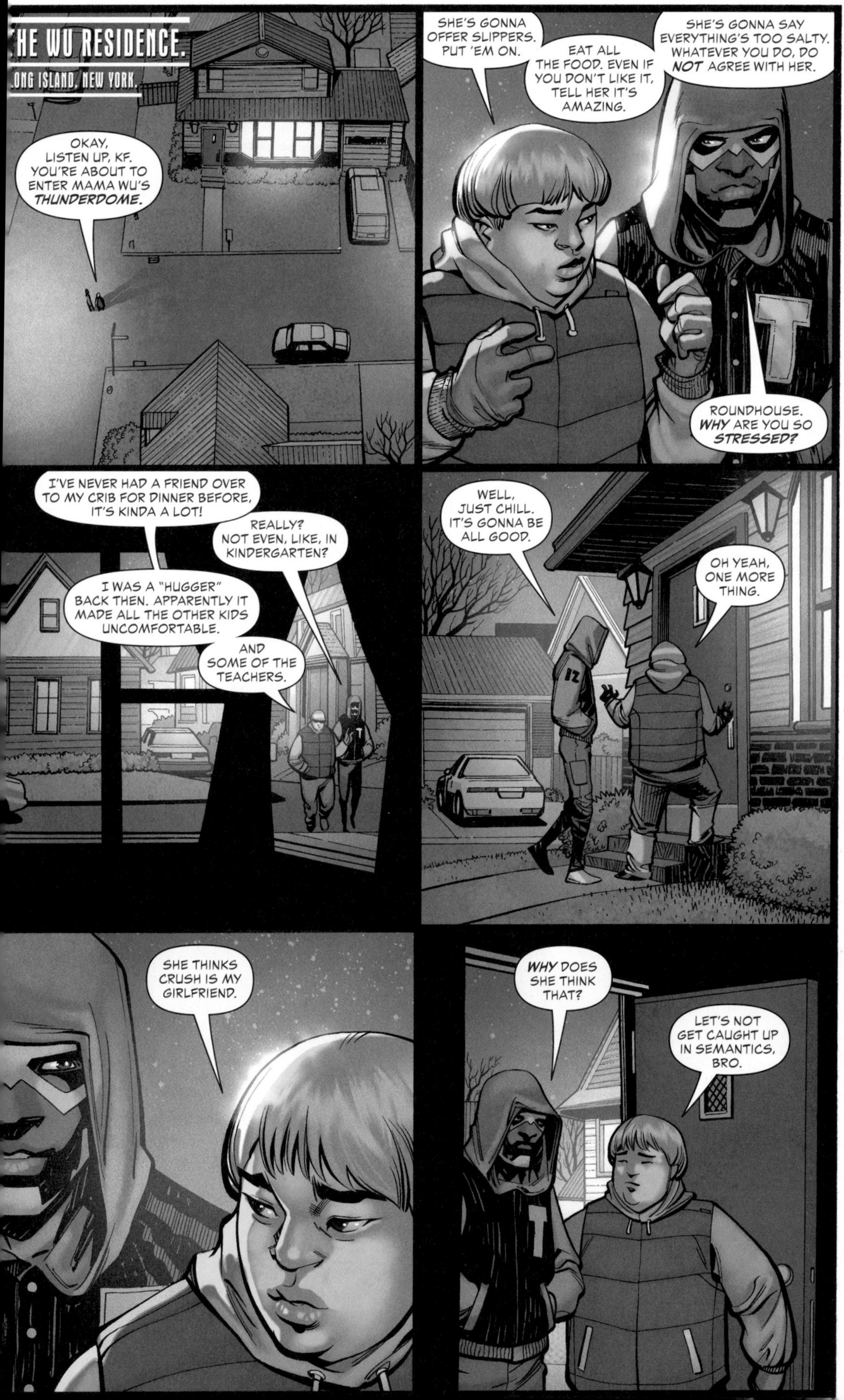
THE WU RESIDENCE.
LONG ISLAND, NEW YORK.
OKAY, LISTEN UP, KF. YOU'RE ABOUT TO ENTER MAMA WU'S THUNDERDOME.
SHE'S GONNA OFFER SLIPPERS. PUT 'EM ON.
EAT ALL THE FOOD. EVEN IF YOU DON'T LIKE IT, TELL HER IT'S AMAZING.
SHE'S GONNA SAY EVERYTHING'S TOO SALTY. WHATEVER YOU DO, DO NOT AGREE WITH HER.
ROUNDHOUSE. WHY ARE YOU SO STRESSED?
I'VE NEVER HAD A FRIEND OVER TO MY CRIB FOR DINNER BEFORE, IT'S KINDA A LOT!
REALLY? NOT EVEN, LIKE, IN KINDERGARTEN?
I WAS A "HUGGER" BACK THEN. APPARENTLY IT MADE ALL THE OTHER KIDS UNCOMFORTABLE.
AND SOME OF THE TEACHERS.
WELL, JUST CHILL. IT'S GONNA BE ALL GOOD.
OH YEAH, ONE MORE THING.
SHE THINKS CRUSH IS MY GIRLFRIEND.
WHY DOES SHE THINK THAT?
LET'S NOT GET CAUGHT UP IN SEMANTICS, BRO.

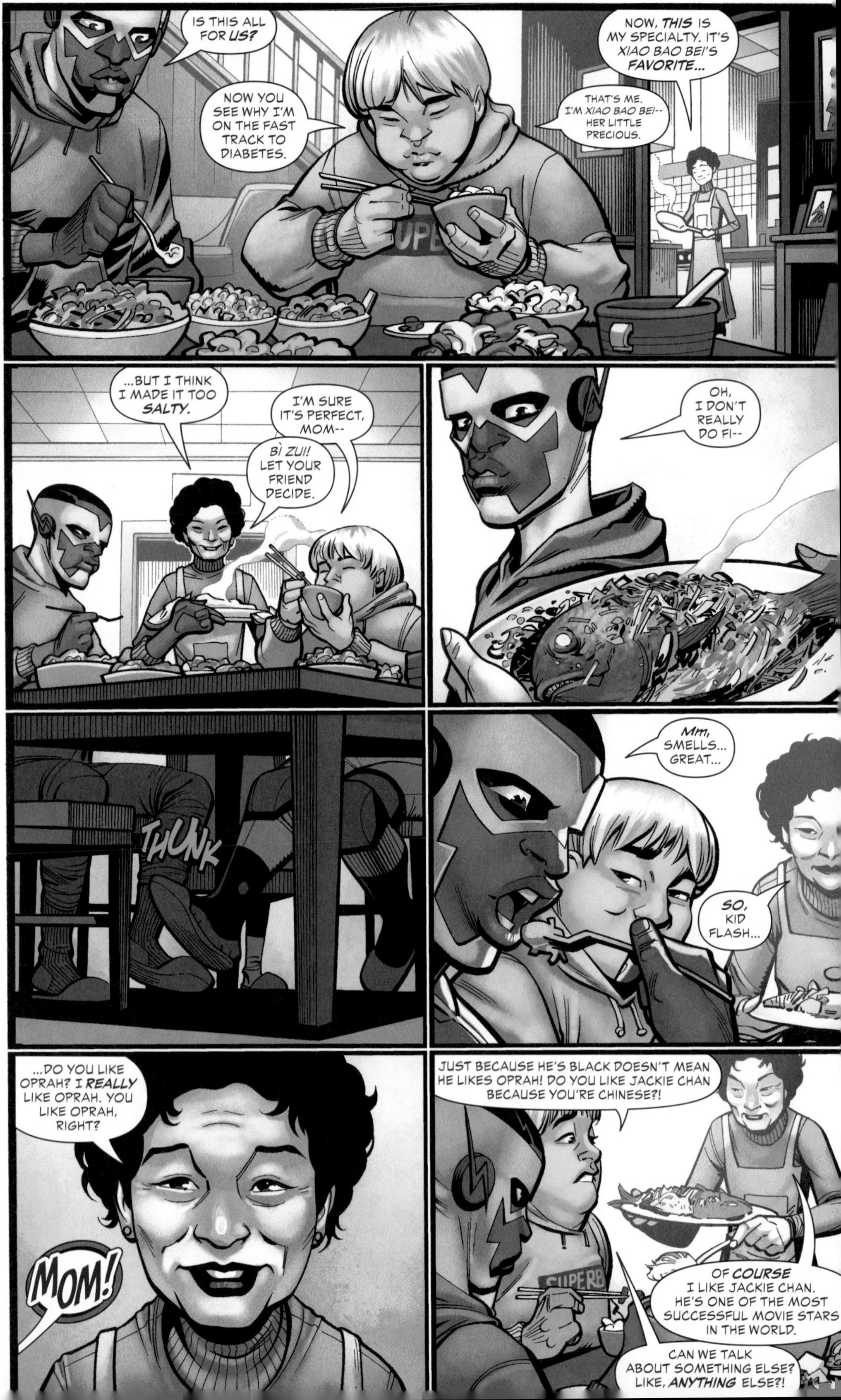
IS THIS ALL FOR US?
NOW YOU SEE WHY I'M ON THE FAST TRACK TO DIABETES.
NOW, THIS IS MY SPECIALTY. IT'S XIAO BAO BEI'S FAVORITE...
THAT'S ME. I'M XIAO BAO BEI-- HER LITTLE PRECIOUS.
...BUT I THINK I MADE IT TOO SALTY.
I'M SURE IT'S PERFECT, MOM--
BÌ ZUI! LET YOUR FRIEND DECIDE.
OH, I DON'T REALLY DO FI--
THUNK
Mm, SMELLS... GREAT...
SO, KID FLASH...
...DO YOU LIKE OPRAH? I REALLY LIKE OPRAH. YOU LIKE OPRAH, RIGHT?
MOM!
JUST BECAUSE HE'S BLACK DOESN'T MEAN HE LIKES OPRAH! DO YOU LIKE JACKIE CHAN BECAUSE YOU'RE CHINESE?!
OF COURSE I LIKE JACKIE CHAN. HE'S ONE OF THE MOST SUCCESSFUL MOVIE STARS IN THE WORLD.
CAN WE TALK ABOUT SOMETHING ELSE? LIKE, ANYTHING ELSE?!

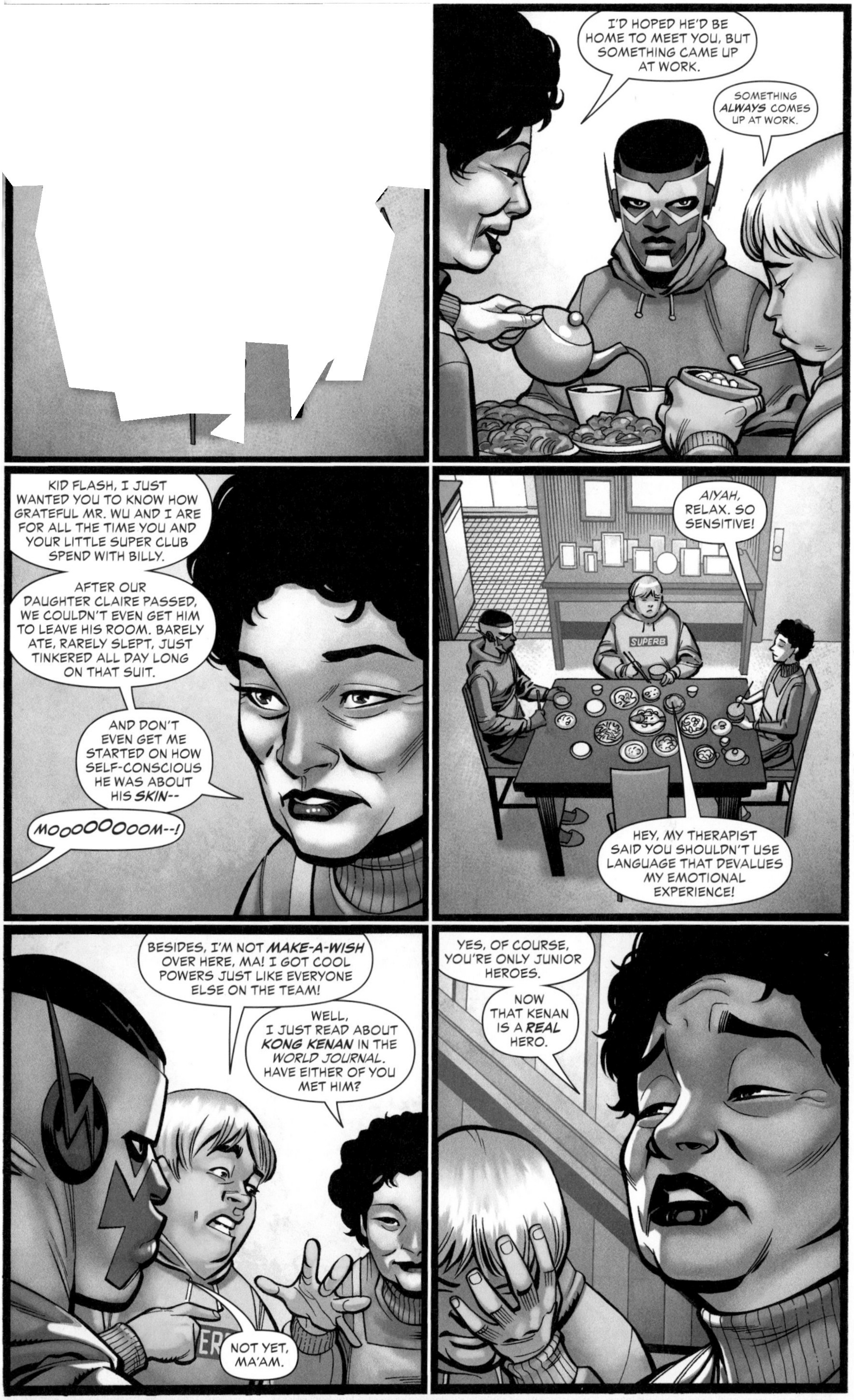

I'D HOPED HE'D BE HOME TO MEET YOU, BUT SOMETHING CAME UP AT WORK.
SOMETHING ALWAYS COMES UP AT WORK.
KID FLASH, I JUST WANTED YOU TO KNOW HOW GRATEFUL MR. WU AND I ARE FOR ALL THE TIME YOU AND YOUR LITTLE SUPER CLUB SPEND WITH BILLY.
AFTER OUR DAUGHTER CLAIRE PASSED, WE COULDN'T EVEN GET HIM TO LEAVE HIS ROOM. BARELY ATE, RARELY SLEPT, JUST TINKERED ALL DAY LONG ON THAT SUIT.
AND DON'T EVEN GET ME STARTED ON HOW SELF-CONSCIOUS HE WAS ABOUT HIS SKIN--
MOOOOOOOOM--!
AIYAH, RELAX. SO SENSITIVE!
SUPERB
HEY, MY THERAPIST SAID YOU SHOULDN'T USE LANGUAGE THAT DEVALUES MY EMOTIONAL EXPERIENCE!
BESIDES, I'M NOT MAKE-A-WISH OVER HERE, MA! I GOT COOL POWERS JUST LIKE EVERYONE ELSE ON THE TEAM!
WELL, I JUST READ ABOUT KONG KENAN IN THE WORLD JOURNAL. HAVE EITHER OF YOU MET HIM?
NOT YET, MA'AM.
YES, OF COURSE, YOU'RE ONLY JUNIOR HEROES.
NOW THAT KENAN IS A REAL HERO.

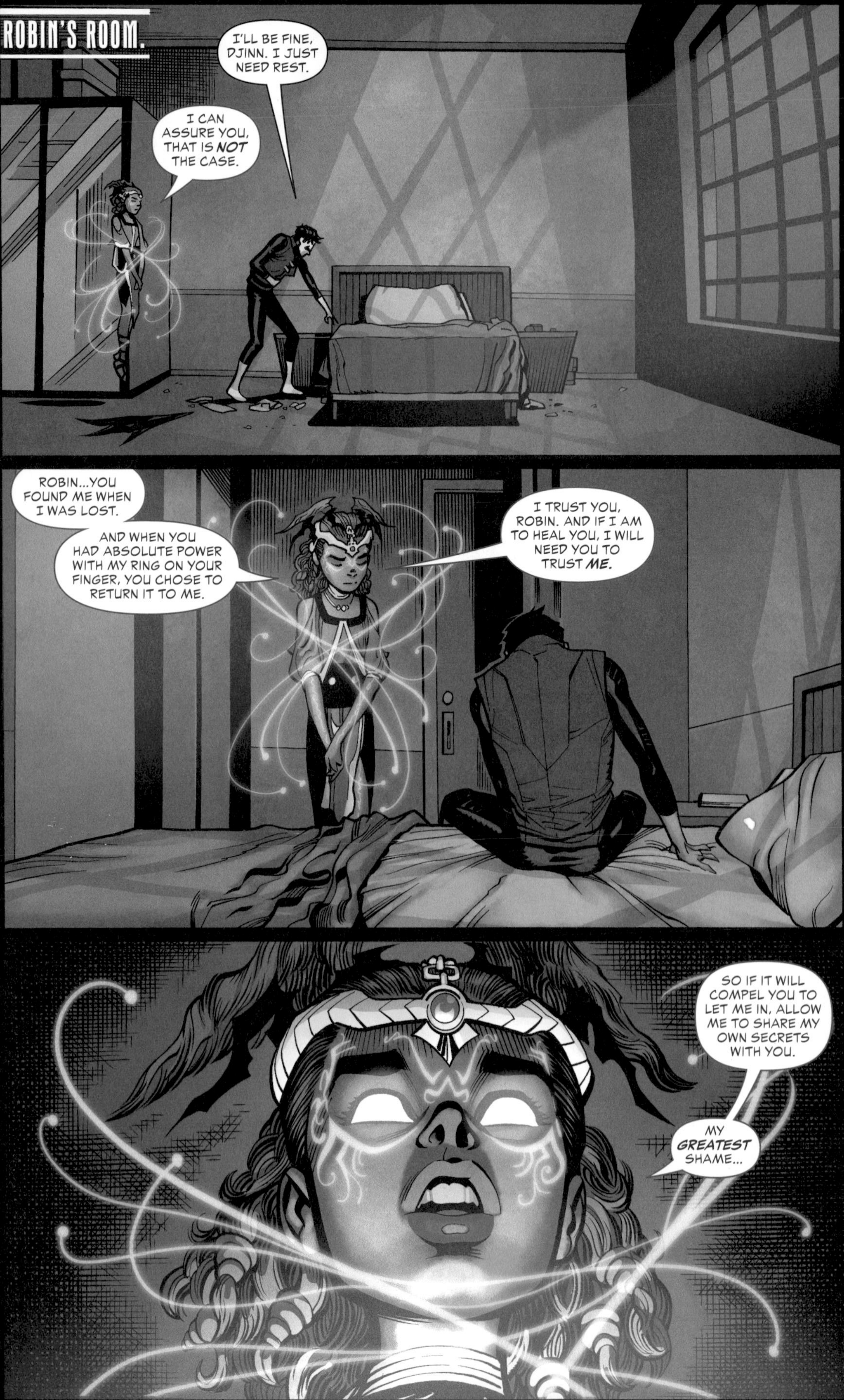
ROBIN'S ROOM.
I'LL BE FINE, DJINN. I JUST NEED REST.
I CAN ASSURE YOU, THAT IS NOT THE CASE.
ROBIN...YOU FOUND ME WHEN I WAS LOST.
AND WHEN YOU HAD ABSOLUTE POWER WITH MY RING ON YOUR FINGER, YOU CHOSE TO RETURN IT TO ME.
I TRUST YOU, ROBIN. AND IF I AM TO HEAL YOU, I WILL NEED YOU TO TRUST ME.
SO IF IT WILL COMPEL YOU TO LET ME IN, ALLOW ME TO SHARE MY OWN SECRETS WITH YOU.
MY GREATEST SHAME...

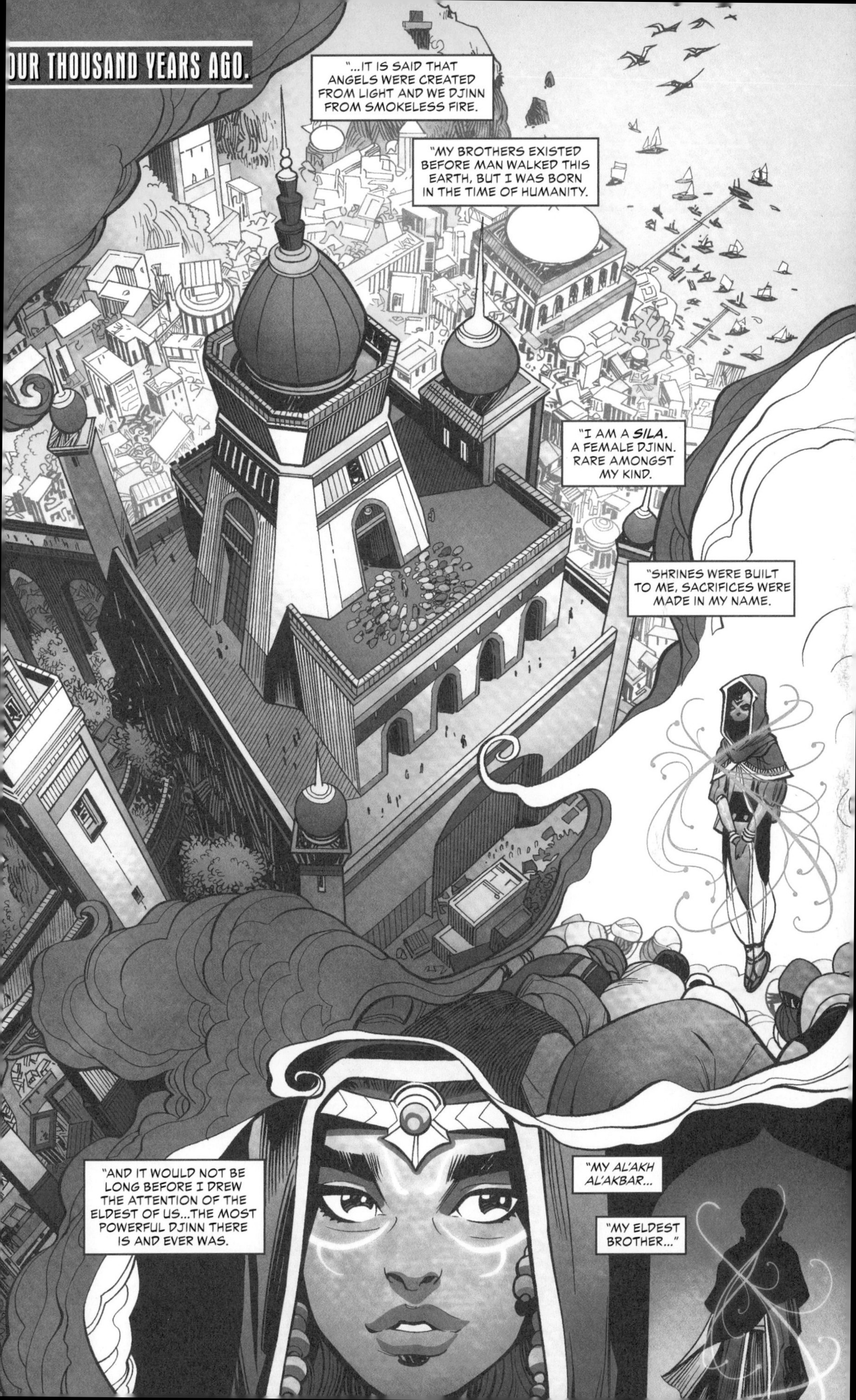
OUR THOUSAND YEARS AGO.
"...IT IS SAID THAT ANGELS WERE CREATED FROM LIGHT AND WE DJINN FROM SMOKELESS FIRE.
"MY BROTHERS EXISTED BEFORE MAN WALKED THIS EARTH, BUT I WAS BORN IN THE TIME OF HUMANITY.
"I AM A SILA. A FEMALE DJINN. RARE AMONGST MY KIND.
"SHRINES WERE BUILT TO ME, SACRIFICES WERE MADE IN MY NAME.
"AND IT WOULD NOT BE LONG BEFORE I DREW THE ATTENTION OF THE ELDEST OF US...THE MOST POWERFUL DJINN THERE IS AND EVER WAS.
"MY AL'AKH AL'AKBAR...
"MY ELDEST BROTHER..."

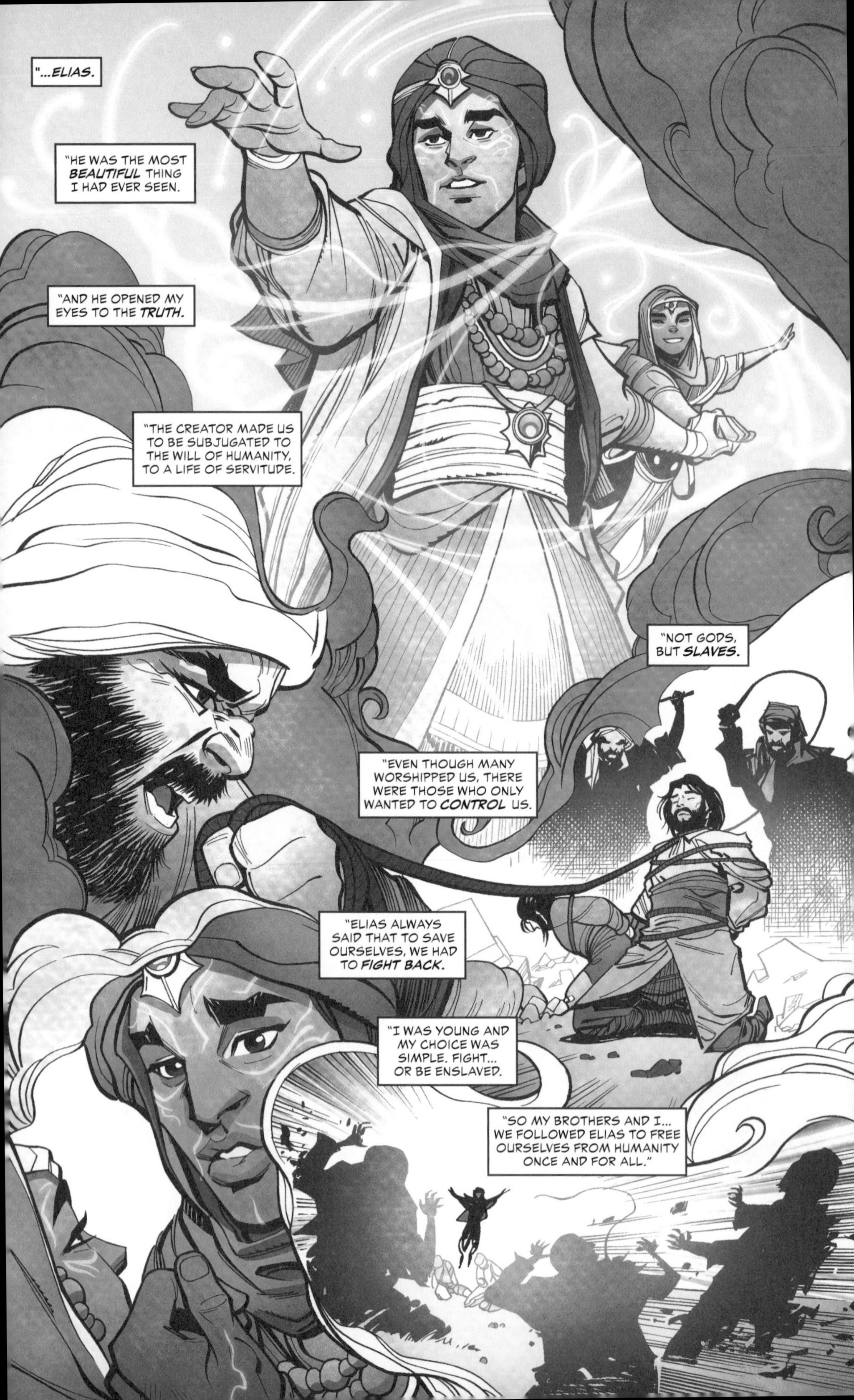
"...ELIAS.
"HE WAS THE MOST BEAUTIFUL THING I HAD EVER SEEN.
"AND HE OPENED MY EYES TO THE TRUTH.
"THE CREATOR MADE US TO BE SUBJUGATED TO THE WILL OF HUMANITY, TO A LIFE OF SERVITUDE.
"NOT GODS, BUT SLAVES.
"EVEN THOUGH MANY WORSHIPPED US, THERE WERE THOSE WHO ONLY WANTED TO CONTROL US.
"ELIAS ALWAYS SAID THAT TO SAVE OURSELVES, WE HAD TO FIGHT BACK.
"I WAS YOUNG AND MY CHOICE WAS SIMPLE. FIGHT... OR BE ENSLAVED.
"SO MY BROTHERS AND I... WE FOLLOWED ELIAS TO FREE OURSELVES FROM HUMANITY ONCE AND FOR ALL."

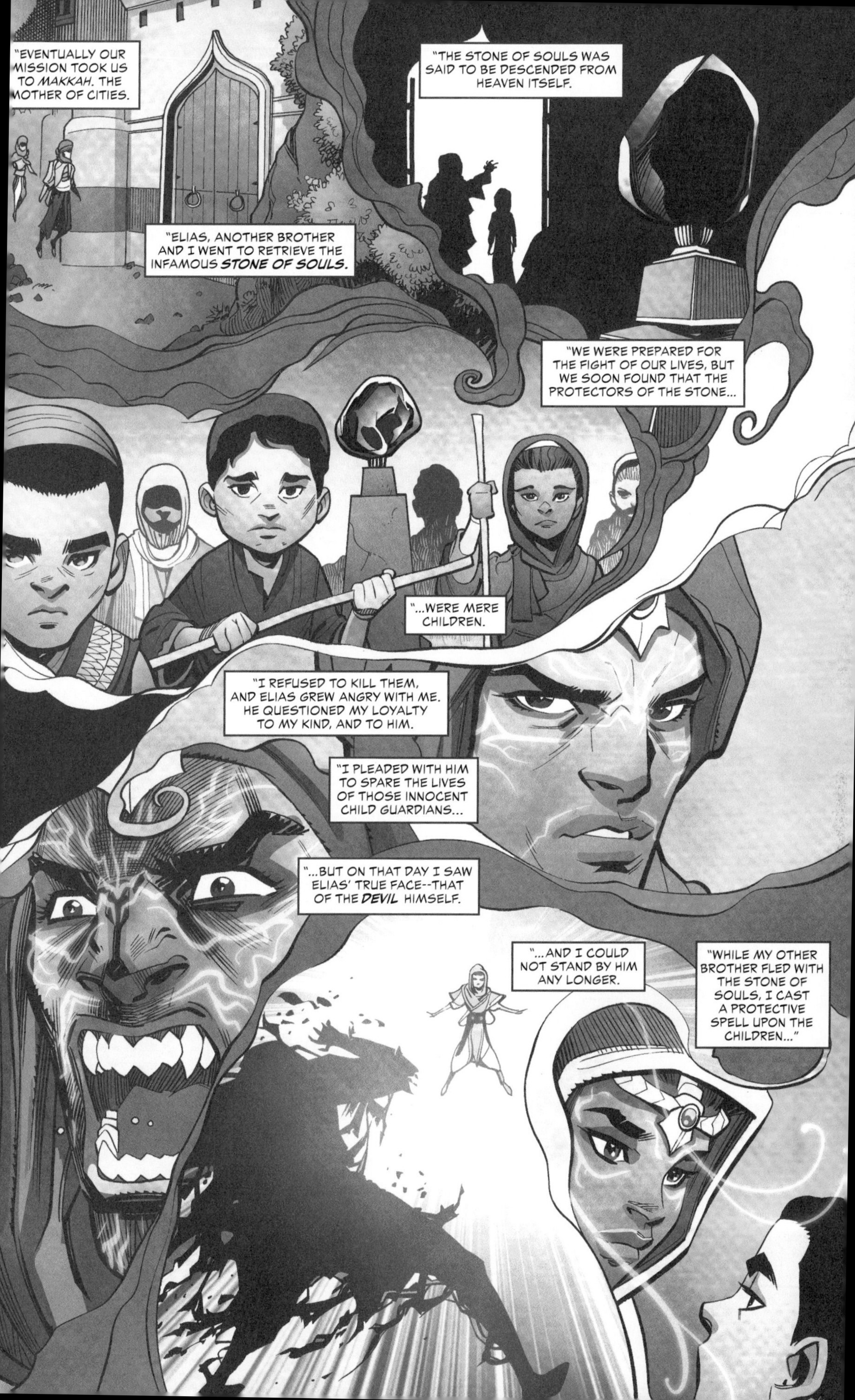
"EVENTUALLY OUR MISSION TOOK US TO *MAKKAH*. THE MOTHER OF CITIES.
"THE STONE OF SOULS WAS SAID TO BE DESCENDED FROM HEAVEN ITSELF.
"ELIAS, ANOTHER BROTHER AND I WENT TO RETRIEVE THE INFAMOUS ***STONE OF SOULS***.
"WE WERE PREPARED FOR THE FIGHT OF OUR LIVES, BUT WE SOON FOUND THAT THE PROTECTORS OF THE STONE...
"...WERE MERE CHILDREN.
"I REFUSED TO KILL THEM, AND ELIAS GREW ANGRY WITH ME. HE QUESTIONED MY LOYALTY TO MY KIND, AND TO HIM.
"I PLEADED WITH HIM TO SPARE THE LIVES OF THOSE INNOCENT CHILD GUARDIANS...
"...BUT ON THAT DAY I SAW ELIAS' TRUE FACE--THAT OF THE ***DEVIL*** HIMSELF.
"...AND I COULD NOT STAND BY HIM ANY LONGER.
"WHILE MY OTHER BROTHER FLED WITH THE STONE OF SOULS, I CAST A PROTECTIVE SPELL UPON THE CHILDREN..."

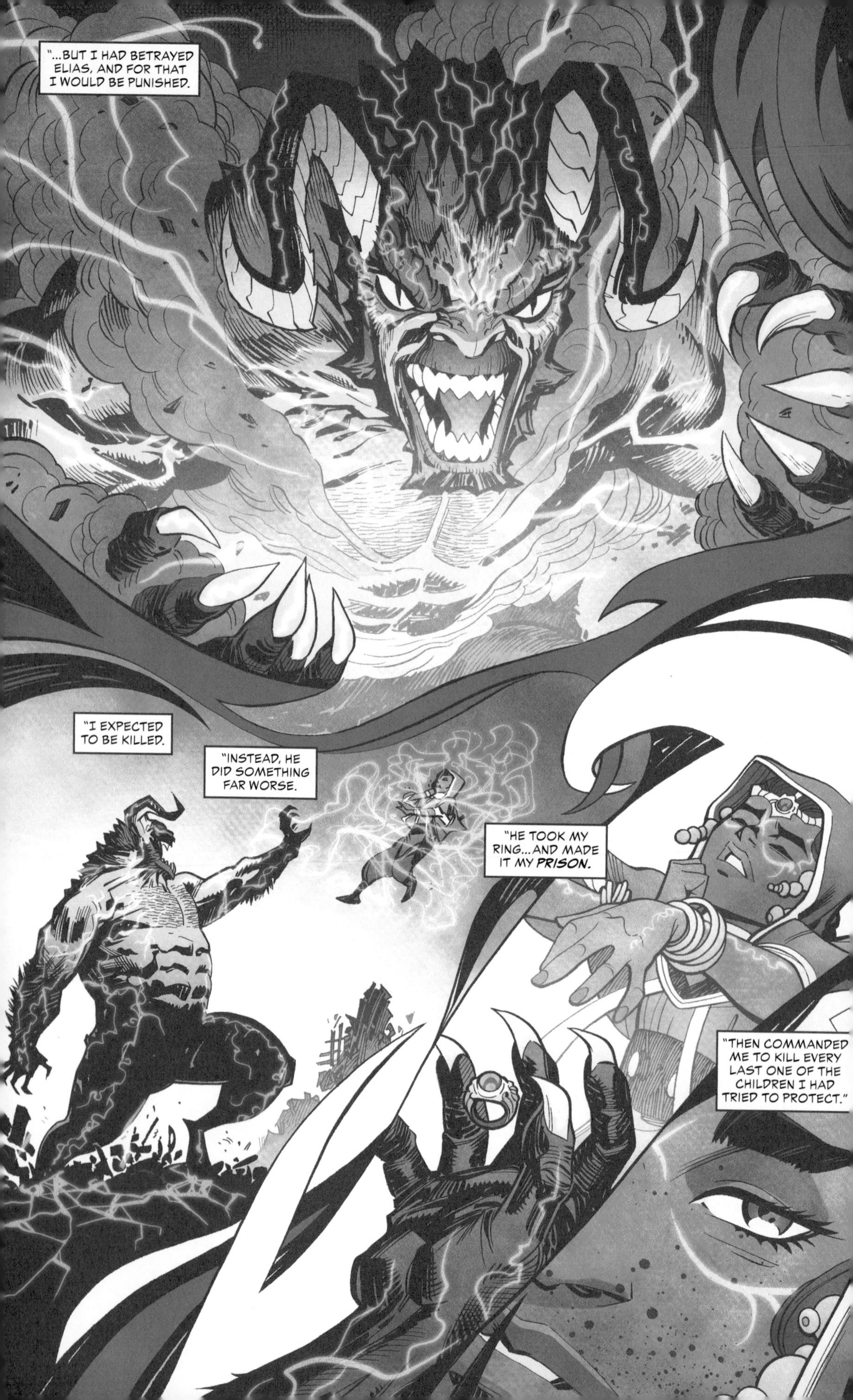
"...BUT I HAD BETRAYED ELIAS, AND FOR THAT I WOULD BE PUNISHED.
"I EXPECTED TO BE KILLED.
"INSTEAD, HE DID SOMETHING FAR WORSE.
"HE TOOK MY RING...AND MADE IT MY *PRISON*.
"THEN COMMANDED ME TO KILL EVERY LAST ONE OF THE CHILDREN I HAD TRIED TO PROTECT."

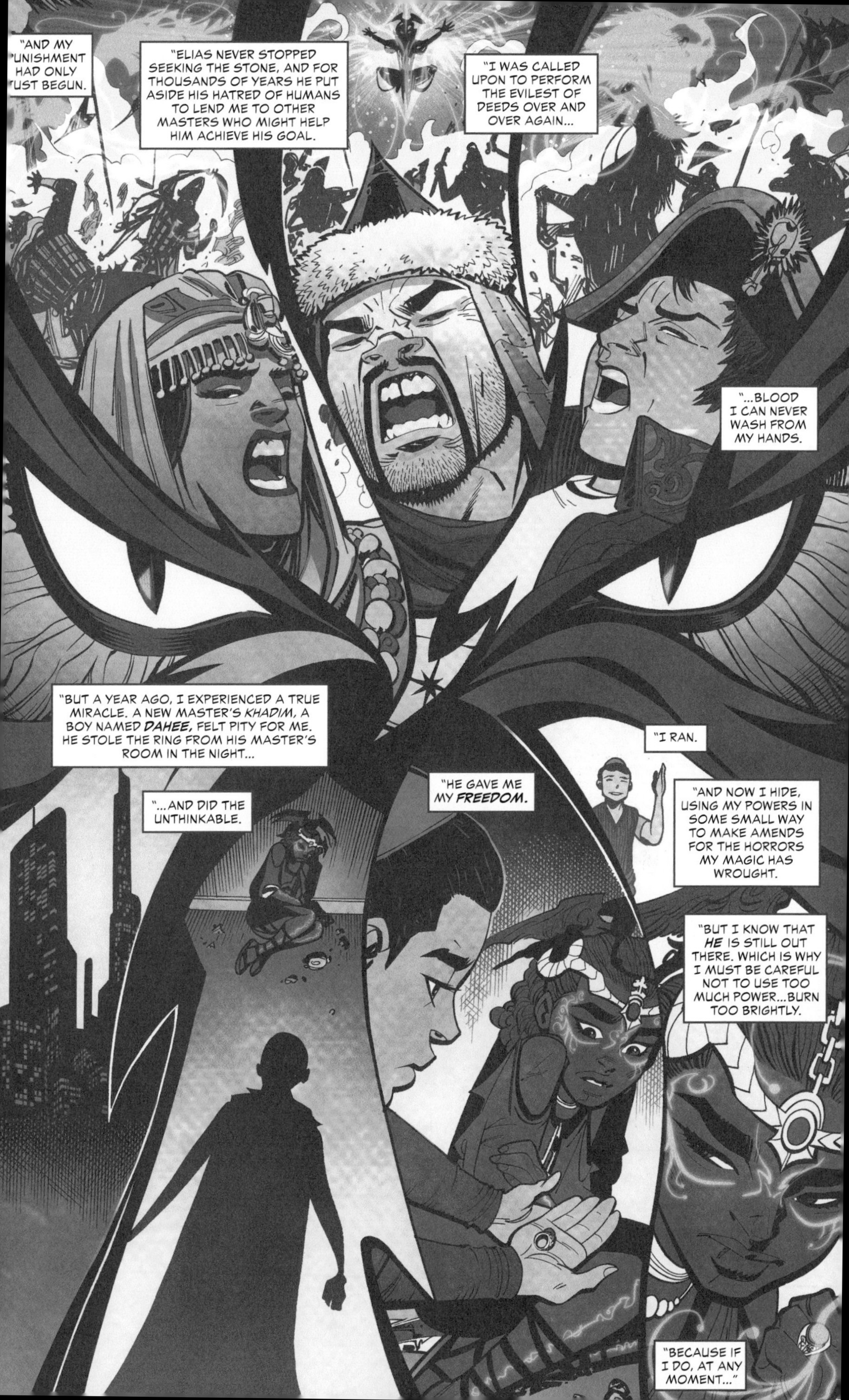
"AND MY
PUNISHMENT
HAD ONLY
JUST BEGUN.
"ELIAS NEVER STOPPED SEEKING THE STONE, AND FOR THOUSANDS OF YEARS HE PUT ASIDE HIS HATRED OF HUMANS TO LEND ME TO OTHER MASTERS WHO MIGHT HELP HIM ACHIEVE HIS GOAL.
"I WAS CALLED UPON TO PERFORM THE EVILEST OF DEEDS OVER AND OVER AGAIN...
"...BLOOD I CAN NEVER WASH FROM MY HANDS.
"BUT A YEAR AGO, I EXPERIENCED A TRUE MIRACLE. A NEW MASTER'S *KHADIM*, A BOY NAMED ***DAHEE***, FELT PITY FOR ME. HE STOLE THE RING FROM HIS MASTER'S ROOM IN THE NIGHT...
"...AND DID THE UNTHINKABLE.
"HE GAVE ME MY ***FREEDOM***.
"I RAN.
"AND NOW I HIDE, USING MY POWERS IN SOME SMALL WAY TO MAKE AMENDS FOR THE HORRORS MY MAGIC HAS WROUGHT.
"BUT I KNOW THAT ***HE*** IS STILL OUT THERE. WHICH IS WHY I MUST BE CAREFUL NOT TO USE TOO MUCH POWER...BURN TOO BRIGHTLY.
"BECAUSE IF I DO, AT ANY MOMENT..."

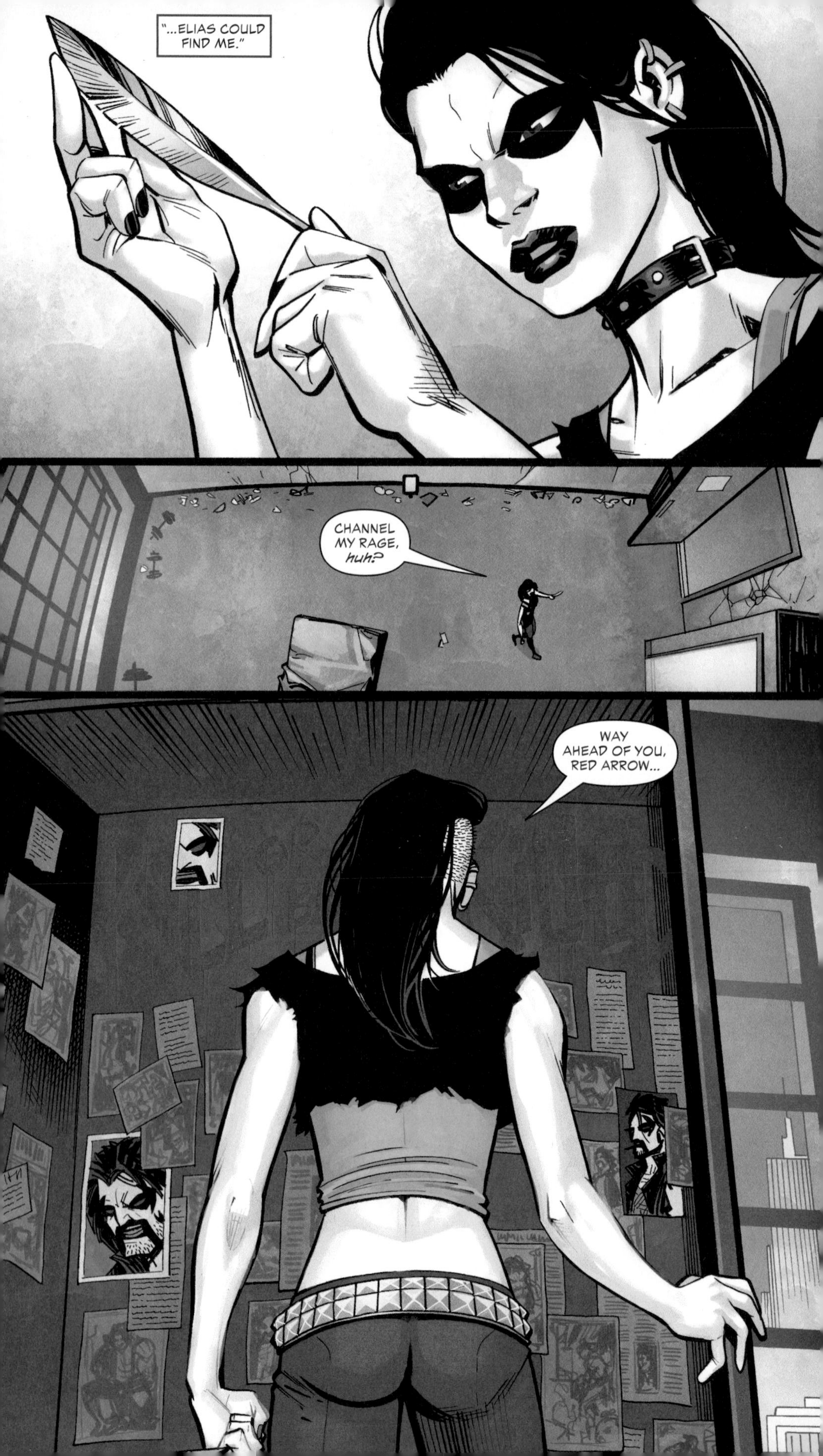
"...ELIAS COULD FIND ME."
CHANNEL MY RAGE, *huh?*
WAY AHEAD OF YOU, RED ARROW...

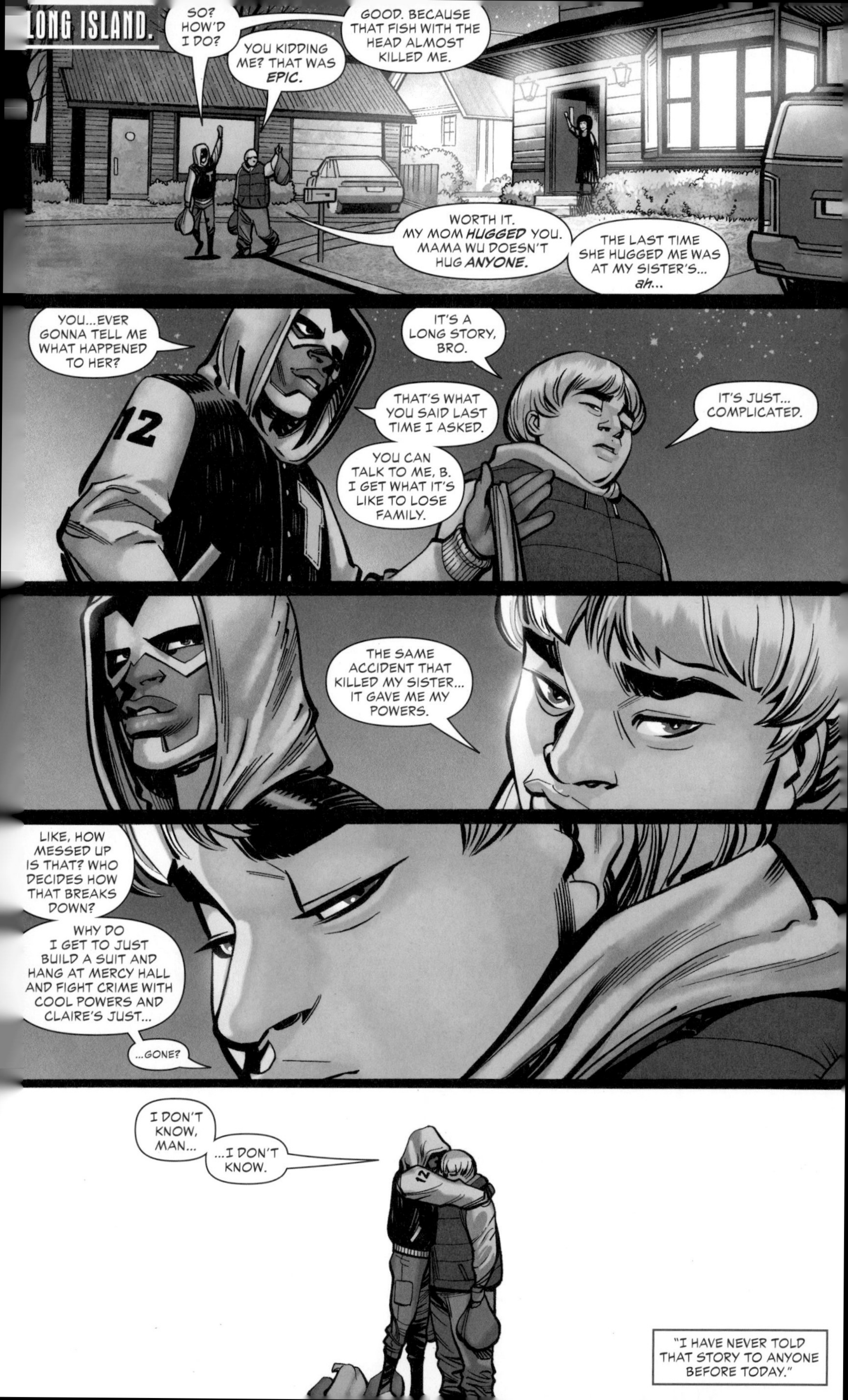
LONG ISLAND.
SO? HOW'D I DO?
YOU KIDDING ME? THAT WAS EPIC.
GOOD. BECAUSE THAT FISH WITH THE HEAD ALMOST KILLED ME.
WORTH IT. MY MOM HUGGED YOU. MAMA WU DOESN'T HUG ANYONE.
THE LAST TIME SHE HUGGED ME WAS AT MY SISTER'S... ah...
YOU...EVER GONNA TELL ME WHAT HAPPENED TO HER?
IT'S A LONG STORY, BRO.
THAT'S WHAT YOU SAID LAST TIME I ASKED.
YOU CAN TALK TO ME, B. I GET WHAT IT'S LIKE TO LOSE FAMILY.
IT'S JUST... COMPLICATED.
THE SAME ACCIDENT THAT KILLED MY SISTER... IT GAVE ME MY POWERS.
LIKE, HOW MESSED UP IS THAT? WHO DECIDES HOW THAT BREAKS DOWN?
WHY DO I GET TO JUST BUILD A SUIT AND HANG AT MERCY HALL AND FIGHT CRIME WITH COOL POWERS AND CLAIRE'S JUST...
...GONE?
I DON'T KNOW, MAN...
...I DON'T KNOW.
"I HAVE NEVER TOLD THAT STORY TO ANYONE BEFORE TODAY."

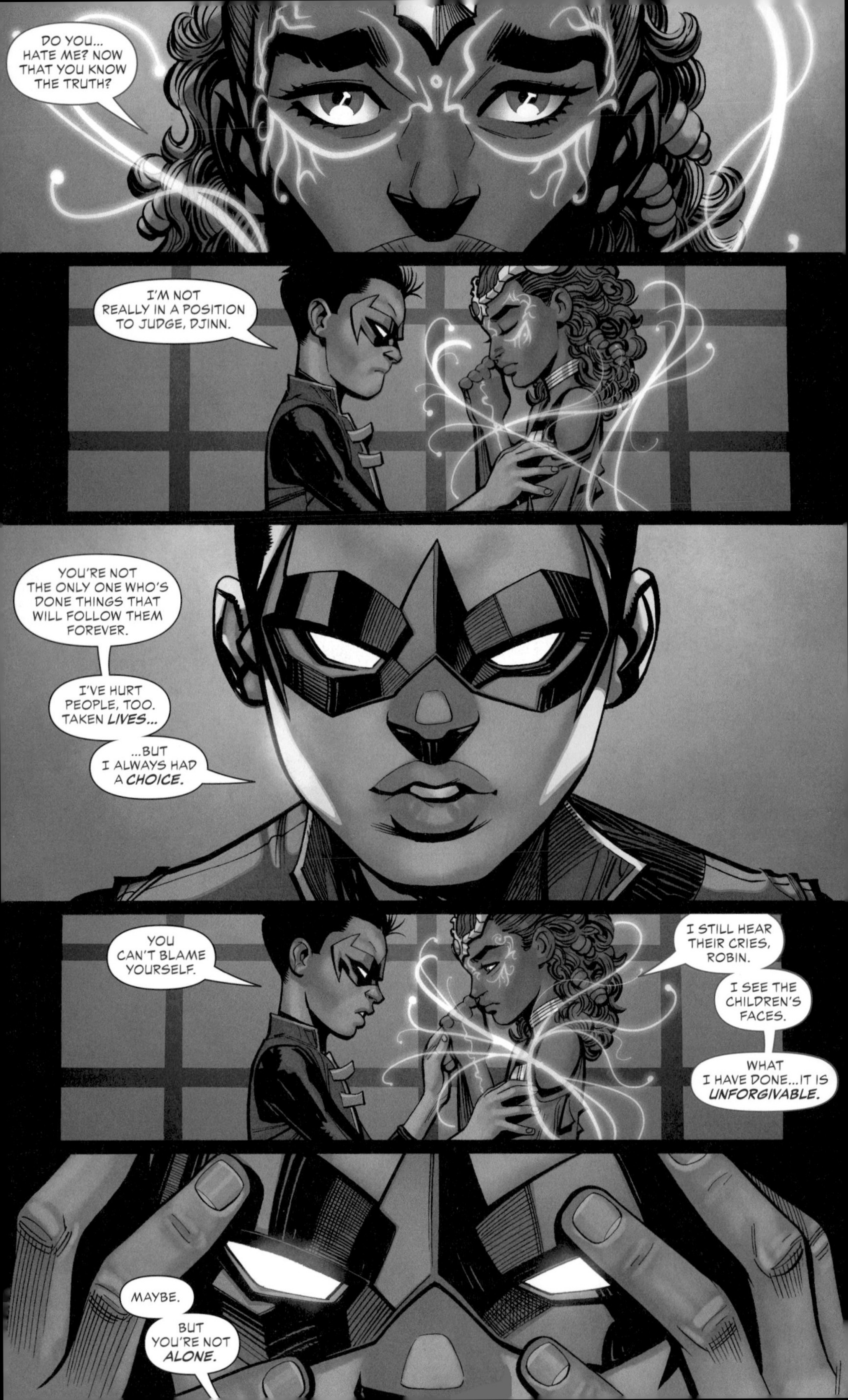

DO YOU... HATE ME? NOW THAT YOU KNOW THE TRUTH?
I'M NOT REALLY IN A POSITION TO JUDGE, DJINN.
YOU'RE NOT THE ONLY ONE WHO'S DONE THINGS THAT WILL FOLLOW THEM FOREVER.
I'VE HURT PEOPLE, TOO. TAKEN *LIVES*...
...BUT I ALWAYS HAD A *CHOICE*.
I STILL HEAR THEIR CRIES, ROBIN.
I SEE THE CHILDREN'S FACES.
WHAT I HAVE DONE...IT IS *UNFORGIVABLE*.
YOU CAN'T BLAME YOURSELF.
MAYBE.
BUT YOU'RE NOT *ALONE*.

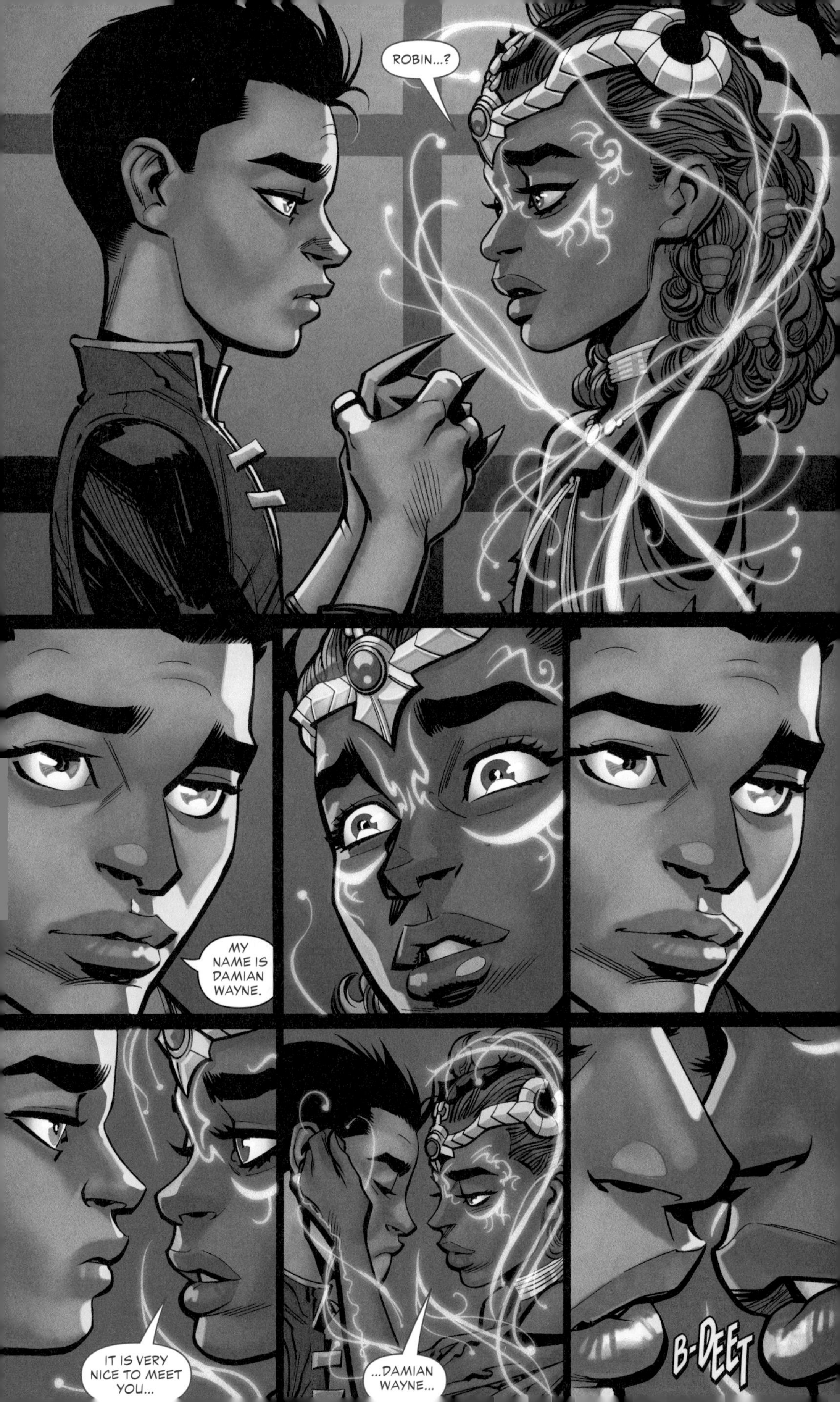
ROBIN...?
MY NAME IS DAMIAN WAYNE.
IT IS VERY NICE TO MEET YOU...
...DAMIAN WAYNE...
B-DEET

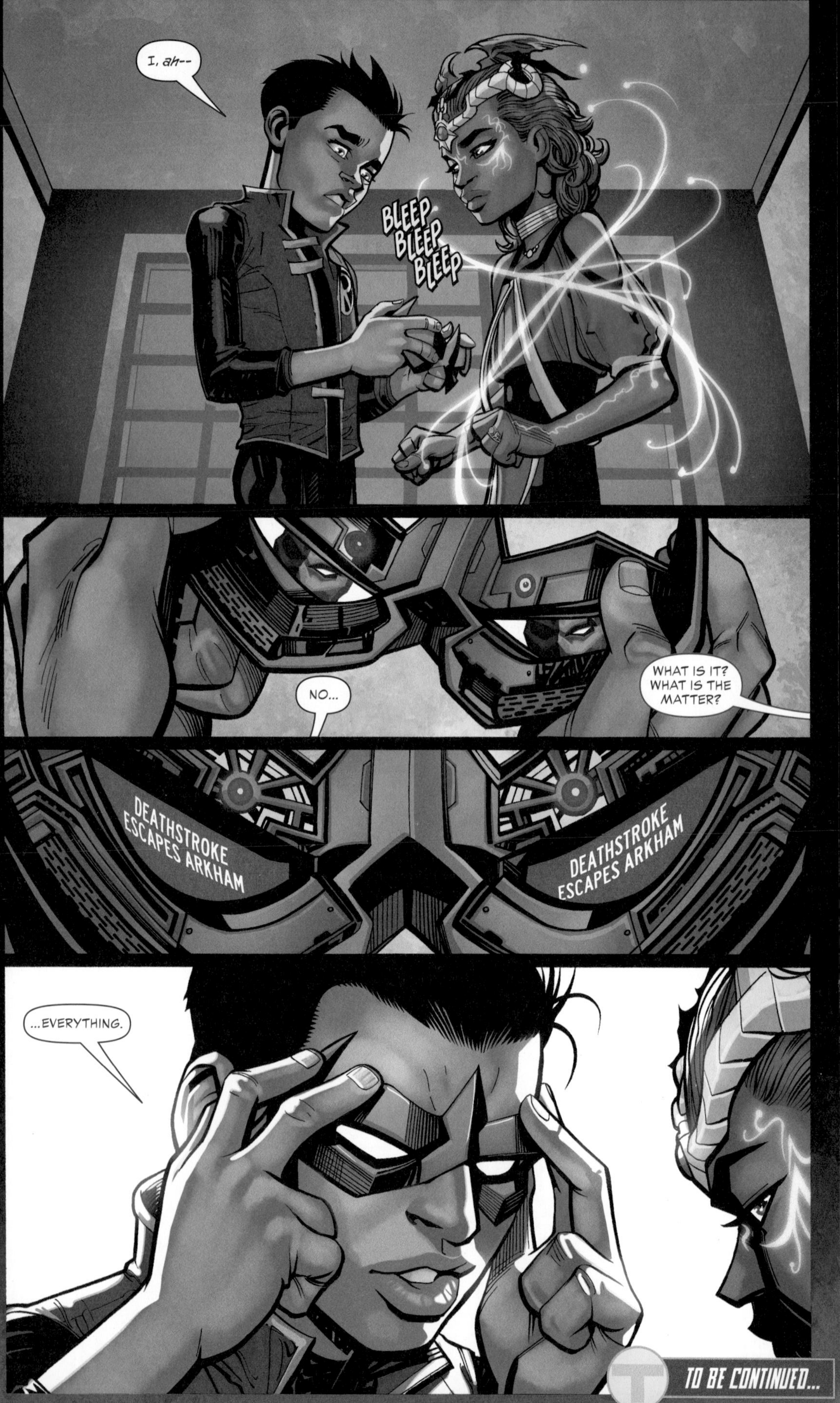
I, ah--
BLEEP BLEEP BLEEP
NO...
WHAT IS IT? WHAT IS THE MATTER?
DEATHSTROKE ESCAPES ARKHAM
DEATHSTROKE ESCAPES ARKHAM
...EVERYTHING.
TO BE CONTINUED...

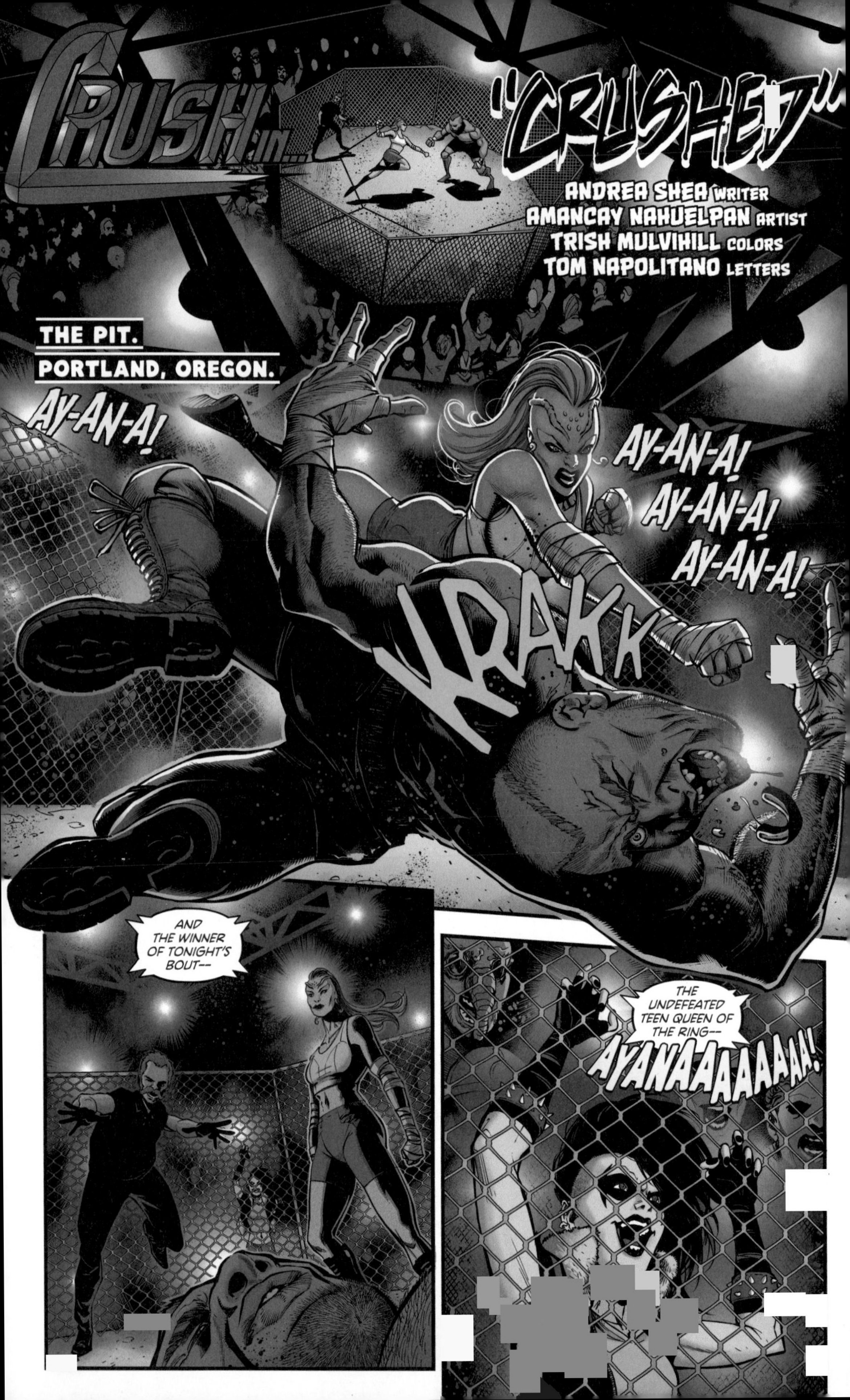
CRUSH IN...
"CRUSHED"
ANDREA SHEA WRITER
AMANCAY NAHUELPAN ARTIST
TRISH MULVIHILL COLORS
TOM NAPOLITANO LETTERS
THE PIT.
PORTLAND, OREGON.
AY-AN-A!
AY-AN-A!
AY-AN-A!
AY-AN-A!
KRAKK
AND THE WINNER OF TONIGHT'S BOUT--
THE UNDEFEATED TEEN QUEEN OF THE RING--
AYANAAAAAAA!

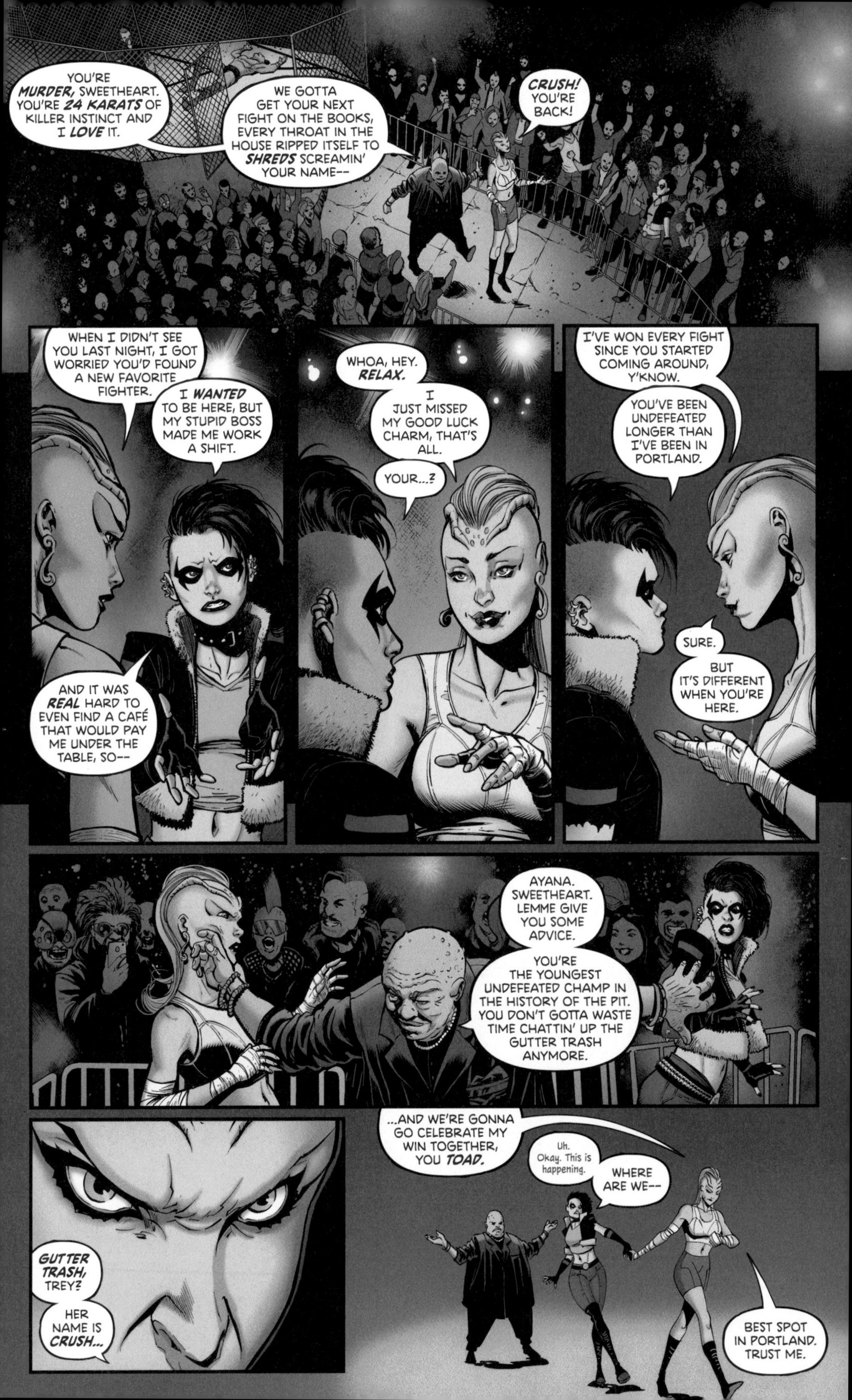
YOU'RE MURDER, SWEETHEART. YOU'RE 24 KARATS OF KILLER INSTINCT AND I LOVE IT.
WE GOTTA GET YOUR NEXT FIGHT ON THE BOOKS, EVERY THROAT IN THE HOUSE RIPPED ITSELF TO SHREDS SCREAMIN' YOUR NAME--
CRUSH! YOU'RE BACK!
WHEN I DIDN'T SEE YOU LAST NIGHT, I GOT WORRIED YOU'D FOUND A NEW FAVORITE FIGHTER.
I WANTED TO BE HERE, BUT MY STUPID BOSS MADE ME WORK A SHIFT.
AND IT WAS REAL HARD TO EVEN FIND A CAFÉ THAT WOULD PAY ME UNDER THE TABLE, SO--
WHOA, HEY. RELAX.
I JUST MISSED MY GOOD LUCK CHARM, THAT'S ALL.
YOUR...?
I'VE WON EVERY FIGHT SINCE YOU STARTED COMING AROUND, Y'KNOW.
YOU'VE BEEN UNDEFEATED LONGER THAN I'VE BEEN IN PORTLAND.
SURE.
BUT IT'S DIFFERENT WHEN YOU'RE HERE.
AYANA. SWEETHEART. LEMME GIVE YOU SOME ADVICE.
YOU'RE THE YOUNGEST UNDEFEATED CHAMP IN THE HISTORY OF THE PIT. YOU DON'T GOTTA WASTE TIME CHATTIN' UP THE GUTTER TRASH ANYMORE.
GUTTER TRASH, TREY?
HER NAME IS CRUSH...
...AND WE'RE GONNA GO CELEBRATE MY WIN TOGETHER, YOU TOAD.
Uh. Okay. This is happening.
WHERE ARE WE--
BEST SPOT IN PORTLAND. TRUST ME.

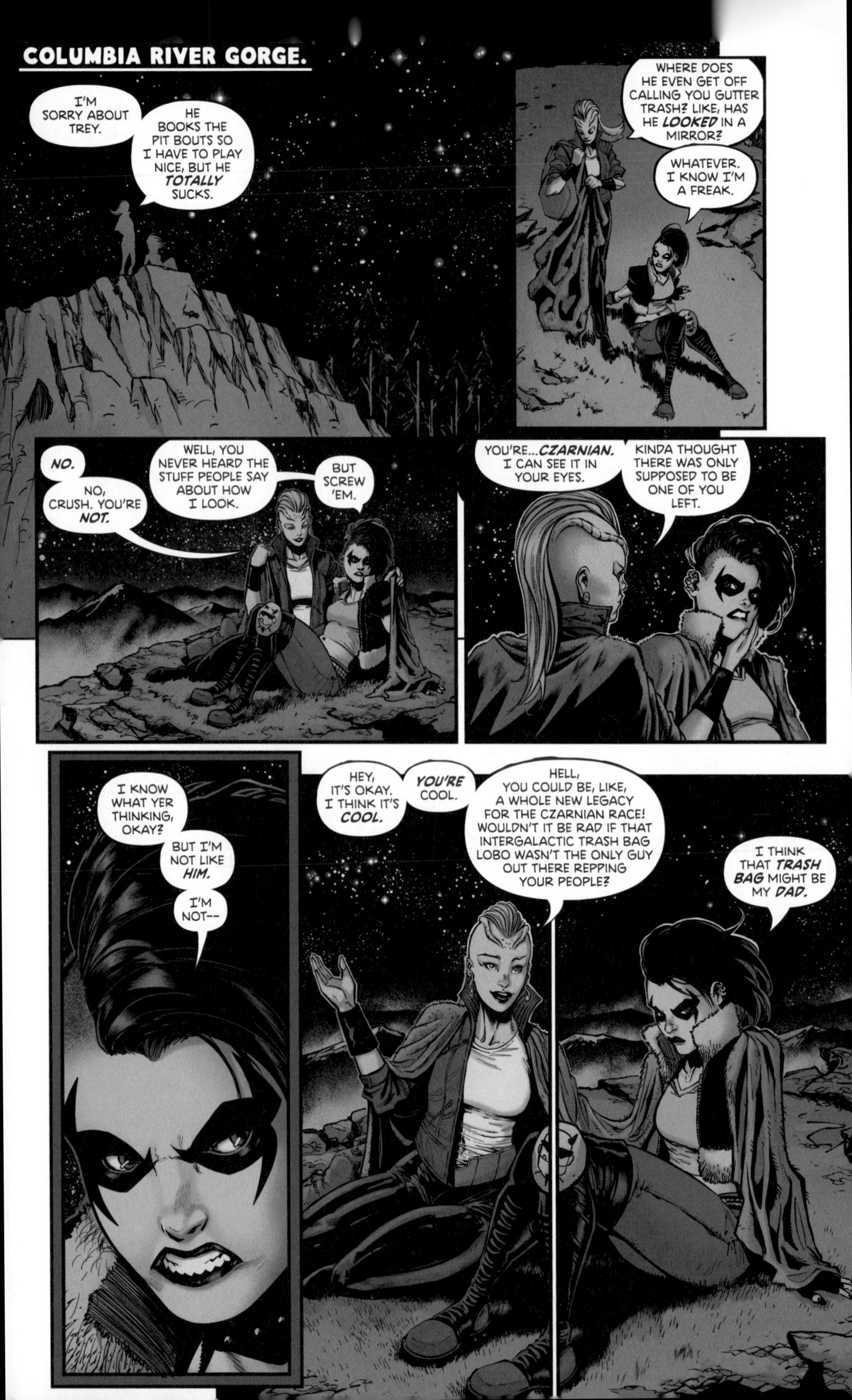
COLUMBIA RIVER GORGE.
I'M SORRY ABOUT TREY.
HE BOOKS THE PIT BOUTS SO I HAVE TO PLAY NICE, BUT HE TOTALLY SUCKS.
WHERE DOES HE EVEN GET OFF CALLING YOU GUTTER TRASH? LIKE, HAS HE LOOKED IN A MIRROR?
WHATEVER. I KNOW I'M A FREAK.
NO.
NO, CRUSH. YOU'RE NOT.
WELL, YOU NEVER HEARD THE STUFF PEOPLE SAY ABOUT HOW I LOOK.
BUT SCREW 'EM.
YOU'RE...CZARNIAN. I CAN SEE IT IN YOUR EYES.
KINDA THOUGHT THERE WAS ONLY SUPPOSED TO BE ONE OF YOU LEFT.
I KNOW WHAT YER THINKING, OKAY?
BUT I'M NOT LIKE HIM.
I'M NOT--
HEY, IT'S OKAY. I THINK IT'S COOL.
YOU'RE COOL.
HELL, YOU COULD BE, LIKE, A WHOLE NEW LEGACY FOR THE CZARNIAN RACE! WOULDN'T IT BE RAD IF THAT INTERGALACTIC TRASH BAG LOBO WASN'T THE ONLY GUY OUT THERE REPPING YOUR PEOPLE?
I THINK THAT TRASH BAG MIGHT BE MY DAD.

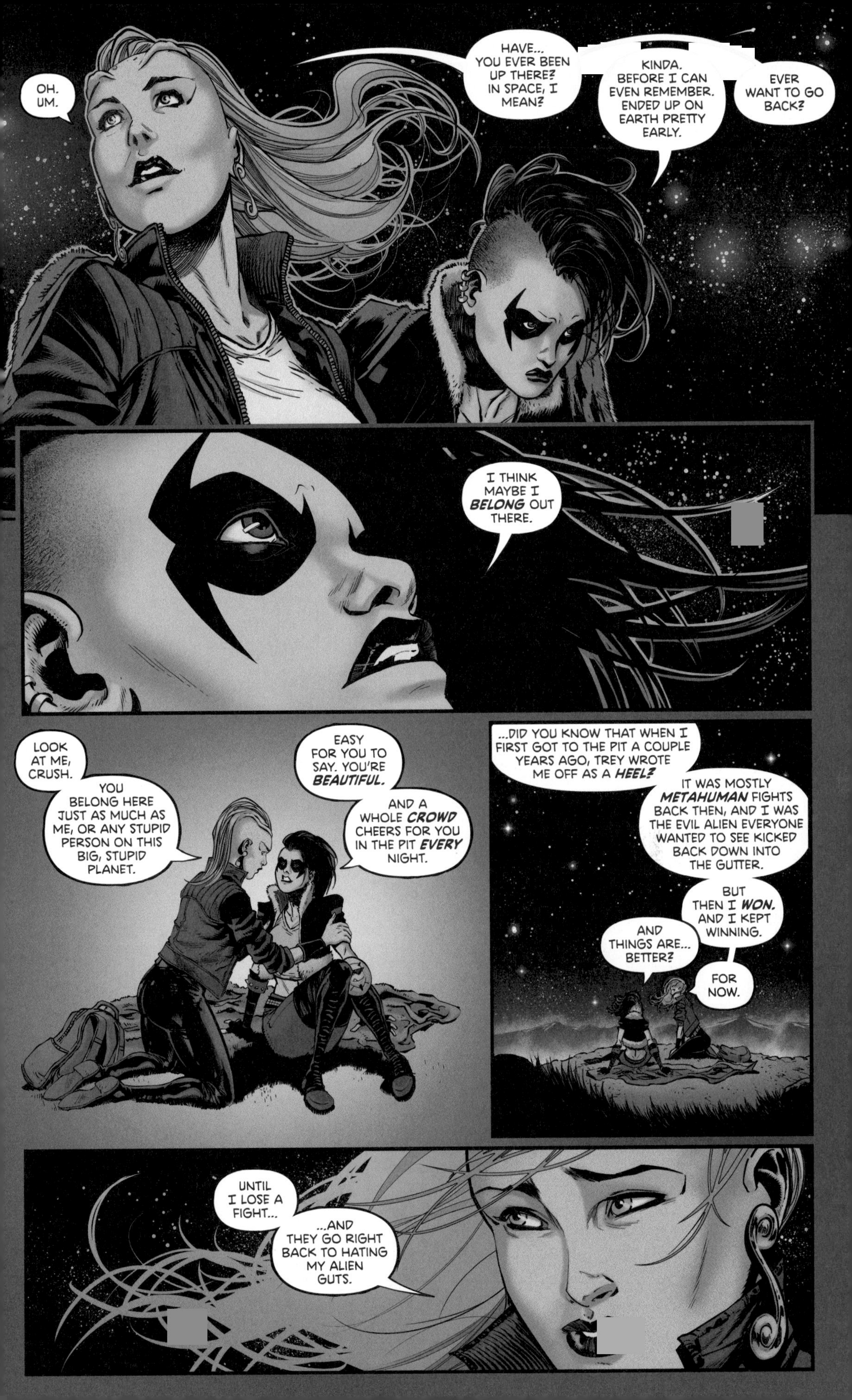
OH.
UM.
HAVE... YOU EVER BEEN UP THERE? IN SPACE, I MEAN?
KINDA. BEFORE I CAN EVEN REMEMBER. ENDED UP ON EARTH PRETTY EARLY.
EVER WANT TO GO BACK?
I THINK MAYBE I BELONG OUT THERE.
LOOK AT ME, CRUSH.
YOU BELONG HERE JUST AS MUCH AS ME, OR ANY STUPID PERSON ON THIS BIG, STUPID PLANET.
EASY FOR YOU TO SAY. YOU'RE BEAUTIFUL.
AND A WHOLE CROWD CHEERS FOR YOU IN THE PIT EVERY NIGHT.
...DID YOU KNOW THAT WHEN I FIRST GOT TO THE PIT A COUPLE YEARS AGO, TREY WROTE ME OFF AS A HEEL?
IT WAS MOSTLY METAHUMAN FIGHTS BACK THEN, AND I WAS THE EVIL ALIEN EVERYONE WANTED TO SEE KICKED BACK DOWN INTO THE GUTTER.
BUT THEN I WON. AND I KEPT WINNING.
AND THINGS ARE... BETTER?
FOR NOW.
UNTIL I LOSE A FIGHT...
...AND THEY GO RIGHT BACK TO HATING MY ALIEN GUTS.

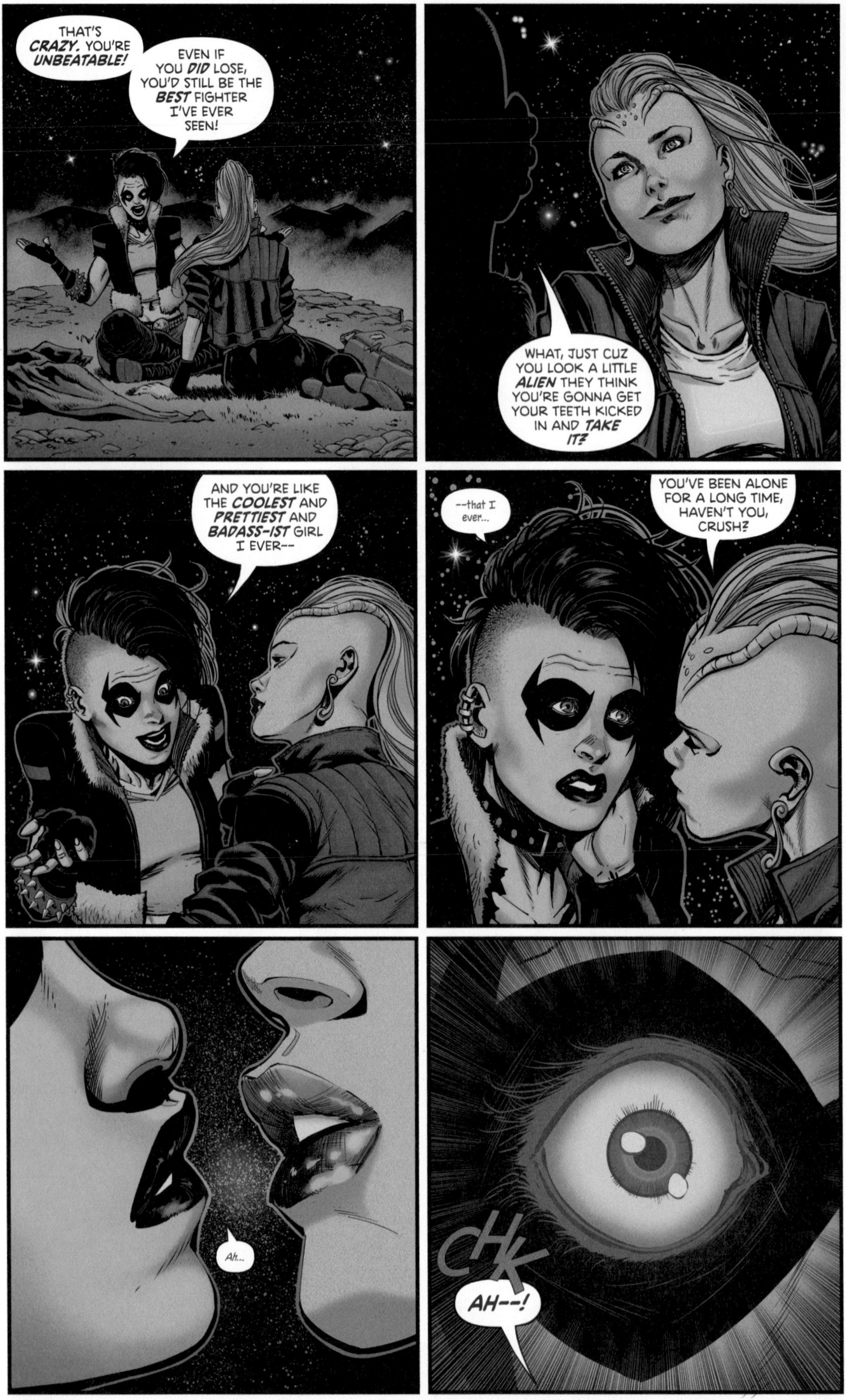

THAT'S CRAZY. YOU'RE UNBEATABLE!
EVEN IF YOU DID LOSE, YOU'D STILL BE THE BEST FIGHTER I'VE EVER SEEN!
WHAT, JUST CUZ YOU LOOK A LITTLE ALIEN THEY THINK YOU'RE GONNA GET YOUR TEETH KICKED IN AND TAKE IT?
AND YOU'RE LIKE THE COOLEST AND PRETTIEST AND BADASS-IST GIRL I EVER--
--that I ever...
YOU'VE BEEN ALONE FOR A LONG TIME, HAVEN'T YOU, CRUSH?
Ah...
CHK
AH--!

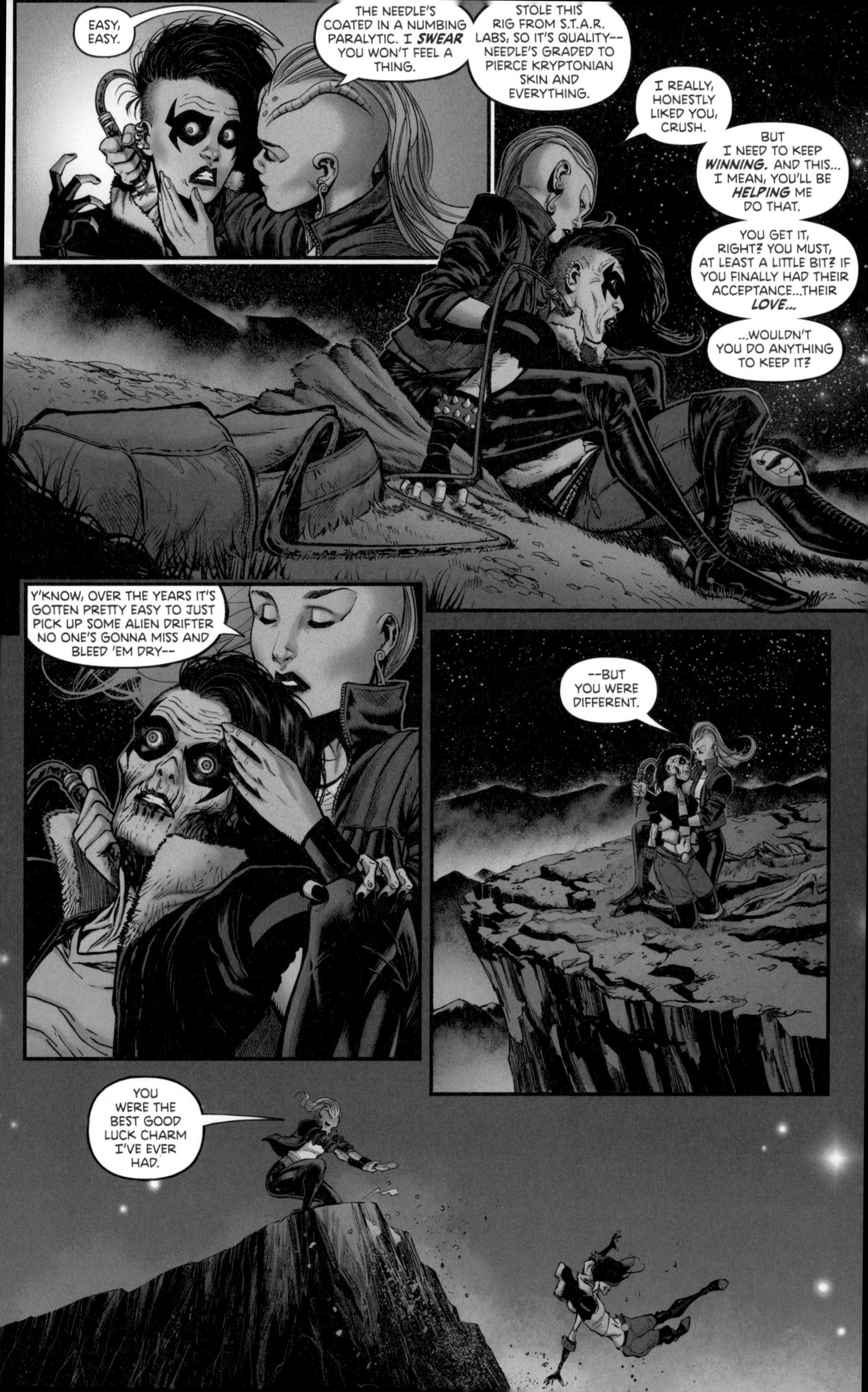
EASY, EASY.
THE NEEDLE'S COATED IN A NUMBING PARALYTIC. I *SWEAR* YOU WON'T FEEL A THING.
STOLE THIS RIG FROM S.T.A.R. LABS, SO IT'S QUALITY-- NEEDLE'S GRADED TO PIERCE KRYPTONIAN SKIN AND EVERYTHING.
I REALLY, HONESTLY LIKED YOU, CRUSH.
BUT I NEED TO KEEP *WINNING.* AND THIS... I MEAN, YOU'LL BE *HELPING* ME DO THAT.
YOU GET IT, RIGHT? YOU MUST, AT LEAST A LITTLE BIT? IF YOU FINALLY HAD THEIR ACCEPTANCE...THEIR *LOVE...*
...WOULDN'T YOU DO ANYTHING TO KEEP IT?
Y'KNOW, OVER THE YEARS IT'S GOTTEN PRETTY EASY TO JUST PICK UP SOME ALIEN DRIFTER NO ONE'S GONNA MISS AND BLEED 'EM DRY--
--BUT YOU WERE DIFFERENT.
YOU WERE THE BEST GOOD LUCK CHARM I'VE EVER HAD.

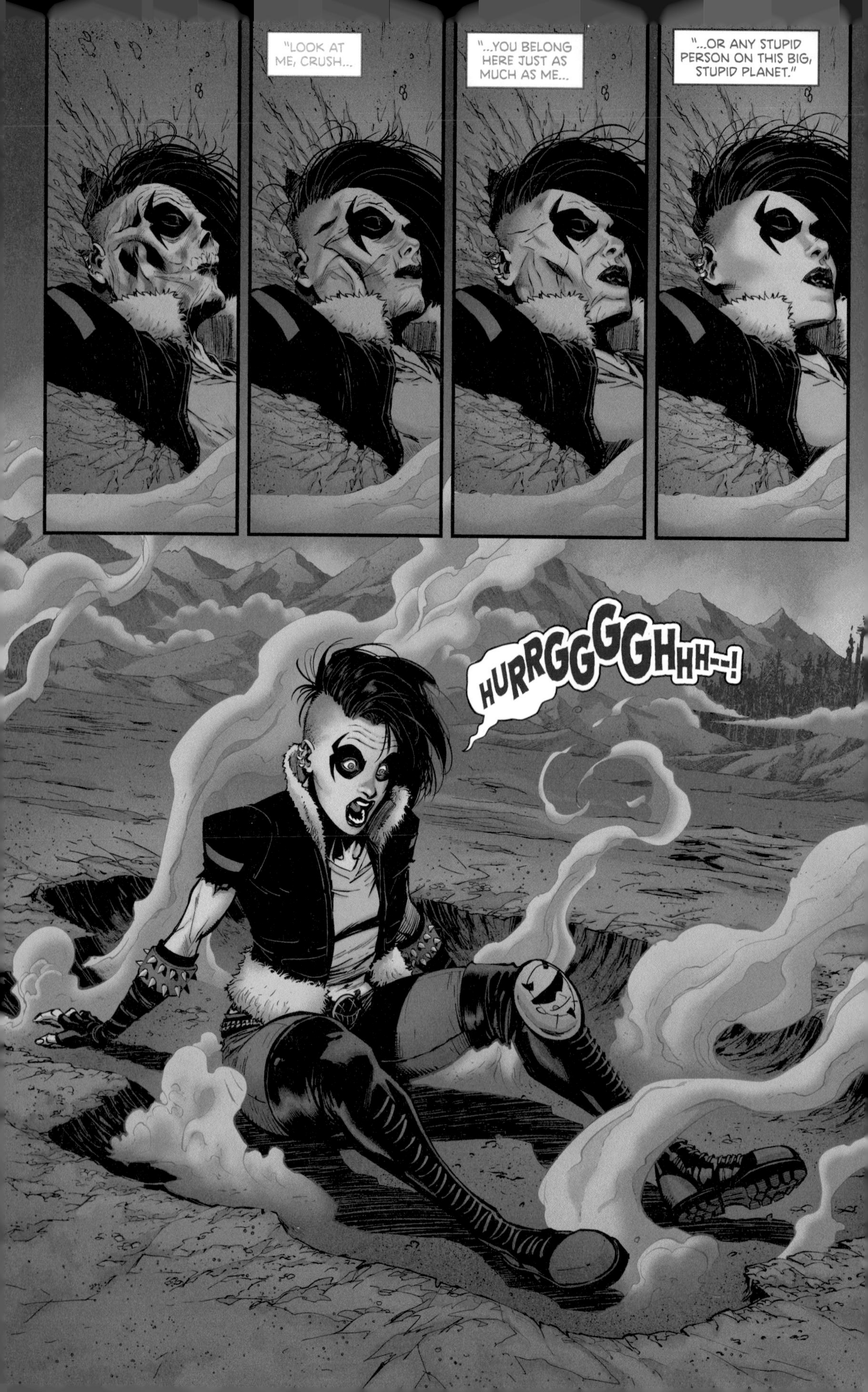
"LOOK AT ME, CRUSH...
"...YOU BELONG HERE JUST AS MUCH AS ME...
"...OR ANY STUPID PERSON ON THIS BIG, STUPID PLANET."
HURRGGGGHHH--!

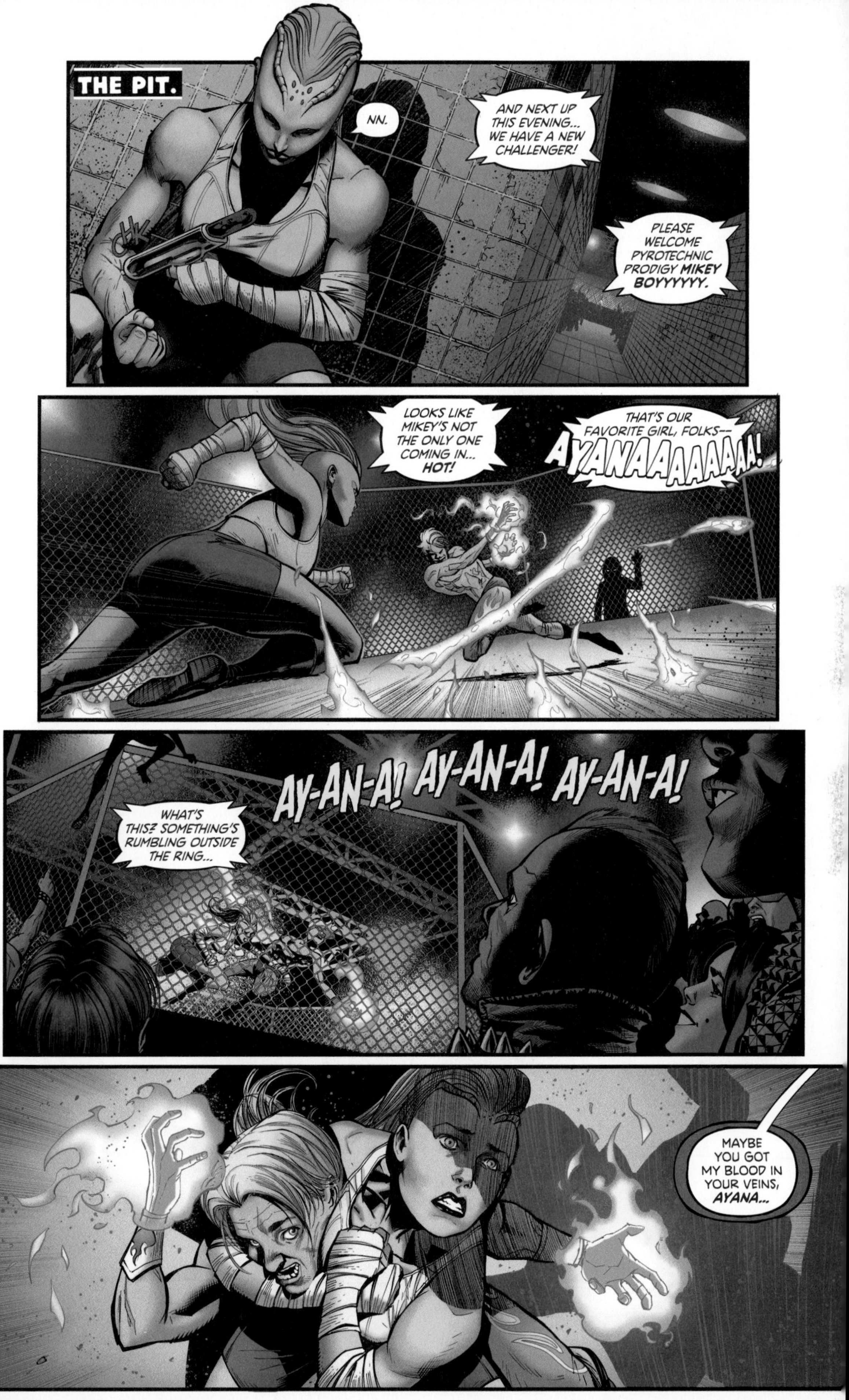
THE PIT.
NN.
AND NEXT UP THIS EVENING... WE HAVE A NEW CHALLENGER!
PLEASE WELCOME PYROTECHNIC PRODIGY MIKEY BOYYYYYY.
LOOKS LIKE MIKEY'S NOT THE ONLY ONE COMING IN... HOT!
THAT'S OUR FAVORITE GIRL, FOLKS-- AYANAAAAAAAA!
AY-AN-A! AY-AN-A! AY-AN-A!
WHAT'S THIS? SOMETHING'S RUMBLING OUTSIDE THE RING...
MAYBE YOU GOT MY BLOOD IN YOUR VEINS, AYANA...

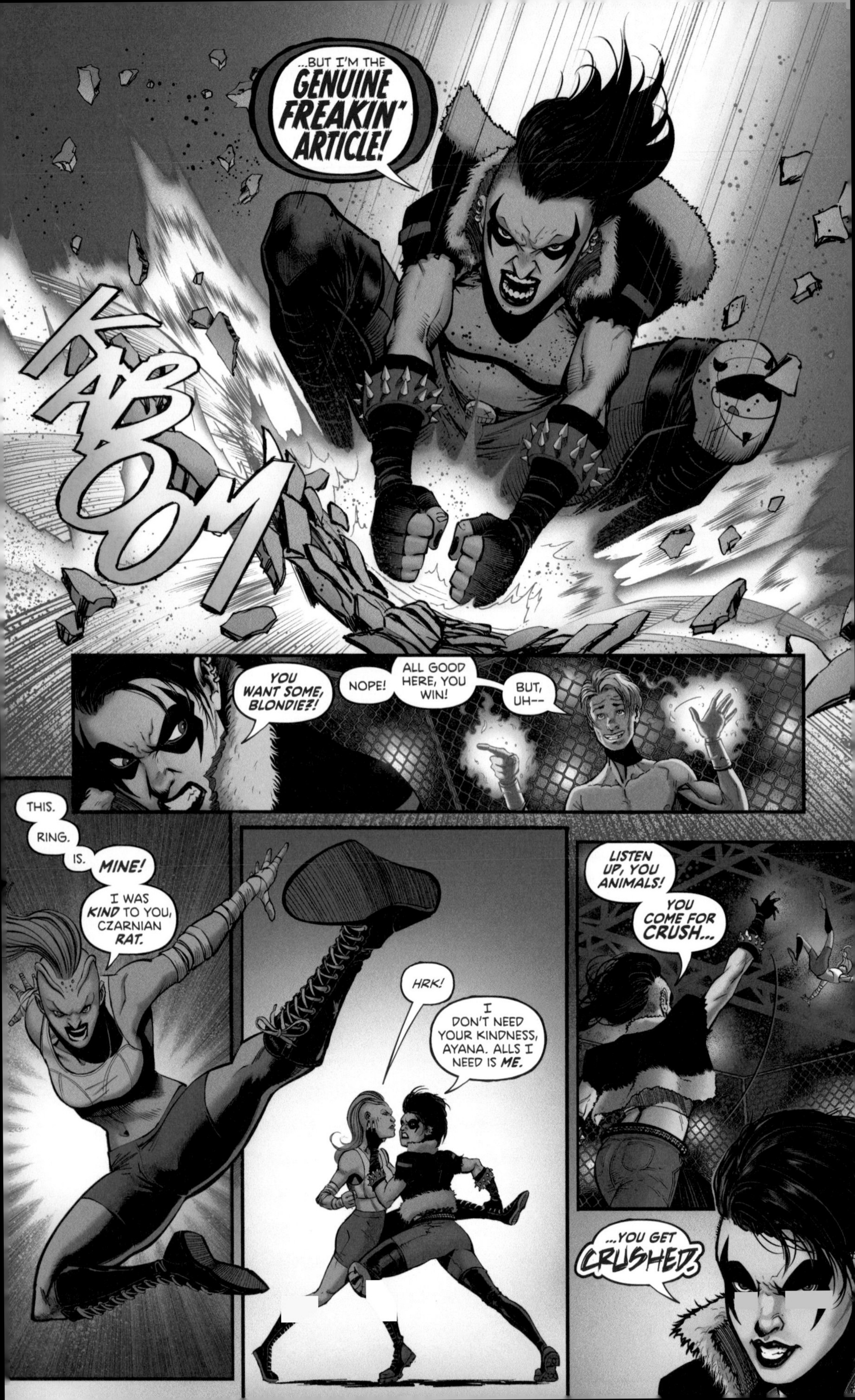
...BUT I'M THE GENUINE FREAKIN' ARTICLE!
KABOOM
YOU WANT SOME, BLONDIE?!
NOPE!
ALL GOOD HERE, YOU WIN!
BUT, UH--
THIS.
RING.
IS.
MINE!
I WAS KIND TO YOU, CZARNIAN RAT.
HRK!
I DON'T NEED YOUR KINDNESS, AYANA. ALLS I NEED IS ME.
LISTEN UP, YOU ANIMALS!
YOU COME FOR CRUSH...
...YOU GET CRUSHED.

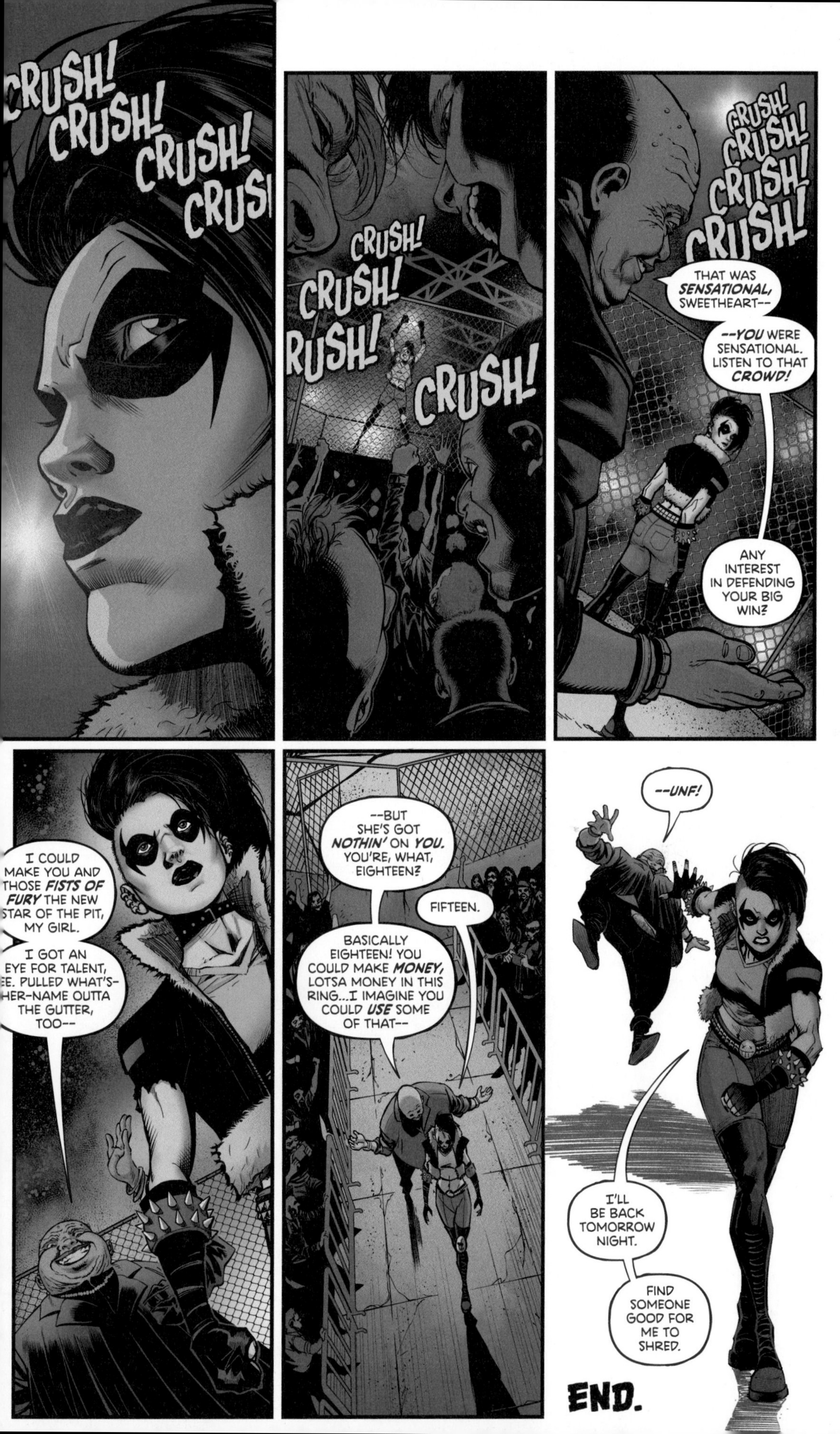
CRUSH!
CRUSH!
CRUSH!
CRUSH!
CRUSH!
CRUSH!
RUSH!
CRUSH!
CRUSH!
CRUSH!
CRUSH!
CRUSH!
THAT WAS SENSATIONAL, SWEETHEART--
--YOU WERE SENSATIONAL. LISTEN TO THAT CROWD!
ANY INTEREST IN DEFENDING YOUR BIG WIN?
I COULD MAKE YOU AND THOSE FISTS OF FURY THE NEW STAR OF THE PIT, MY GIRL.
I GOT AN EYE FOR TALENT, SEE. PULLED WHAT'S-HER-NAME OUTTA THE GUTTER, TOO--
--BUT SHE'S GOT NOTHIN' ON YOU. YOU'RE, WHAT, EIGHTEEN?
FIFTEEN.
BASICALLY EIGHTEEN! YOU COULD MAKE MONEY, LOTSA MONEY IN THIS RING...I IMAGINE YOU COULD USE SOME OF THAT--
--UNF!
I'LL BE BACK TOMORROW NIGHT.
FIND SOMEONE GOOD FOR ME TO SHRED.
END.

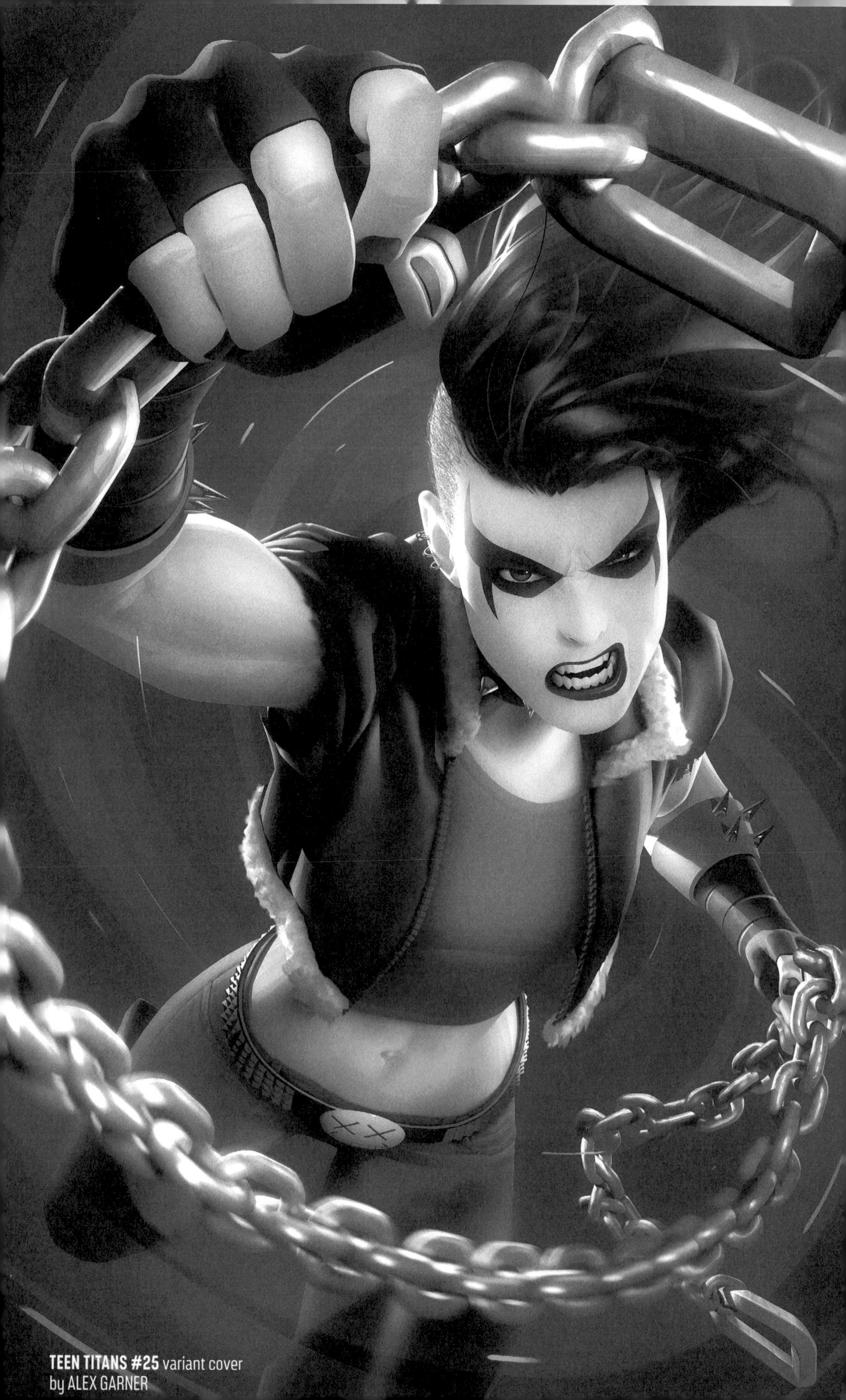

TEEN TITANS #25 variant cover
by ALEX GARNER

TEEN TITANS #26 variant
by ALEX GARNER

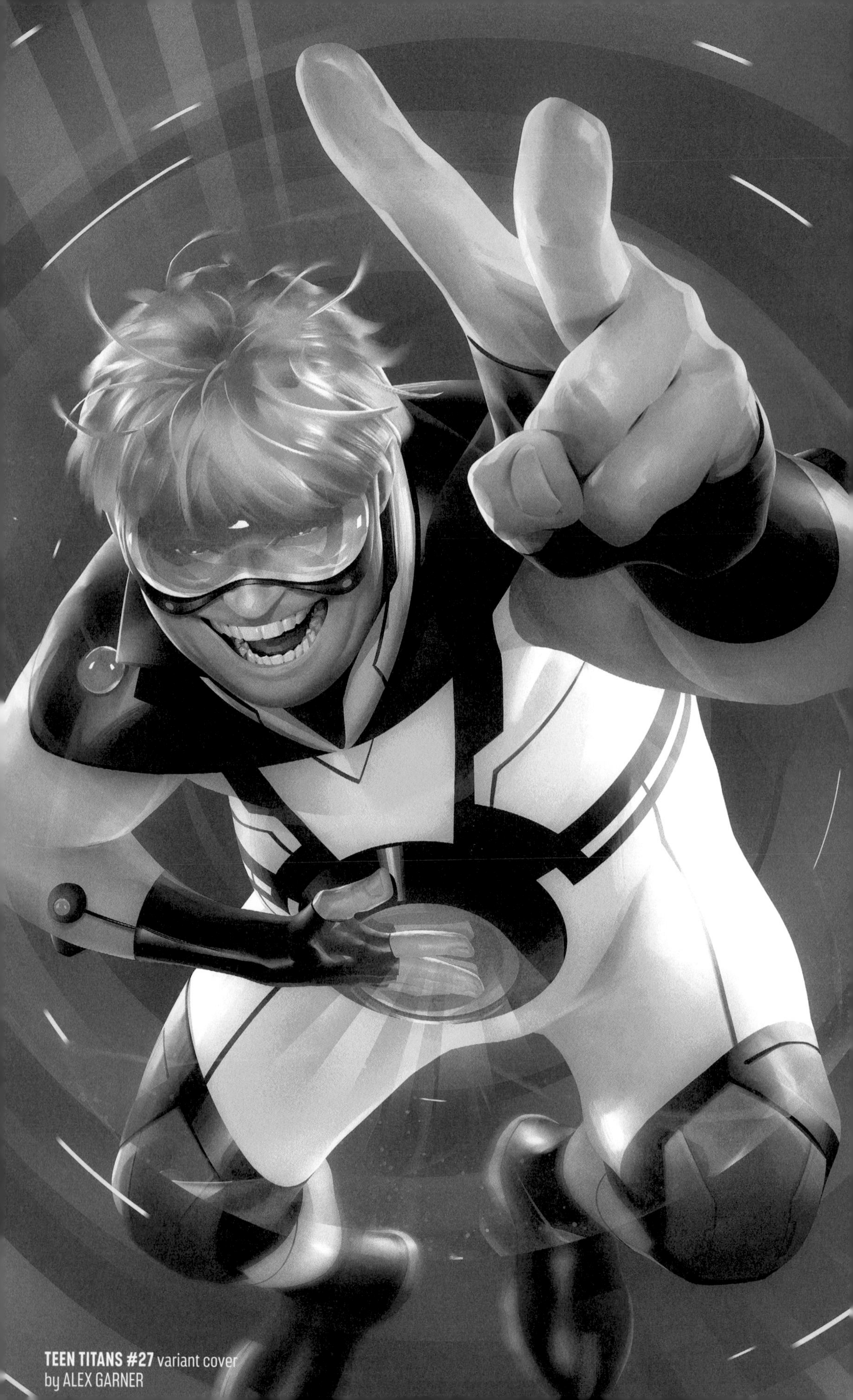

TEEN TITANS #27 variant cover
by ALEX GARNER

JOYSTICK character study by JOSE LUIS

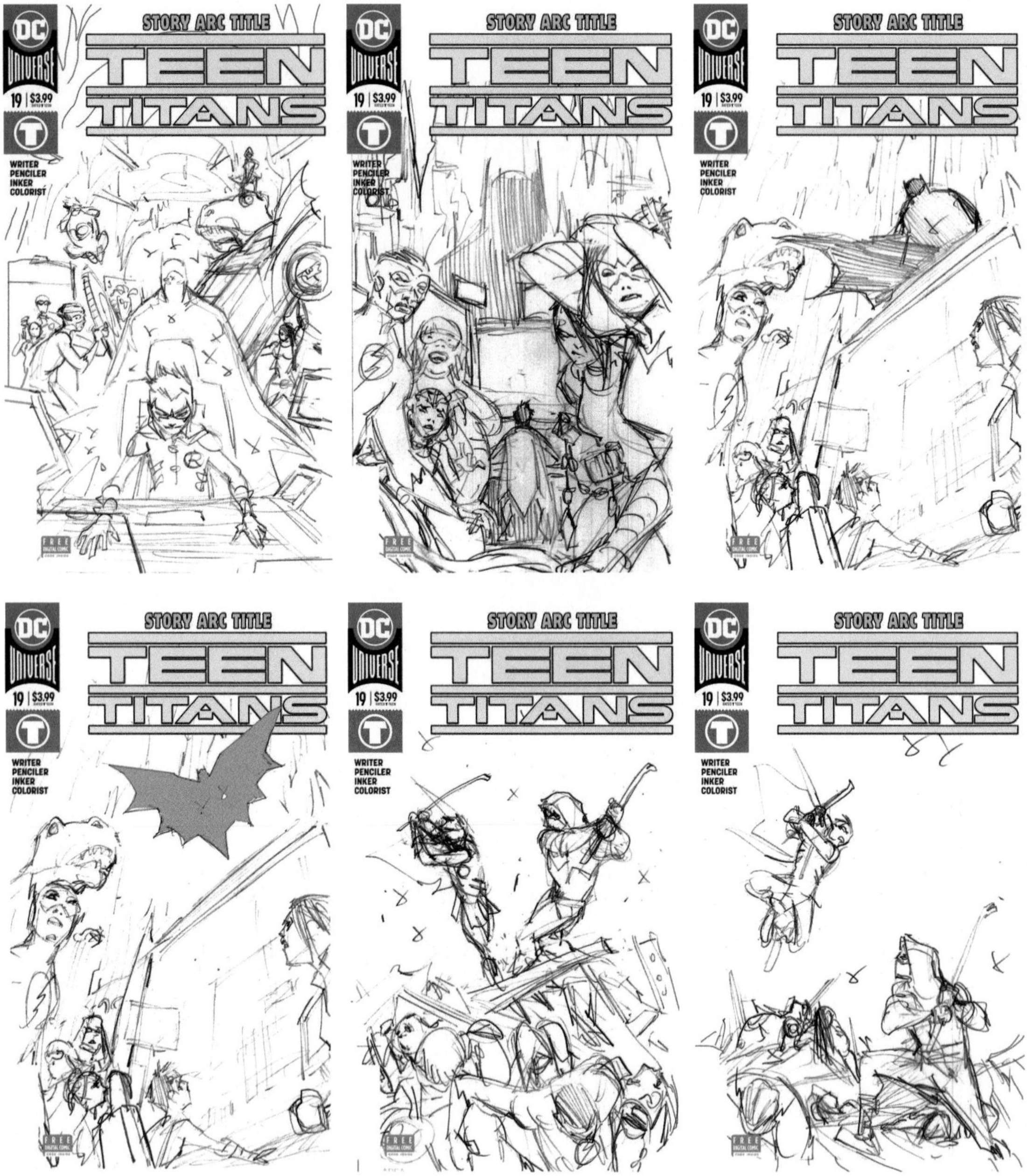
DC UNIVERSE
STORY ARC TITLE
TEEN TITANS
19 | $3.99
WRITER
PENCILER
INKER
COLORIST

TEEN TITANS cover sketches by GIUSEPPE CAMUNCOLI